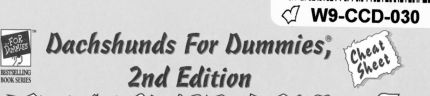

Dachshunds For Dummies, 2nd Edition

Cheat Sheet

W9-CCD-030

Choosing a Vet: A Checklist

When deciding on a vet, fill out the following good-vet checklist to help you make your decision. Make several copies and fill one out after each vet visit you make:

- Was it easy to make an appointment?
- Was the person who answered the phone friendly and accommodating?
- Does the reception area look and smell clean? (A doggy smell is natural, but you shouldn't smell anything unpleasant.)
- Is the office staff friendly and polite?
- Is the staff willing to give you a tour of the facility?
- Does your Dachshund seem interested when you visit, or does he seem nervous?
- Do you have a good feeling about the vet? Is she friendly, open, and easy to talk to?

- Does the vet seem to have a genuine interest and love for animals?
- Does the vet seem to bond with you and your dog?
- Is the vet ready and willing to answer all your questions?
- Does the vet make you feel like she has plenty of time for you?
- Is the vet willing to give you references?
- Is the vet open and forthcoming about her training?
- Does the vet have any experience with Dachshunds?
- Do you have a good feeling about the whole experience?

The Warning Signs of Back Problems

Dogs have differing pain thresholds and an instinct not to reveal when they're in pain. But if you pay attention, you can tell whether your Dachshund is having back pain. Look for the following signs; if you notice any, call your vet:

- Shivering — especially when combined with unusual inactivity
- Refusal to get up and play, even for food
- A yelp when you pet your Dachshund or try to pick him up
- A pulled-in head, arched back, or any other strange position
- A refusal to bend down to the food or water dish to eat or drink
- Limping of any kind
- A "drunken" rear end, which moves but looks as if it isn't completely under control

If your Dachshund drags his back legs or shows any other sign of paralysis or severe pain, go immediately to the vet's office or nearest pet emergency facility. Place a call on the way.

For Dummies: Bestselling Book Series for Beginners

Dachshunds For Dummies, 2nd Edition

Dachsie Must-Haves

Following is a list of pet-supply staples that are pretty much nonnegotiable. Your dog needs them. You can spend a little or a lot, or you can borrow them from a friend who no longer has a small dog. But be sure to find these things, one way or the other:

- **Food:** Buy the best food you can afford.
- **Leash or lead:** Four-foot lengths are good for puppies. When your dog is older, a 6-foot length is perfect. Choose leather or nylon, whichever you prefer.
- **Collar or harness:** Harnesses are nice for Dachshunds because you won't risk pulling on their necks.
- **Food and water bowls:** Any bowl will do, as long as it's unbreakable and heavy enough to prevent capsizing.
- **Shampoo:** Use shampoo made for pets, not for people.
- **Toothbrush and toothpaste made for dogs:** It may seem silly to you, but brushing your dog's teeth is essential for her good health.
- **Nail clippers:** Buy clippers made for dogs, not for humans. Or, use a power tool with a sanding barrel or nail grinder. This way, you won't cut the quick and it leaves the nail tips smooth — trimming and filing in one quick step (as long as you're careful)!
- **Brush and comb:** Your dog's grooming needs depend on what coat your Dachshund has.
- **ID tags:** Nobody thinks they'll lose their dog; if you lose yours, an ID tag tells people where she lives.
- **Pet gate:** A must-have if you have rooms where your Dachshund isn't allowed or stairs you want to keep her from descending or climbing.
- **Toys:** Dachshunds just want to have fun. A few toys are a must-have, even if they're homemade.
- **Pet odor remover:** Accidents happen, but if your dog smells a previous mistake on your carpet, accidents will happen again and again.

For Dummies: Bestselling Book Series for Beginners

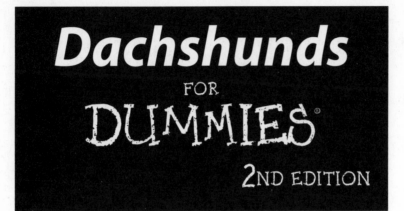

Dachshunds

FOR

DUMMIES®

2ND EDITION

Dachshunds FOR DUMMIES®

2ND EDITION

by Eve Adamson

Wiley Publishing, Inc.

Dachshunds For Dummies®, 2nd Edition
Published by
Wiley Publishing, Inc.
111 River St.
Hoboken, NJ 07030-5774
www.wiley.com

WILEY

About the Author

Eve Adamson has been a Dachshund fan since childhood and a contributing editor for *Dog Fancy* magazine. Eve has written or co-authored over 45 books, including *Adopting a Pet For Dummies, Shih Tzu For Dummies,* and *Labrador Retrievers For Dummies.* She has won many dog writing awards and is a member of the Dog Writer's Association of America. Eve lives in Iowa City with her family, which includes her dogs, Jack and Sally.

Dedication

To Sally, who taught me more about dogs than any book.

Author's Acknowledgments

Many people assisted in helping to bring this book to fruition. First and foremost, thanks to Dr. Carey Wasem for providing knowledge, enthusiasm, information, and for tech-editing the manuscript. Thanks to Adrian Milton for providing wonderful pictures. Damian must be proud! Thanks to Darryl E. McDonald, DVM, MS, Diplomate ACVS of the Dallas Veterinary Surgical Center in Dallas, Texas, for his expertise on Dachshund orthopedics. Thanks to the Dachshund Club of America for lending expertise via its excellent illustrated breed standard; informative Web site (www.dachshund-dca.org); its *Canine Intervertebral Disk Disease* booklet (available on the Web site) prepared for the DCA by Patricia J. Luttgen, DVM, MS, Diplomate, American College of Veterinary Internal Medicine, Specialty of Neurology, in Denver, Colorado; and via the friendly and helpful efforts of Andra O'Connell, Ann Gordon, and Jan Oswald. Thanks to Bob Brennert up in Canada, who, along with his wonderful Wiener Dogs Web site (www.wienerdogs.org), was also a great source of information and support. And thanks, of course, to all those smooths, longhairs, and wirehairs out there, mighty, mini, and in-betweeny, for inspiring such great love and devotion in their two-legged human servants.

Publisher's Acknowledgments

We're proud of this book; please send us your comments through our Dummies online registration form located at www.dummies.com/register/.

Some of the people who helped bring this book to market include the following:

Acquisitions, Editorial, and Media Development

Project Editor (Previous Edition): Tim Gallan

Acquisitions Editor: Tracy Boggier

Copy Editor: Josh Dials

Technical Editor: Dr. Carey Wasem

Editorial Manager: Jennifer Ehrlich

Editorial Supervisor & Reprint Editor: Carmen Krikorian

Editorial Assistants: Erin Calligan Mooney, Joe Niesen, Leeann Harney, David Lutton

Cover Photo: © Mark Raycroft/Getty Images

Cartoons: Rich Tennant (www.the5thwave.com)

Composition Services

Project Coordinator: Erin Smith

Layout and Graphics: Stacie Brooks, Carl Byers, Reuben W. Davis, Melissa K. Jester, Stephanie D. Jumper, Barbara Moore, Christine Williams

Anniversary Logo Design: Richard Pacifico

Proofreader: Evelyn Still

Indexer: Sherry Massey

Special Help: Natalie Faye Harris

Publishing and Editorial for Consumer Dummies

Diane Graves Steele, Vice President and Publisher, Consumer Dummies

Joyce Pepple, Acquisitions Director, Consumer Dummies

Kristin A. Cocks, Product Development Director, Consumer Dummies

Michael Spring, Vice President and Publisher, Travel

Kelly Regan, Editorial Director, Travel

Publishing for Technology Dummies

Andy Cummings, Vice President and Publisher, Dummies Technology/General User

Composition Services

Gerry Fahey, Vice President of Production Services

Debbie Stailey, Director of Composition Services

Contents at a Glance

Table of Contents

Introduction

● ●

Dachshunds: What's not to love? They're cute, cuddly, smart, and friendly, and they're shaped like hot dogs — which is why people occasionally call them wiener dogs! (I don't think they mind.) They come in all kinds of different colors and patterns, and you'll even find them in different sizes. If you like small- to medium-size dogs with plenty of spunk and compassion, you'll love Dachshunds.

You don't have to know diddly-squat about Dachshunds to use this book. If you know nothing about dog care, this book has plenty of information for you to start a rewarding relationship with a Dachshund.

And if you're a seasoned dog-care veteran, I bet you'll find this book plenty useful. It's filled with tips, tricks, and advice for life with Dachshunds, including a good bit of technical information about keeping your Dachshund healthy in all stages of its life.

About This Book

This book is your easy-to-understand primer on Dachshund care. I describe what Dachshunds are, not only in shape, size, and color — the things described in the official breed standard — but also in terms of personality and temperament so that you can decide if a Dachshund is the right dog for you. I help you discover the best ways to find a great Dachshund, and I show you how to take care of your Dachshund from the day you bring him home. I cover housetraining, feeding, pest prevention, vet care, obedience training, and much more. If you have a Dachshund or are considering buying one, this book has all the information you need.

But this book doesn't do *everything*. For one thing, it isn't a boring reference book. It isn't a textbook on Dachshund history, medical issues, or training (although it covers all those subjects). And it isn't a guide on breeding (which I don't recommend for most pet owners), on showing dogs, or on the complex ins and outs of dog competition (although I do talk about plenty of fun dog sports and activities you can enjoy with your Dachshund). This is a fun book, a sometimes irreverent book, a user-friendly book, and most of all a book that celebrates Dachshunds. You find out who and what they are and how you can make the most of your relationship by choosing the best one for you and taking the best possible care of your new pet.

Conventions Used in This Book

Every *For Dummies* book follows certain conventions, and in this book, I do a few things to make your reading easier and more fun. These conventions include the following:

- ✔ I use *italics* to highlight words I go on to define for you, and when I include key words in a list, I put them in **boldface.**

- ✔ You'll find all Web and e-mail addresses in monofont.

- ✔ Sometimes I call Dachshunds by their common nickname, "Dachsies." Some people also spell this nickname "Doxies."

- ✔ When you see "Mini," don't think that I'm just being playful with the Dachshund's small size. This is a shortened version of Miniature, which is a type of Dachshund.

- ✔ In general, when referring to Dachshunds, I alternate between male and female pronouns between chapters. In other words, Dachsies will be "he" in some chapters and "she" in others.

What You're Not to Read

Okay, you can read the whole book if you want to — every word. I won't mind one bit! But this book does include some information that isn't absolutely essential. For one thing, the sidebars (shaded gray boxes) contain non-essential but fun facts or extra information that may interest you. Skip them if you like. And when you see a Technical Stuff icon, that means I'm getting more, well, technical, so if you aren't into that kind of thing, you can skip those, too.

But I do hope that you'll read the rest of the book, because that's where the really important stuff lies — the information that will help you and your Dachshund have a happier and more successful life together.

Foolish Assumptions

They say a fool and his assumptions are soon parted . . . or maybe they say that about money. Anyway, I *do* make some assumptions about you, which may or may not be foolish. For one thing, I assume you *love* Dachshunds, or are thinking about falling in love soon. I assume you're interested in being the best possible dog owner, whether you've already brought home your new Dachshund or you're about to. I assume you have the time, the will, and the way to bring a Dachshund into your life, or that you have a Dachshund you love and cherish and you want to learn how to improve your relationship and dog-care skills. I also assume you're interested in training your dog — maybe doing some dog sports or possibly just having the best possible little cuddly lap dog you can have.

I also assume you aren't interested in becoming a Dachshund breeder, and that you aren't picking up a Dachshund to help you train for a triathlon, herd sheep, or be your hunting retriever. (Hunting *hound* is a different story; your Dachshund can probably play that role without a hiccup.) You know what Dachshunds are — or you think you do — but you want to know more. Am I right?

How This Book Is Organized

This book is divided into parts, each containing related chapters on a Dachsie topic. The following sections show what I cover in each part.

Part 1: Preparing to Live with a Dachshund

I start out by defining the Dachshund and I describe the different varieties of Dachshunds that you're likely to encounter. I then provide advice on where to find the Dachshund that may become your new friend, and I include a discussion on the pros and cons of working with rescue shelters.

Part 11: Starting Out on the Right Paw at Home

Find out how to prepare your home, yourself, and your family for the fun-filled life with a Dachshund. I help you Dachshund-proof your home and family, suggest what things to buy to be fully supplied, and explain what to expect when you bring your wiener-shaped friend home on that very first day.

Part III: The Obedient Dachshund (Not an Oxymoron)

After describing the Dachshund personality and helping you understand your role as a trainer, I show you how to housetrain your Dachshund. Then I provide helpful advice on how to teach your Dachsie basic good manners and all the behaviors that any good dog should know. I conclude this part with coverage of dog shows and other fun competitions like agility and earthdog trials.

Part IV: Helping Your Dachshund Stay Healthy

In this part, you find out what it takes to keep your Dachshund happy and healthy, from vaccinations to good grooming to regular exercise. I also describe in detail the back problems that many Dachshunds develop, as well as a few other health problems some Dachshunds could experience. I then discuss the health needs of — and joys of owning — older dogs.

Part V: The Part of Tens

Every *For Dummies* book ends with top-ten lists, and this one is no exception. I present ten Dachshund books and ten Dachshund-centric Web sites that you can peruse. Also, I list ten great people foods Dachshunds can enjoy safely and ten foods no Dachshund should ever eat.

Icons Used in This Book

Look for the following icons next to tidbits of useful information:

Here you'll find dog-related tips and common-sense hints to make life with your Dachshund easier and more enjoyable.

I place this icon next to information that will help you prevent mistakes or warn you against actions that may potentially cause problems.

When you see this icon, expect to find interesting tidbits, lore, and information about Dachshunds and dogs in general.

This icon pops up when I'm describing technical terms and dog information.

 I use this icon when I want you to, um, remember an important concept. Knowing this information will help you down the road.

Where to Go from Here

The great thing about *For Dummies* books is that they are references rather than tutorials. I've organized this book into self-contained chapters that you can read in pretty much any order you wish. So skip around if that's what you want to do. Of course, the progression of chapters in the book is logically arranged just in case you want to read the book from cover to cover.

So you can pick a topic out of the Table of Contents and start reading, or you can flip to the first page of Chapter 1 and read till you get to the end. Either way, I'm sure you'll enjoy the experience.

If you already know a lot about dog care, feel free to skip around and check out whatever Dachshund-related topics catch your fancy. The detailed Table of Contents and Index should help you out. If you don't really know much about Dachshunds, be sure to read the first part of this book to get the lowdown.

Part I

Preparing to Live with a Dachshund

The 5th Wave   By Rich Tennant

"Okay, I'll let him play as long as you stop saying, 'You can't take an old dog's new tricks.'"

In this part . . .

1 begin this book by telling you what the heck a Dachshund actually is (as defined by the breed standard), and then I describe the different kinds of Dachshunds you're likely to encounter. I also provide advice on where to find the Dachshund that may become your new friend, including a discussion on the pros and cons of working with rescue shelters and other adoption agencies.

Chapter 1

Is a Dachshund Right for You?

*E*verybody loves a Wiener dog! Those funny bodies, those short little legs, those floppy ears, those pleading eyes, and those *antics*. Dachshunds are clowns. They can keep a room in stitches, and they can coax even the most stolid disciplinarian into slipping them just one more dog cookie. Dachshunds aren't big dogs, so they don't take up much room. And they're so darned *cute*. Who can resist a pet like that?

Apparently, not many of us. As of 2006 (the most current statistics available at the time of this printing), Dachshunds were the sixth most popular dog breed in terms of registrations with the American Kennel Club (AKC). They've been a little higher on the list and a little lower at times, but for more than a decade, the diminutive Dachsie has sat comfortably in the top ten.

Many people own Dachshunds, so they can't be too much trouble, can they? Of course, a cute face and a good sense of humor aren't reasons in and of themselves to take on the 15-year-or-so responsibility of owning a dog. Too many people don't give pet ownership in general, and Dachshund ownership in particular, a lot of thought. But you're not like them, because you've already begun research by picking up this book. Good for you! Before you proceed further in your quest for the Dachshund of your dreams, read this chapter to look closely at the responsibilities of Dachshund servitude (because, as you'll soon see, Dachsies own you, not the other way around). But what if you already have a Dachsie pup curled in your lap? Better late than never: You're still at the right chapter!

Examining the Pros and Cons of Dachshund Ownership

Dachshund ownership is easy to romanticize: You and your cute little wiener dog, together forever. You see yourself taking leisurely walks through the park with your Dachsie by your side; relaxing with a good book and his warm body on your lap; having a loyal companion and friend, and a playmate for the kids; and having friends comment on how well-behaved, well-trained, and intelligent your dog is.

Well, guess what? Life with a dog isn't always like that. From sleepless nights with a new puppy to expensive medication to treat health problems in your aging pet (see Chapter 18), having a dog as a family member is a lot like having a child. It takes a lot of work and a lot of time. It takes a physical, emotional, and financial commitment. And it often ends in heartbreak, even when your dog lives to a ripe old age, because humans usually outlive dogs, and no one wants to say goodbye to a best friend.

On the flip side, living with a Dachshund *will* fill your life with fun. You'll always be the object of your Dachshund's colossal affection. You just need to be realistic and decide whether you're ready to take on the responsibility. This section helps you put your feelings in perspective.

Dachshund pros

Here are some major benefits to owning a Dachshund:

- Dachshunds love you unconditionally.
- Studies show that having a pet lowers blood pressure and helps to manage stress.
- Fulfilling your dog's exercise needs may keep you in shape (see Chapter 16).
- Dachshunds are great companions and listeners.
- Dachshunds can help teach children to respect and be kind to animals.
- Dachshunds are good at warning you if someone is outside the house — welcome or not.
- If you bring home a rescued Dachshund, you can feel good about saving a life. And your dog will show his gratitude every day (see Chapter 5).

A word about the AKC

The American Kennel Club (AKC) is a nonprofit organization, established in 1884, that's devoted to the advancement of purebred dogs. The AKC maintains a record of all registered dogs; publishes ideal standards for each recognized breed; sponsors a variety of dog events, including conformation shows, obedience and field trials, agility competitions, and the Canine Good Citizen program; and produces educational information. (See Chapter 2 for more information on the AKC's Dachshund standards.)

Dachshund cons

A hard fact of life is that the drawbacks to owning a Dachshund can outweigh the benefits for some people:

- Dachshunds need plenty of attention and affection. They want to be with you, not tied to a chain in the backyard.

- Dachshunds aren't people (even though they may think they are!) and must be taught how to live with people. Without proper and consistent teaching and socialization efforts, your dog may end up becoming an annoyance to you, your family, or your neighbors. He may even inflict damage on your possessions, other people, or himself.

- Dachshunds must be housebroken, and until they are, your carpet or other household surfaces may suffer. (And housetraining a Dachshund is no picnic; for more, see Part III.)

- Dachshunds cost money. Most people can expect to spend around $1,000 in the first year to give their new puppies the proper care and supplies.

- Dachshunds need your time. They require walking, feeding, training, grooming, and attention *every single day* to stay healthy and happy.

- Dachshunds aren't a commitment to be taken lightly. Many live to be 15 years old or more.

- Your Dachshund will probably grow old and die before you do. You have to make decisions about your Dachsie's health care and quality of life, and eventually you must deal with your own grief.

- Your Dachshund requires regular preventive veterinary care. If he becomes ill or injured, you're also responsible for his care and treatment. Dachshunds are prone to several serious health conditions (see Chapters 16 and 17), and the medical costs to treat these problems can be high.

  ✔ Dachshunds tie you down. You can't just fly off on a sponta-
    neous vacation for a long weekend, or decide not to come
    home after work without arranging for your dog's care.

  ✔ Dachshunds don't speak English. You have to learn to
    communicate with your dog in a way he understands.

How's that for a reality check? Think long and hard about the
commitment you're about to make before you bring home
a Dachshund.

Dachshunds are more stubborn than some breeds, so training
efforts can be frustrating for the beginner. Don't give up. When
in doubt, talk to your vet, hire a trainer, and practice, practice,
practice — every day. Eventually, you'll be speaking the same
language, and your Dachshund will understand what you want.
He really does live to please you, even if it sometimes seems like
you live to please him.

Dachshunds: Not Just Any Dog

It's one thing to prepare for a dog; it's another thing to prepare for
a Dachshund. Dachshunds have all the basic needs of a dog, but they
come with a few of their own special quirks and considerations. If
you have your heart set on owning a Dachsie — who can blame you
after seeing a cutie like the pup shown in Figure 1-1? — you must
be ready to handle a few extras. The following list presents the
common characteristics of Dachshunds:

  ✔ **Dachshunds have fragile backs.** Because of their dwarfism
    (big dog, short legs), Dachshunds are genetically predisposed
    to have faulty spines, which can become injured when handled
    incorrectly, or sometimes for no apparent reason. Certain
    things can be hard on a Dachshund's back and can even
    result in a paralyzing disk rupture:

      • Going up and down stairs

      • Jumping off furniture

      • Even running quickly around a sharp corner.

    Get ready to carry your Dachshund up and down the stairs!

  ✔ **Dachshunds love to jump.** But because jumping is so hard
    on a Dachshund's back, you need to keep an eye on your
    Dachsie to keep him from jumping off high places like beds,
    couches, porches, and so on. Some people install ramps in
    their homes so their dogs can ascend and descend from high
    places without jarring their spines. (For more on making your
    home Dachshund-friendly, see Chapter 6.)

The Dachsie name game

The name *Dachshund* is German for "badger dog." Although plenty of people pronounce it like *dash-hound,* the word is correctly pronounced *docks-hoont.* Yet, in Germany, the Dachshund isn't called a Dachshund at all. The dog is a *Teckel* or *Dackel.* (Back in the 19th century, the Dachshund was even called the Royal Teutonic Dog by some.)

The name *Dachshund* is somewhat misunderstood. *Dachs* means "badger" in German; *hund* doesn't, contrary to what you may think, mean "hound." It simply means "dog." Although Dachshunds are, to this day, classified in the Hound group according to the American Kennel Club, they could arguably fit just as well with the Terriers. *Terrier* means "earth dog," and going underground is what Dachshunds do best (well, one of the many things they do best). Dachshunds hunt by scent and have keen noses like their Hound brothers and sisters, but if you're on the other side of a door, that bark sounds an awful lot like a Terrier.

In any case, categories don't really matter. What matters is knowing that your Dachshund will display characteristics of the Hound *and* the Terrier. You can call him anything you like! (How about "good dog"?)

✔ **Dachshunds live to eat.** Obesity puts further strain on a Dachshund's back — not to mention his heart and entire body. Cute and pleading as he may be, you must be prepared to keep your Dachshund's eating under control. No, your Dachshund shouldn't eat that quarter-pound burger with cheese, let alone too many extra dog treats!

Dachshunds (like all dogs) have fewer taste buds than humans, so the taste of food isn't as intense for them as it is for us. For this reason, dogs are more likely to eat just about anything, taste not withstanding.

✔ **Dachshunds bark.** Barking is part of their *modus operandi.* They were bred to hunt badgers or other small game underground (see Chapter 2). When the game was cornered, a Dachshund would bark to alert his human. Although you can train any dog not to bark excessively, Dachshunds bark pretty frequently. Get used to it, or don't get a Dachshund.

✔ **Dachshunds are manipulative.** They're cute, and they know it. They're clever, too. They can get you to do just about anything, unless you have rules and you stick to your guns. Your dog has to know that rules are rules and that what you say goes. If you're a big marshmallow when it comes to consistency and rule enforcement, you can't get angry at your dog for making his own rules. Somebody has to do it!

So, what would your Dachsie's rules be? Here's a good guess:

- I can do whatever I want to do, whenever I want to do it.
- If I touch it, lick it, chew it, shred it, smell it, or see it, it's mine.
- Humans live to serve me.

Unless those rules sound reasonable to you (Hint: They shouldn't!), prepare to accept your role as pack leader.

Photo courtesy of Gail Painter.

Figure 1-1: Dachsies, although cute, love to bark, jump, and manipulate.

Understanding a Dachshund's Special Needs

Dachshunds have special-care needs related to preserving the integrity of their spinal cords. Dachshunds are *chondrodystrophic,* an inherited condition that results in dwarfism and makes the Dachshund's spine vulnerable to disc rupture. One hard jump off a high bed, a fall from a porch, or even a sudden twisting movement to catch a ball can rupture a disk. The result can range from severe pain to paralysis — temporary or permanent. (For a more detailed discussion of disk disease, see Chapter 17.)

"How common is this flimsy disk problem?"

According to the Dachshund Club of America, Inc. — in its must-have publication *Canine Intervertebral Disk Disease* (available from the DCA for free — see Chapter 20 for contact information) — approximately one in four Dachshunds will experience a disk problem. Evidence suggests that Intervertebral Disk Disease (IVDD) is a genetic condition. The University of California, Davis, is currently investigating the genetic nature of this disease. If the link can be determined, scientists may be able to develop a test to predict which dogs are most likely to suffer from IVDD. Meanwhile, experts do know that most incidents occur between the ages of 3 and 7, with age 4 being the most common age of occurrence.

Of course, not every Dachshund is doomed to suffer this debilitating and painful condition, and I hope you won't be dissuaded from bringing a Dachshund into your life out of fear. But caution is warranted. Here are some steps you can take to care for your dog:

- ✔ Avoid long or steep flights of stairs and jumps off high places.

- ✔ Steer clear of any activities, like vigorous tug-of-war games, that can twist the spine.

- ✔ Keep your dog slim (for more on diet, see Chapter 8).

- ✔ Exercise for fun and for preventive measure. Daily walks and plenty of activity are important to keep a Dachshund's muscles strong and stable so they can support the spine.

Just be sure that the activities you choose are the kinds a Dachshund excels in — brisk walks and hikes, organized field-trial or earth-dog competitions (see Chapter 15), or just playing in the park.

In other words, just like a human with a weak back, Dachshunds need to exercise properly, eat a healthy diet, and avoid certain movements to minimize the possibility of injury. If you follow these responsible Dachsie-owner rules, chances are your Dachshund will never have a problem.

What's Your PQ (Patience Quotient)?

Living with a Dachshund requires a degree of patience. Let me emphasize this one: *Patience.*

Do you have the patience required not to lose your cool when your Dachshund steals your pot roast right off your plate? Or eats the last half of your book before you get to the exciting conclusion? Or has an accident in the house *again?* I'm not saying you can't get irritated — or even downright angry — at your Dachshund. But yelling, screaming, flailing your arms around, and, dog-forbid, hitting your pup are activities that will do more harm than good every single time.

Every time your Dachshund makes a mistake — accidentally or on purpose — you have an opportunity to teach him something. This is especially true when you catch him in the act. But this teaching has to be performed calmly and rationally. Teaching a Dachshund is a lot like teaching a child: Losing your temper will only scare and confuse your charge. Keeping your cool will prove that you're the pack leader and the one with all the power. (For more on training your Dachshund, head to the chapters of Part III.)

Think long and hard about whether you have a short fuse or a long one before bringing home a Dachshund. And then, who knows? You may end up with a perfect little angel, and the whole discussion will be moot. Better to be prepared, however, because most Dachshunds are about half-angel, and half-, well . . . you know.

Dachshund Dollars: The Financial Commitment

Before you purchase any dog, whether Dachshund or Great Dane, be aware that you'll have to make a financial commitment as well as emotional and time commitments. Sure, you don't *have* to take your pet to the vet. You won't be breaking any law if you don't. But without regular veterinary visits, puppies have a much higher chance of becoming sick and dying from a serious disease, like parvovirus or distemper. And throughout their lives, adult and senior dogs need regular checkups, vaccinations (it is, in fact, against the law to skip the rabies vaccine), and tests to maintain their health and to catch health problems in the early stages. In addition, your vet can help you with wormings, flea control, and heartworm prevention, and can give you advice on general issues of care, behavior, and training. Worth every penny!

Puppies are immune to many diseases while nursing on mother's milk. As soon as a puppy is weaned and you take him home, however, his immunity quickly disappears and he's vulnerable to a number of serious diseases until he can build up his own immune system. Vaccinate your puppy according to your veterinarian's recommendations to keep him safe during this gap of time. (For more on the first vet visit and which vaccinations your puppy really needs, see Chapter 16.)

Canine parvovirus is a quick-spreading, highly contagious viral disease that comes in two forms: enteric (diarrheal) and myocardial (affecting the heart). Young puppies are particularly vulnerable, and the disease often is fatal. *Distemper* is also a virus that spreads quickly and is highly contagious. In advanced stages, distemper affects the brain and can cause permanent neurological damage and often death. Distemper is the principal cause of disease and death in unvaccinated dogs.

In addition to a lifetime of regular veterinary care and vaccinations, you need to spend some of your hard-earned cash on supplies. Dogs need food — probably your most significant expense, all told — as well as feeding supplies, collars and leashes, dens (a crate or kennel), chew toys, and a number of other necessities and luxuries (see Chapter 8 for a major discussion on Dachshund necessities and accessories).

So how much money are we talking? Consider the theoretical breakdown of expenses shown in Table 1-1. Although expenses can vary dramatically from region to region, I list the approximate costs somewhere in the middle of the extremes. I also assume that you'll buy your puppy from a good breeder for an average price of $600

Table 1-1   First-Year Expenses for Dachsie Puppy Owners

Item	Cost
The dog	**$600.00**
Veterinary	
First office visit	$50.00
Four vaccinations at $35.00 each	$140.00
Rabies shot	$15.00
Bordatella vaccine	$15.00
Leptospirosis vaccine (x2) and/or Lyme disease vaccine (x2), depending on where you live	$15.00 each
Spay/neuter operation	$150.00
Registration	$20.00

(continued)

Table 1-1 *(continued)*

Item	Cost
Total vet cost	**$420.00**
Prevention	
Heartworm prevention at $3.50/month	$42.00
Flea control spot-on at $8.00/month	$96.00
Total prevention cost	**$138.00**
Obedience classes	
Puppy class (6–8 sessions)	$50.00
Basic obedience (6–8 sessions)	$50.00
Total obedience classes cost	**$100.00**
Services	
Pet sitter/boarding for one-week vacation at $20.00/day	$140.00
Professional grooming (for longhairs and wirehairs), 6 times/year at $25.00/ session	$150.00
Total services cost	**290.00**
Pet supplies	
Food	$400.00
Leash	$20.00
Retractable Leash	$25.00
Collar or harness	$12.00
Food and water bowls	$10.00
Dog bed (although Dachsies will probably prefer to sleep with you)	$50.00
Crate	$75.00
Shampoo (two bottles)	$20.00
Toothbrush/paste	$5.00
Nail clippers	$10.00
Brush	$5.00

Item	Cost
Comb	$6.00
ID tags	$4.00
Pet gate	$40.00
Toys (chew toy, squeaky toy, ball, and plush toy)	$50.00
Treats, one box/month	$30.00
Chewing/teething treats (rawhides, hooves, and so on), one purchase/month	$50.00
Poop scoop	$10.00
Breed book	$15.00
Training book	$15.00
Pet odor remover, 1 gallon	$20.00
Total pet supplies cost	**$872.00**
GRAND TOTAL	**$2,420.00**

Not cheap — and this grand total assumes that your pup is healthy. If your puppy suffers from serious health problems, you can add quite a bit to the grand total. Are you ready for this?

Sure, you can cut corners here and there, but if you have to cut so many corners that you compromise the health and welfare of your dog — or if you aren't willing to spend money on your pet because he's "just a dog" — perhaps you should reconsider bringing a dog into your life right now. Dogs deserve proper care and a comfortable existence just like you do.

The Size of Love: Standards versus Minis

A Dachshund decision you need to consider is what size will work best for you. Dachshunds come in two sizes — Standard and Miniature — according to the official breed standard published by the American Kennel Club and the Canadian Kennel

Club. Although the AKC doesn't officially consider the two sizes as separate classifications, the sizes are divided by weight for the purpose of competition:

> Miniatures are 11 pounds and under at 12 months of age and older; Standards are over 11 pounds, usually falling between 16 and 32 pounds.

Unofficially, many people call Dachshunds between 11 and 16 pounds *tweenies,* because they're between the two preferred Dachshund sizes. Tweenies may not be preferable in the show ring, but they're just as good as the larger Standards and the smaller Miniatures as pets. Some pet owners even prefer the medium size.

In Europe, Dachshunds officially fall into three sizes: Standard, Miniature, and Rabbit. These sizes are determined not by weight, but by chest circumference. Rabbits are what Americans would consider the smallest Miniatures.

What size suits your fancy? Maybe you've seen only Standard Dachshunds, or you like a sturdier dog. Maybe your heart melts at the sight of a Mini pup, and you can't wait to hold one in the palm of your hand. Maybe you aren't sure. No matter what, Dachshunds are a surprisingly sturdy dog and tend to believe they're much bigger than they are. Here are some general considerations:

- ✔ If you live in an apartment or a house without a fenced-in yard, a Miniature Dachshund may be best for you. Smaller dogs can fulfill much of their exercise needs inside the house.

- ✔ Minis may need more help with stairs and ledges because every jump is bigger for them than for a Standard, and they're just as prone to disk disease.

- ✔ If you like the idea of participating in outdoor activities with your Dachshund — things like hiking or long walks, for example — you may want to consider a Standard. I'm not saying Minis can't go on walks. On the contrary, they have a lot of energy and love to exercise. They may not be able to keep up with your fast strides, however. Remember how short their legs are!

The size matter is largely a personal one. Some people just like smaller or larger dogs — although Standards can hardly be considered large, even at their biggest and most roly-poly. Whatever size you choose, a Dachshund is a Dachshund — challenging and fun, full of mischief, and brimming with love for you (yes, even when he tips over that trash can). A Dachshund wants only your care, loving authority, and devoted attention in return.

Are You Ready to Be Owned by a Dachsie?

I can almost hear you: "Yes, yes, I'm ready to own a Dachshund! Sure, Dachshunds have minds of their own, but I can handle one. How tough could it be with a dog that short?" Ah, but Napoleon was short, too. Take the following quiz to make sure you're truly prepared and ready to be owned by a Dachshund; I'll address the answers afterward:

1. **Dachshunds believe they should**

    A. Guard the house.

    B. Rule the house.

2. **A Dachshund loves to please you**

    A. No matter what.

    B. When you're holding a doggy treat.

3. **Dachshund training sessions should be**

    A. Fastidiously structured.

    B. Cleverly disguised as playtime.

4. **When your Dachshund really, really wants that (third) oatmeal cookie, you should**

    A. Just give it to him.

    B. Close your eyes tightly, take a deep breath, try not to think about that cute little cocked head, and just say no.

5. **Dachshunds are obedient**

    A. After you've trained them.

    B. When the spirit moves them.

6. **When it comes to crowds, Dachshunds**

    A. Are a little shy and would rather blend.

    B. Love to be the center of attention and will do just about anything for applause (even if it's naughty).

7. **When it comes to the power of destruction, a Dachshund**

    A. Doesn't do much damage after the initial teething stages.

    B. Can rival a Labrador Retriever in his ability to dismantle a sofa.

8. Dachshunds often keep their noses to the ground because

   A. They're surveying their environment through scent.

   B. They're hoping beyond hope that they'll run across a piece of food.

9. If you don't allow your Dachshund on the furniture, he'll

   A. Never get on the furniture.

   B. Quickly learn to get off the furniture when he hears you coming.

10. To a Dachshund, a fence is

   A. A safe enclosure.

   B. Something to dig under.

11. To a Dachshund, the outside world is

   A. An intimidating place.

   B. His personal playground.

12. A Dachshund likes to perch in high places in the room because

   A. He doesn't want to get stepped on.

   B. He likes to survey his kingdom.

13. Dachshunds bark

   A. Only when a true threat is approaching.

   B. When anyone approaches — or just for fun.

14. To a Dachshund, any animal under 10 pounds is

   A. Not worth noticing.

   B. Absolutely worth chasing (hamsters beware!).

15. Dachshunds love

   A. People.

   B. Kids.

   C. Other Dachshunds.

   D. Other dogs.

   E. The occasional cat.

   F. All the above

DACHSIE MOXIE

Body of a hot dog; eye of a tiger

Dachshunds are big fans of adults (although not necessarily strangers), well-behaved children, other Dachshunds, and often other dogs. A Dachshund may even befriend the family cat. Everything else, however, is quite literally "fair game." Neighborhood cats, rabbits, squirrels, birds, field mice, hamsters, and other small animals look like prey to your Dachshund. And being bred to hunt, a Dachshund *will* pursue.

Count up all your responses. If you answered mostly As, you may not be ready for a Dachshund. Your ideas of what a dog should be and do may be better fulfilled with another breed. Of course, to grasp that special Dachshund mode of thinking, you may just need to give this book a once-through and then try the quiz again. Converts abound.

If you answered mostly Bs, you're already talkin' Dachsie. You already know, or can guess at, what life will be like with a Dachshund in the house. Challenging? Yes. Fun? Oh, yes. Easy? Oh, no! But as long as you know what you're getting into and are ready to trade in the easy parts for some great fun, you may be just the kind of companion a Dachshund needs.

And as for Number 15: Although the answer is F (all the above), *you* will be tops on your Dachshund's list.

Chapter 2

Defining the Dashing Dachshund

In This Chapter

▶ Understanding why Dachshunds look like they do

▶ Reviewing the Dachsie body

▶ Exploring the AKC's breed standard

*Y*ou know one when you see one. You can easily describe one. But can you actually define what a Dachshund is? If you read this chapter, you'll be able to do just that.

The definition of a breed can mean several things. For example, it can mean the *breed standard,* which is (and this is a mouthful) a description of the nonexistent, ideal specimen of a particular breed, against which actual dogs of the breed are measured for the purposes of improving the breed through breeding programs and for judging the conformation of dogs in dog shows. The definition can also mean, simply, the qualities that make a breed unique. I cover both definitions throughout this chapter.

Hey, Who Stretched Out My Dog?

If you ask anyone on the street to describe a Dachshund, chances are you'll get some version of "those long dogs," "those wiener-shaped dogs," or "those short, stretched-out dogs." Most people know Dachshunds have unusually short legs and unusually long bodies (see Figure 2-1). But why on earth would anyone try to "make" a dog like that?

Dachshund-shaped dogs are nothing new. Some historians claim that the Dachshund shape existed 4,000+ years ago in ancient Egypt. But the Dachshunds people know and love today were developed primarily for one purpose: to hunt. The following sections take you through the Dachshund's shape and how a Dachshund is meant to use that unusual body.

Figure 2-1: Short legs and a long body: That's a dachshund.

Photo courtesy of Ronald Globus.

The right stuff for hunting

Although they share many features (and plenty of ancestors) with the Basset Hound, Dachshunds certainly are unique. Lighter, smaller, finer-boned, and quicker than their Basset cousins (although some sources say that, originally, the Dachshund was the larger of the two breeds), Dachshunds can fit into places a Basset can't, and they usually can move with greater agility.

Dachshunds also have a keen scenting ability, facilitated by their low stance and long ears. But it's the Dachshund personality that's even more highly prized. Their energy, eagerness, and Terrier-like feistiness in the pursuit of small game have historically distinguished Dachshunds as excellent hunting companions.

Why Dachshunds have long bodies

The Dachshund's long body is unusual but useful for its original purpose: hunting. Dachshunds had to be large enough to contend with badgers and other game that could put up a fierce counterattack. On the other hand, Dachshunds had to be low to the ground and compact to be able to follow the badger into its burrow without getting stuck. The Dachshund's long, slender body was the perfect solution. Adding length gave the dog more power and weight while maintaining its low height.

DACHSIE MOXIE

How breeds are "made"

All purebred dogs are made, to some extent. A tiny Chihuahua and a giant Tibetan Mastiff are both variations on the same theme, created by humans through selective breeding to serve a specific purpose. Dachshunds, too, were designed to serve a specific purpose: to follow a badger, or other burrowing game, into its tunnel and flush it out or bark to alert an accompanying human of its whereabouts. German hunters probably crossed short-legged, long-bodied French hounds like Basset Hounds and Beagles with Terriers that liked to dig underground and chase vermin, although nobody knows for sure. We do know they developed Miniature Dachshunds during the 1800s by crossing in smaller dogs and breeding the smallest Dachshunds together, specifically for hunting purposes, too. The Mini's tiny body could fit into even smaller holes in pursuit of small game. Of course, the Minis also made (and still make) charming lap dogs, too.

At first, the Dachshund's long body may seem more of an impediment to agile movement, but Dachshunds are surprisingly lithe and light-footed. Their spines are flexible (although they don't respond well to sudden movements, hard jolts, or twists — see Chapter 17). And although Dachshunds are a fairly deep-chested breed, their bodies are perfect for wriggling. If you have a Dachshund at home, you've probably already seen this wriggling as your Dachshund slyly makes her way to the foot of your bed underneath the covers.

Why Dachshunds have short legs

Another distinguishing feature of the Dachshund is its short legs. Dachshunds have short legs to best fit into badger dens and burrows of other small game. But Dachshunds have been used for all sorts of hunting, not just burrowing, and its characteristically short legs serve the Dachshund well in several ways:

✔ Short legs allow a Dachshund to move quickly through dense brush and into spaces that, even though above ground, would be tight fits for a taller dog. In fact, Dachshunds have been used to flush out wild boar, because after the boar is on the loose, the Dachshunds can hide, protected, under the dense underbrush.

✔ Underground, the Dachshund's short legs allow her to maneuver well in a burrow. If the game being pursued turns to attack, short legs allow the Dachshund to back up.

✔ The Dachshund's compact legs serve as powerful excavators. Dachshunds can dig out anything and dig into or out of anywhere.

✔ A Dachshund's short legs keep her closer to the ground and enhance her ability to catch and follow a scent

Dachshund Anatomy 101

Although the Dachshund's unusual form makes it an ideal hunting dog, and many Dachsies are still used for this purpose (see the previous section), the Dachshund's more common role today is one of companion, friend, and resident court jester. But the Dachshund's unusual shape is worth understanding even if you don't plan to hunt a day in your life. Knowing your Dachsie's anatomy will help you understand her health needs and prevent or prepare for potential problems.

Talking dog anatomy means using plenty of terms that many folks may not be familiar with, so Figure 2-2 shows a boy Dachshund with all his parts labeled. And following is a list — a mini Dachs-tionary — that defines the anatomical terms shown in the figure.

This Dachs-tionary comes in mighty handy when you're reading the section "Evaluating the Perfect Dachsie."

- ✔ **Cheek:** The fleshy area behind the corners of a Dachshund's mouth.

- ✔ **Muzzle:** The part of the dog's head in front of the eyes, including the nose and jaws.

- ✔ **Stop:** The place where the muzzle meets the skull.

- ✔ **Skull:** The head bone, of course.

- ✔ **Crest:** The back of the skull where it begins its descent.

- ✔ **Neck:** The area attaching the head to the shoulders and upper chest.

- ✔ **Withers:** The highest point of the dog's shoulder blades, used to measure a Dachshund's height.

- ✔ **Back:** The top of the dog, from withers to tail.

- ✔ **Loin:** The section of the dog between the ribs and hipbones.

- ✔ **Rump:** The area above the hipbones, in front of the base of the tail.

- ✔ **Hock:** The joint on the rear legs between the second thigh and the *metatarsus* (the area between the heel and toes, or *rear pastern*), corresponding to the human heel. In a Dachshund, this joint sticks out from behind.

- ✔ **Toes:** The digits at the ends of the paws.

- ✔ **Stifle:** The dog's knee — the first leg joint between the thigh and what's called the second thigh (see "Hock").

✔ **Elbow:** The joint between the front arm and forearm.

✔ **Forearm:** The lower part of the front leg, between the elbow and wrist. In a Dachshund, the forearm should be relatively straight but comfortably shaped around the chest.

✔ **Dewclaw:** A functionless fifth toe, which is often — but not necessarily — removed.

✔ **Pastern:** The area of the foot between the wrist and the toes.

✔ **Wrist:** The joint between the forearm and the toes.

✔ **Shoulder:** The top end of the front legs, connecting the legs to the body.

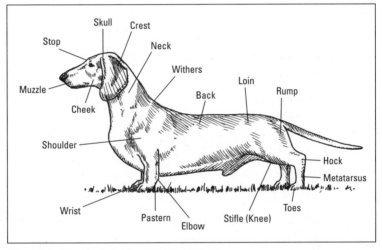

Figure 2-2: The Dachsie's anatomy in all its glory.

Evaluating the Perfect Dachsie

The American Kennel Club publishes a standard for the Dachshund that was developed by the Dachshund Club of America, Inc. (DCA), and that defines and describes — in great detail — the *ideal* Dachshund. Every so often, this standard has been updated to further improve the breed. The most recent revision officially took effect in March 2007, the first change to the standard since 1992.

Of course, what's ideal for one person may not be ideal for all people. But the breed standard has a specific purpose for all Dachsie lovers:

✔ The standard is designed to guide breeders in their pursuits so that they don't bring puppies into the world with faults (some with serious consequences, and others with mostly cosmetic faults). The standard can further the good health and good looks of the Dachshund breed.

✔ The standard serves as a guide for dog-show judges, who are judging, in essence, the work of the breeders. Judges in dog shows measure each Dachshund they see against an imaginary perfect Dachshund, and the dogs that come closest to the ideal do the best in competitions. (Chapter 15 goes into greater detail about competitions your Dachshund could enter.)

✔ Some aspects of the breed standard detail important qualities that happen to be particularly relevant for pet owners. For instance, the breed standard says that a Dachshund should appear "neither crippled, awkward, nor cramped in his capacity for movement" and that his temperament should be "clever, lively, and courageous . . .". In other words, a sound body and mind make for a wonderful pet as well as a technically correct Dachshund.

That said, some people do like to know that their dogs are as close to perfect as possible. And, because it never hurts to understand the ideal for your breed, this section goes over the AKC breed standard for the Dachshund in detail. The standard is largely based around qualities that ensure good health and the betterment of the breed (the goals of any good breeder). For more on all the characteristics of a Dachshund, jump over to Chapter 3.

Don't be too critical of your beloved pet if she doesn't fit the breed standard very well. Who cares if your Dachshund's eyes aren't perfectly "almond-shaped and dark-rimmed," if your smooth Dachshund's coat is a little too thick, or if your Standard Dachshund is the biggest one you've ever seen; she can still be the most perfect pet you've ever had. Plenty of love, attention, and care — coupled with proper management and training — are the things that make a good pet, *not* the perfect coat texture or profile.

Reviewing the AKC's official breed standard

The AKC's official Dachshund breed standard was approved on January 9, 2007, and became effective on March 1, 2007. Here it is, divided into a few specific categories.

✔ **General Appearance:** Low to ground, long in body and short of leg with robust muscular development. The skin is elastic and pliable without excessive wrinkling. Appearing neither crippled, awkward, nor cramped in her capacity for movement, the Dachshund is well balanced with bold and confident head carriage and intelligent, alert facial expression. Her hunting spirit, good nose, loud tongue, and distinctive build make her well suited for below-ground work and for beating the bush. Her keen nose gives her an advantage over most other breeds for trailing. ***Note:*** Inasmuch as the Dachshund is a hunting dog, scars from honorable wounds shall not be considered a fault.

✔ **Size, Proportion, Substance:** Bred and shown in two sizes, Standard and Miniature, Miniatures aren't a separate classification but compete in a class division for "11 pounds and under at 12 months of age and older." Weight of the Standard size is usually between 16 and 32 pounds.

✔ **Head:** Viewed from above or from the side, the head tapers uniformly to the tip of the nose. The eyes are of medium size, almond-shaped, and dark-rimmed, with an energetic, pleasant expression; not piercing; and very dark in color. The bridge bones over the eyes are strongly prominent. Wall eyes, except in the case of dappled dogs (see the following section), are a serious fault. The ears are set near the top of the head, not too far forward; of moderate length, rounded; not narrow, pointed, or folded. Their carriage, when animated, is with the forward edge just touching the cheek so that the ears frame the face. The skull is slightly arched, neither too broad nor too narrow, and slopes gradually with little perceptible stop into the finely formed, slightly arched muzzle, giving a Roman appearance. Lips are tightly stretched, well covering the lower jaw. Nostrils well open. Jaws opening wide and hinged well back of the eyes, with strongly developed bones and teeth.

✔ **Teeth:** Powerful canine teeth; teeth fit closely together in a *scissors bite*. An *even bite* is a minor fault. Any other deviation is a serious fault.

Different breeds have different bites. In other words, their upper and lower jaws and teeth meet in different ways. In many breeds, including Dachshunds, a scissors bite is the preferred bite. In this bite, the outside of the lower teeth touches the inner side of the upper teeth when the dog's mouth is closed. In an even bite, also called a *level bite,* the top and bottom teeth meet with no overlapping.

✔ **Neck:** Long, muscular clean-cut, without dewlap, slightly arched in the nape, flowing gracefully into the shoulders without creating the impression of a right angle.

The *dewlap* is the name for loose, pendulous skin that hangs down from a dog's throat and neck. Dachshunds shouldn't have one.

✔ **Trunk:** Long and fully muscled. When viewed in profile, the back lies in the straightest possible line between the withers and the short, very slightly arched loin. A body that hangs loosely between the shoulders is a serious fault.

✔ **Abdomen:** Slightly drawn up.

✔ **Forequarters:** For effective underground work, the front must be strong, deep, long, and cleanly muscled.

✔ **Forequarters in detail, Chest:** The breastbone is strongly prominent in front so that on either side a depression or dimple appears. When viewed from the front, the thorax appears oval and extends downward to the mid-point of the forearm. The enclosing structure of the well-sprung ribs appears full and oval to allow, by its ample capacity, complete development of heart and lungs. The keel merges gradually into the line of the abdomen and extends well beyond the front legs. Viewed in profile, the lowest point of the breast line is covered by the front leg.

The *keel* is the outline of the lower chest (in profile), stretching from the top of the breastbone to the bottom of the ribs.

✔ **Forequarters in detail, Shoulder Blades:** Long, broad, well laid-back and firmly placed upon the fully developed thorax; closely fitted at the withers; furnished with hard yet pliable muscles.

✔ **Forequarters in detail, Upper Arm:** Ideally the same length as the shoulder blade and at right angles to the latter; strong of bone and hard of muscle; lying close to the ribs, with elbows close to the body, yet capable of free movement.

✔ **Forequarters in detail, Forearm:** Short in stature; supplied with hard yet pliable muscles on the front and outside, with tightly stretched tendons on the inside at the back, slightly curved inward. The joints between the forearms and the feet (wrists) are closer together than the shoulder joints, so that the front doesn't appear absolutely straight. The inclined shoulder blades, upper arms, and curved forearms form parentheses that enclose the ribcage, creating the correct "wraparound front." Knuckling over is a disqualifying fault.

Knuckling over refers to a faulty wrist joint that flexes forward when a dog stands. Knuckling over is a serious fault in Dachshunds. It weakens what should be strong front legs and disqualifies any Dachshund from the show ring.

✔ **Forequarters in detail, Feet:** Front paws are full, tight, compact, with well-arched toes and tough, thick pads. They may be equally inclined a trifle outward. There are five toes — four in use — close together with a pronounced arch and strong, short nails. Front dewclaws may be removed.

- ✔ **Hindquarters:** Strong and cleanly muscled. The pelvis, the thigh, the second thigh, and the rear pastern are ideally the same length and give the appearance of a series of right angles. From the rear, the thighs are strong and powerful. The legs turn neither in nor out.

- ✔ **Hindquarters in detail, Rear Pasterns:** Short and strong, perpendicular to the second thigh bone. When viewed from behind, they're upright and parallel.

- ✔ **Hindquarters in detail, Feet/Hind Paws:** Smaller than the front paws, with four compactly closed and arched toes with tough, thick pads. The entire foot points straight ahead and is balanced equally on the ball and not merely on the toes. Rear dewclaws should be removed.

- ✔ **Hindquarters in detail, Croup:** Long rounded and full, sinking slightly toward the tail.

  The *croup* is the entire pelvic girdle region.

- ✔ **Hindquarters in detail, Tail:** Set in continuation of the spine, extending without kinks, twists, or pronounced curvature; not carried too gaily.

- ✔ **Gait:** Fluid and smooth. Forelegs reach well forward, without much lift, in unison with the driving action of the hind legs. The correct shoulder assembly and well-fitted elbows allow the long, free stride in front. Viewed from the front, the legs don't move in exact parallel planes, but incline slightly inward. Hind legs drive on a line with the forelegs, with the hock joints and rear pasterns turning neither in nor out. The propulsion of the hind leg depends on the dog's ability to carry the hind leg to complete extension.

  Viewed in profile, the forward reach of the hind leg equals the rear extension. The thrust of correct movement is seen when the rear pads are clearly exposed during rear extension. Rear feet don't reach upward toward the abdomen and there is no appearance of walking on the rear pasterns. Feet must travel parallel to the line of motion with no tendency to swing out, cross over, or interfere with each other. Short, choppy movement, rolling or high-stepping gait, and close or overly wide coming or going are incorrect.

  The Dachshund must have agility, freedom of movement, and endurance to do the work for which she was developed.

- ✔ **Temperament:** The Dachshund is clever, lively, and courageous to the point of rashness, persevering in above- and below-ground work, with all the senses well developed. Any display of shyness is a serious fault.

The most important things to worry about with a Dachshund are temperament and health. Buying a Dachshund from a breeder can be a good move, because good breeders breed that classic friendly, funny, brave Dachshund temperament. They also want dogs that are sound and free of health problems. For the average pet owner, those are the really important priorities.

Brushing over special characteristics of the coat varieties

The Dachshund is bred with three varieties of coat — smooth, wire-haired, and longhaired — and is shown in two sizes — Standard and Miniature. All three varieties and both sizes must conform to the characteristics specified in the previous section. The features in the following sections are applicable for each variety.

Smooth Dachshunds

Here are the defining characteristics of the smooth Dachshund:

Coat: Short, smooth and shining. Should be neither too long nor too thick. Ears not leathery.

Tail: Gradually tapered to a point; not too richly haired. Long, sleek bristles on the underside are considered a patch of strong-growing hair, not a fault. A brush tail is a fault, as is a partly or wholly hairless tail.

A *brush tail* is a tail that's bushy and heavy with hair. Dachshunds shouldn't have one.

Color of hair: Although base color is immaterial, certain patterns and basic colors predominate. One-colored Dachshunds include red and cream, with or without a shading of interspersed dark hairs. A small amount of white on the chest is acceptable, but not desirable.

Nose and nails: Black.

Two-colored Dachshunds

The two-colored smooth coat variety includes black, chocolate, wild boar, gray (blue), and fawn (Isabella). Each has deep, rich tan or cream markings over the eyes, on the sides of the jaw and underlip, on the inner edge of the ear, front, breast, inside and behind the front legs, on the paws and around the anus, and from the anus to about one-third to one-half the length of the tail on the underside. Undue prominence or extreme lightness of tan markings is undesirable. A small amount of white on the chest is acceptable, but not desirable.

Colors voted *out*

Double-dappled Dachshunds are dappled Dachshunds with an additional sprinkling of pure white patches. This used to be an allowed pattern in the breed standard, but unusual and interesting as they may appear, double dapples are associated with multiple health problems. In 2007, the Dachshund Club of America voted to remove the double-dappled pattern from the standard.

Piebald Dachshunds are white with large spots of any color; this color pattern also isn't allowed in the breed standard. The Dachshund Club of America voted to add it in 2007, but the motion failed, with 316 votes for and 431 against.

Dachshund colors, such as red or black, are easy to picture, but other colors are less well known. *Wild boar* is more common on wirehaired Dachshunds but can also occur on smooths. It refers to a black or dark outer coat over a lighter-colored undercoat. *Isabella* is a fancy word for a fawn color. Some two-color Dachshunds are fawn with tan markings, called *Isabella and tan.*

The nose and nails for two-colored dachshunds are as follows: in the case of black dogs, the two are black; for chocolate and all other colors, dark brown, but self-colored is acceptable.

Dappled Dachshunds

The dapple (*merle*) pattern is expressed as lighter-colored areas contrasting with the darker base color, which may be any acceptable color. Neither the light nor the dark color should predominate. The nose and nails are the same as for one- and two-colored Dachshunds. Partial or wholly blue (wall) eyes are as acceptable as dark eyes. A large area of white on the chest of a dapple is permissible.

Brindle is a pattern (as opposed to a color) in which black or dark stripes occur over the entire body, although in some specimens the pattern may be visible only in the tan points.

The sable pattern consists of a uniform dark overlay on red dogs. The overlay hairs are double-pigmented, with the tip of each hair much darker than the base color. The pattern usually displays a widow's peak on the head. The nose, nails, and eye rims are black. Eyes are dark — the darker the better.

Wirehaired Dachshunds

Here are the defining characteristics of the wirehair Dachshund:

Coat: With the exception of the jaw, eyebrows, and ears, the whole body is covered with a uniform tight, short, thick, rough, hard, outer coat, but with finer, somewhat softer, shorter hairs (undercoat) distributed between the coarser hairs. The absence of an undercoat is a fault. The distinctive facial furnishings include a beard and eyebrows. On the ears, the hair is shorter than on the body, almost smooth.

The general arrangement of the hair is such that the wirehaired Dachshund, when viewed from a distance, resembles the smooth. Any sort of soft hair in the outer coat, wherever found on the body — especially on the top of the head — is a fault. The same is true of long, curly, or wavy hair, or hair that sticks out irregularly in all directions.

Tail: Robust, thickly haired, gradually tapering to a point. A flag tail is a fault.

A *flag tail* is a relatively long tail carried high, with feathering on it. Dachshunds shouldn't have one.

Color of hair: Although the most common colors are wild boar, black and tan, and various shades of red, all colors and patterns listed in the smooth hair section are admissible. Wild boar appears as banding of the individual hairs and imparts an overall grizzled effect, which is most often seen on wirehaired Dachshunds but may also appear on other coats. Tan points may or may not be evident. Variations include red boar and chocolate-and-tan boar.

A small amount of white on the chest, although acceptable, isn't desirable.

Nose and nails: Same as for the smooth variety in most cases. Nose, nails, and eye rims are black on wild-boar and red-boar Dachshunds. On chocolate-and-tan-boar Dachshunds, nose, nails, eye rims, and eyes are self-colored — the darker the better.

Longhaired Dachshunds

Here are the defining characteristics of the longhaired Dachshund:

Coat: The sleek, glistening, often slightly wavy hair is longer under the neck and on the forechest, the underside of the body, the ears, and behind the legs. The coat gives the dog an elegant appearance. Short hair on the ear isn't desirable. Too profuse a coat — which masks type — equally long hair over the whole body, a curly coat, and a pronounced parting on the back are all faults.

Tail: Carried gracefully in prolongation of the spine; the hair attains its greatest length here and forms a veritable flag.

Color of hair: Same as for the smooth Dachshund variety.

Nose and nails: Same as for the smooth variety.

Chapter 3

The Long and Short of Dachshund Varieties

*O*ne of the great things about bringing home a Dachshund is that you have so many options: Big or small; longhaired, short-haired, or wirehaired; and plenty of colors to choose from, too. Do you want a boy or a girl? A puppy or an older dog? You have some important choices ahead of you, and you need to think about some issues and weigh some options before you can choose the Dachsie that best suits your life. This chapter will help you consider your options. I also help shed some light on which Dachshund differences don't really make any, well, difference, as well as those options that can make all the difference in the world.

The bottom line when choosing your new family member? All the cosmetic considerations don't really matter that much (assuming you aren't planning on breeding/showing your dog). *Health and temperament, health and temperament, health and temperament* are what matter. Make that your mantra as you visit breeders and meet puppies and their parents (see Chapter 4). The best dogs have two healthy parents — better yet, four healthy grandparents as well. They're raised in a family home by a breeder who makes an effort to socialize them. They're given proper medical care from the beginning of their lives and are bred to exhibit the classic Dachshund personality: fun, funny, feisty, fearless, and fantastic (see Chapter 2). Need I say more?

Size Matters (Or Does It?)

When it comes to Dachshunds, size does matter — at least in some ways. By North American standards, Dachshunds come in two sizes: Standard and Miniature, as shown in Figure 3-1. Dachshunds that fall right in between the Miniature and Standard weights are unofficially called *tweenies* by some. Sizes are divided according to weight, not height.

By European standards, Dachshunds come in three sizes: Standard, Miniature, and Rabbit; the Rabbits, the smallest size, are approximately equivalent to a Miniature Dachshund, and sizes are distinguished by chest circumference rather than weight.

Figure 3-1: A Standard and a Miniature Dachshund, in their model poses.

But what difference does size really make? It depends. Standards and Minis were bred differently, and their personalities and needs, although similar, aren't interchangeable. Also, one size may fit your lifestyle better than another.

The following sections run down the differences between micro- and macro-wiener dogs (and those that fall somewhere in between). But before you dive into the details, take a minute to answer some questions to get a feel for which Dachshund size may best suit you.

Determining your size match before you get the details

Answering the following questions may help you decide which type of size to focus on in your search for a new pup:

1. **When you imagine yourself bonding with your new Dachshund puppy, what qualities do you picture yourself treasuring most?**

    A. Energy, playfulness, and the Romp Factor.

    B. The clowning, the hilarity of the big watchdog in a little package, and, of course, the Cute-as-a-Button Factor.

    C. The combination of independent thinker and devoted companion.

2. **The quality you're least looking forward to dealing with in your new Dachshund is**

    A. Shedding — you can't stand the thought of dog hair everywhere.

    B. Barking — shrill noises really get to you.

    C. Housetraining — yuck. There's nothing worse than cleaning up a dog mess.

3. **The other members of your family include**

    A. Kids under 5.

    B. One other adult.

    C. Another dog and/or a cat.

4. **You live**

    A. On a farm.

    B. In an apartment.

    C. In a house with a fenced backyard.

5. **Your activity level is**

    A. Pretty high. You like to go on walks, and you like to keep moving. You wonder, "Can Dachshunds catch a Frisbee?"

    B. Pretty low. You're housebound or can't move too quickly, for whatever reason. Or maybe you just don't like to move more than you have to!

    C. About average. You plan to walk your dog every day, but you're no athlete.

6. **Your house has**

    A. Plenty of high places — high couches, steep stairs, high beds, and so on.

B. Plenty of low and level places — futon beds and couches, for example, but no stairs.

C. Some high places and some low places, but the high places and steep stairs can be modified if necessary with ramps or some obstacles.

7. **You worry most about**

A. The costs associated with your Dachshund. You're willing to do what it takes, but you wonder, "How much is this going to run me, anyway?" (Check out Chapter 8 for some common Dachsie expenses.)

B. Accidentally injuring your Dachshund. "They look so delicate."

C. Training your Dachshund. You've heard the breed is pretty darned stubborn.

8. **Above all, you're looking for**

A. A playmate that can really play. "No wimpy, sissy dogs for me!"

B. A precious little lap dog to dote on and spoil.

C. A companion to be with you throughout your days and nights, sharing your life as much as possible.

Now, tally up how many As, Bs, and Cs you have. If you have mostly As, a Standard is probably the dog for you. Mostly Bs? Consider a Miniature. If your tally is heavy on the Cs, it probably doesn't matter what size you choose. Any size, including tweenies, will work for you, because you're just glad to have a Dachshund, period.

But each of the preceding questions brings up some specific issues, so you need to look closely at each size, one at a time. Pay particular attention to the size that interests you the most, according to the quiz. If size truly doesn't matter to you, read all three of the following sections to prepare for any type of dog may you end up with.

In general, your preference for a Standard or a Mini is largely a matter of personal taste, but if you aren't sure, visit several breeders and meet plenty of Dachsies. One size or the other will probably capture your heart.

If your main concern is to have a dog with the classic Dachshund personality — an independent and devoted Dachsie, a clown, a chow hound, a dog that's full of mischief and love — it really doesn't matter which size you choose. All sizes reflect the classic Dachshund personality. But other issues beyond personality may concern you. Read on to discover how other factors may impact your decision.

Kids and Dachshunds

Kids and Dachshunds are made for each other — especially when the Dachshund is the more durable Standard size (Miniature Dachshunds can be too small and fragile for very young children). Encourage your children to take an active part in the care, socialization, and training of your Dachshund. Draw up a feeding schedule and let your kids measure out or prepare the dog food. Make walks a family affair. Look for local puppy- or dog-training courses for kids. If your child is a natural, he or she can even compete as a junior handler in a dog show. (Contact your local dog club or the AKC for info on how to become a junior handler. Chapter 19 contains the AKC's contact info.)

The Standard Dachshund

Standards are bigger and more boisterous than Miniatures; they can keep up with you on a walk a little more easily; and they can probably run farther and play harder than most Minis, too. That's not to say that Minis aren't little balls of Dachshund dynamite. But the larger size of the Standard (although keep in mind that even Standards aren't all that big compared to, say, a Labrador Retriever) may be better suited for a very active lifestyle.

You need to consider a few things with a Standard Dachshund:

- ✔ Because they're bigger, Standards will leave more dog hair on the furniture, although having a Standard Dachshund around is nothing like having a large dog when it comes to shedding. A daily brush-through helps a lot (for more on grooming, see Chapter 16).

- ✔ Standards typically are great with other dogs and with kids, although all children should learn how to treat a dog and should be instructed in the proper way to pick up a Dachshund. This is important in order to avoid causing a back injury (see Chapter 17).

- ✔ Standards need more room to exercise than Minis. Standards do best with a daily walk or two and some time to romp in a fenced backyard — and I mean fenced *well.* "Earth dog" isn't a misnomer when it comes to Dachsies. They love to dig and dig and dig, and the bigger, stronger Standards are most efficient at burrowing their way out of a yard that you thought was secure (although many Minis excel at digging, too).

- ✔ Standards cost more to feed than Minis because they're larger, but still, a 30-pound dog doesn't eat too much (see Chapter 8).

The Miniature Dachshund

All Dachshunds are clowns, but there's something particularly hilarious about the antics of the Miniature Dachshund. Of course, that may depend on your sense of humor. Small-dog aficionados are particularly charmed by the Mini's attitude, obstinacy, independence, and over-confident, rapid-fire barks. And, of course, if you love small dogs, a Mini Dachshund really is as cute as they come.

Love cats? Miniature Dachshunds make great cat companions — as long as you introduce the two carefully and give each pet its space until they accept each other. Some people with successful cat-Dachshund households claim that it helps if the Dachshund is second on the scene. If the cat has the home-field advantage, the Dachshund puppy is more likely to afford his new feline housemate the respect she deserves.

Not everyone is fond of Minis, however. Although their personalities are essentially the same as the Standard's, a few differences exist. Here are some unique Mini characteristics:

✔ Minis bark, and their bark can be shrill (particularly the long-haired Minis). If you've had Toy dogs in the past, you know that many of them like to bark. Perhaps they compensate in volume for what they lack in size. Perhaps they want to make sure that you see them. Whatever the reason, if you really, really hate barking, you may be better off with a Standard (although all Dachshunds like to bark, really).

✔ If you have young children, you're probably better off with a Standard. Children under 5 (some breeders even say under age 10) usually aren't able to understand how to properly treat a dog, and a very small dog can get injured if it's dropped, fallen on, or pushed.

Likewise, Minis like to be the center of attention and don't take kindly to poking, prodding, and pulling. Small dogs can injure a small child if they lose patience and decide to snap at those curious fingers (or that inquisitive face). Parents should never leave dogs and small children together unsupervised.

Miniature Dachshund puppies are very small, and although they can act pretty feisty, they're much more fragile than a Standard-sized puppy. If you have a Mini puppy around, watch where you step, watch where you sit, and always put the puppy firmly onto the ground after holding him. Letting him jump out of your arms can result in a back injury or even a broken leg. It has happened.

✔ The Miniature Dachshund's size makes it particularly suited to life in an apartment or a small house. When paper-trained, a Mini Dachshund doesn't necessarily even need to go outside at all, which is an advantage for people who are housebound or who live somewhere that makes forays outdoors inconvenient (such as in a high rise). Minis get plenty of exercise dashing around the house, so you don't need to feel guilty if you can't quite muster a daily walk.

A big thing to consider if you have a Mini is the layout of your home. If you have a lot of stairs, be prepared to cart your Mini up and down. Too much stair walking, especially if the risers are steep, can be dangerous for your Mini's back. Stairs are no picnic for a Standard Dachsie, either, but the back strain is less severe. You should also try to keep your Mini from jumping down off tall beds, chairs, and couches. Consider ramps made for dogs.

✔ If cost is a concern, Minis cost less to feed, and vet bills may be lower because the Mini's small size requires less medication.

Do I have a tweeny?

You may want to consider what some breeders and fanciers are calling *tweenies* — especially if you like a smaller dog but are intimidated by the very small size of a Mini. Tweenies don't exactly fit into the breed standard for show dogs (see Chapter 2). They aren't big enough to be Standards or small enough to be Minis. But as a pet, the tweeny is a wonderful size — not too heavy, not too fragile.

Pick a Coat, Any Coat

Dachshunds come in three coat varieties: smooth, longhaired, and wirehaired, as shown in Figure 3-2. Coat type makes a difference. Each type has different grooming needs and subtle differences in personality. You may have picked which coat you like best at first glance, but read this section to make sure that you're prepared for the necessary responsibilities.

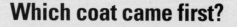

Which coat came first?

Some historical accounts claim that the smooth Dachshund was the original version, with the longhaired developing later and the wirehaired developing later still. Other accounts put the development of the smooth, longhaired, and wirehaired at about the same time. In any case, all three coats are well established now and breeders tend to specialize instead of interbreeding the coat types.

Figure 3-2: The many coats of the Dachshund.

Smooth Dachshunds

The smooth Dachshund is the quintessential Dachshund. If you say *Dachshund*, the smooth is what most people picture. The sleek, shiny coat best shows off the Dachshund's form, and grooming takes little effort — an occasional brush along with regular nail clipping and teeth scrubbing (see Chapter 16.)

When it comes to personality, the smooth is similarly representative. Breeders like to describe the smooth as the most consistent personality type, and many agree that the smooth is the most Dachshund-like. Incomparable to any other breed, the smooth-coated Dachsie *is* the Dachshund incarnate.

Smooths are perfect for people who don't have the time or patience for grooming, who love the stereotypical Dachshund look, and who simply prefer a sleek, short coat. Smooths do shed but don't noticeably drop their coats to grow in new ones (like the longhairs do). Daily grooming sessions may seem like overkill on your smooth.

Here's a trick to add some serious sheen to your smooth Dachshund's coat: After brushing, rub a drop or two of baby oil in your palms and then smooth the oil over your Dachshund's coat. *Gorgeous!*

Longhaired Dachshunds

If you like to groom, or you don't mind it and think it's worth the time to have a dog with a lovely, silky, flowing coat, a longhaired Dachshund may be the dog for you. Longhairs are beautiful, and a longhaired Dachshund puppy is totally adorable. But keeping a longhaired Dachshund requires a significant grooming commitment. That gorgeous coat will soon become a mess of tangles and mats if left unattended. And if your dog likes to romp outside, his coat will pick up leaves, sticks, burrs, and, yes, ticks (see Chapter 16).

During your daily brushing — a requirement — you may feel that you're constantly picking out tangles, but keeping up the task is essential. A matted coat can result in skin problems, a more difficult time with parasite control, and a dog with an unkempt and sorry appearance. If you aren't prepared for the commitment, please don't invest in a longhair. Some Dachshund owners find the daily grooming session to be a joy.

Longhairs are notoriously sweet, gentle creatures that love to spend time with their owners. Yours may revel in the attention he gets from you as you brush, comb, and tend to his personal beauty routine. Grooming sessions are a great opportunity for you to bond with your Dachshund, and you'll feel good about keeping your dog looking so lovely.

Longhairs were probably developed by blending the Dachshund with the Cocker Spaniel, and the longhaired Dachsie has something of the Spaniel about him. Crazy for the hunt, the longhair has the endurance of a Spaniel in the field. But he's also crazy for your attention and loves to cuddle — some people say he's the mellowest of the Dachshunds. Longhairs like nothing better than to have you stroke that long, luxurious coat. You may sometimes wonder if yours has Velcro under all that hair, because he practically sticks to you!

The longhaired Dachshund's hair isn't naturally the same length all over. The longest hair grows on the Dachshund's underside — on the throat and chest — as well as on the ears and behind the legs. You should groom a longhair to accentuate the areas where his hair is long, smooth, silky, and flowing. However, the longhair should never look messy; his coat should lie smooth and flat instead of appearing curly or in any way inelegant.

Wirehaired Dachshunds

If you like Terriers, you'll love the wirehaired Dachshund. Influenced by various Terrier stock, the wirehair takes the Terrier characteristics of the Dachshund to the max. Although all Dachsies make great earth dogs (see Chapter 15), who better to maneuver through the bracken than a dog with a wiry coat that's impervious to wind, rain, burrs, and brush? Add to that the wirehair's feisty spirit and a bark that can cow any small creature into submission, and you have a mighty hunter — not to mention a pet that will keep you laughing.

Wirehairs shed the least of the three coats, but they require a fairly extensive grooming regimen several times a year. Their coats must be *stripped* — a process in which the loose, dead undercoat is plucked out to make room for new growth. Some people like to strip themselves, but others would rather pay groomers. Wirehairs have a distinctive look. They're typically groomed to keep their eyebrows and beard long. The rest of the coat stays short.

Wirehairs have a distinctive personality. You want to see energy? Obstinacy? Hilarity? Wirehairs have it all. They're little extremists — always on the go, always vocalizing their opinions, and always ready for a game of catch or a romp around the yard. They're plenty cuddly, too, so don't be surprised to find your wirehair under the covers at your feet when you retire for the night.

Choosing from a Rainbow of Color and Pattern Options

Color and pattern are subjects of some controversy among Dachshund lovers, but they probably matter the least in terms of choosing your pet. You like red? Black and tan? Cream? Brindle? Fine. If you find a dog in the color you like, great. Color and pattern don't influence personality, so the choice is purely aesthetic.

Dachshunds can come in just about any color typical of dogs and can also come in several different patterns — and any color can occur in any pattern. Wirehairs tend to come in fewer colors, with one of the more common being a color called *wild boar,* which means that the shorter undercoat is lighter and that the longer outer coat is black.

Color and pattern *are* two different things, though. For the sake of clarity, check out the following sections for a description of the colors and patterns that most often occur in Dachshunds.

Spinning the Dachsie color wheel

Dachshunds come in many different colors and color combinations. (The more typical colors are usually more successful in the show ring; see Chapter 15). Here's the color scoop:

- **Red (from strawberry blonde to deep chestnut):** Some shades of red look pretty much like brown, but Dachshund people still call these dogs red.

- **Wheaten:** This is really just a very light red.

- **Cream:** Cream Dachshunds can range from gold to almost white.

- **Wild boar:** This is a double color common on wirehaired Dachshunds. The shorter, softer undercoat is lighter in color, and the longer, dense, wiry outer coat is black.

- **Sable:** Similar to the wild boar coat, the sable coat is marked like a black and tan, but up close you can see that under the black base coat is a layer of red. In some dogs, the tan points on the face are so exaggerated that they appear to form a mask around the eyes or a widow's peak on the forehead.

- **Black and tan:** This common color combination is found on many dogs — from Rottweilers and Dobermans to Chihuahuas. The Dachshund is black with tan points.

- **Chocolate and tan:** This combo is just like black and tan, but the base color is a chocolate-brown color.

- **Isabella and tan:** A grayish beige or rosy fawn color with tan points.

Noticing a marked difference: The patterns

From solid to dappled to brindled, Dachshund markings or patterns have no influence on a dog's personality — only his appearance.

Pick what you like or don't worry about it at all. The subtleties are only relevant to breeders and dog-show judges. Here are the many patterns a Dachshund can wear with pride:

- ✔ **Solid:** A solid color is really an absence of markings rather than a marking itself. Solid means the whole dog is one color. The most common solid color is red, followed by wheaten and cream.

- ✔ **Solid with points:** Black, chocolate, fawn, and Isabella dogs commonly have tan points on their eyebrows, chin, feet, and tail.

- ✔ **Dappled:** *Dappling,* also called *merling,* is a pattern in which random, ragged patches of a lighter color (not white) occur over a darker color. Any color can have dappling on it, and the dappled patches typically are lighter shades of the base color.

   Dapples come in many colors. Black and tan-dappled Dachsies are dappled with gray. Reds are dappled with lighter red. Chocolates are dappled with cream. Isabella and tan-dappled Dachsies are dappled with a lighter silver-gray. The double-dappled dog has white patches in addition to the colored dappling. In the extreme, these dogs are called *piebald* and have very large patches of white (usually considered undesirable).

- ✔ **Brindled:** *Brindling* is a striped pattern. The stripes typically are thin and somewhat ragged, not clear and sharp like a tiger's.

Male or Female? The Battle of the Sexes

Another consideration when choosing your new Dachsie friend is whether you want a boy or a girl. In some breeds, gender seems to make a difference. You hear that the boys are sweeter and more affectionate, or that the girls are gentler and better with kids — or that either gender is more standoffish, yippy, aggressive, or independent.

Some breeders describe Dachshunds as *bitch-dominant* (and they don't even giggle when they say it). That means the females sometimes are more independent or seem less needy than the males (something common in many smaller breeds, I've found). But others claim that any differences in personality are related to individual dogs, not to gender.

Generally in Dachshunds, both sexes are equally sweet, equally stubborn, and equally devoted. Females cost more to spay than males cost to neuter, but this is a one-time expense and probably shouldn't figure much into your decision. Also, a neutered boy isn't likely to spray or wander, and a spayed female isn't likely to have a weight problem, despite what you may have heard or read.

Your best bet is to find a healthy, well-bred litter and then see which puppy you feel a connection with. Or, better yet, let the puppy pick you, with the breeder's guidance. (The breeder can also help you find a puppy whose temperament best matches your lifestyle.) Boy or girl really doesn't matter. The match between you and the puppy is the most important thing, and either sex may be best suited for you.

Although gender doesn't affect personality significantly, it becomes more of a factor when you bring home two Dachshunds. Unneutered males and unspayed females may not get along well with the same sex, but they may get along perfectly with a dog of the opposite sex. Of course, that means you risk the chance of becoming a breeder without meaning to. But you are going to neuter or spay your dog or dogs anyway, right? Don't delay! (See Chapter 16 for more on the procedure.)

Chapter 4

May the Best Breeder Win: Finding the Dachshund for You

In This Chapter

▶ Taking action to find the right breeder for you

▶ Distinguishing the good breeders from the not-so-good

▶ Understanding why you need a contract

▶ Choosing your pup from the breeder's litter

▶ Developing a relationship with your breeder of choice

▶ Considering buying from a pet shop

*R*eady to go hunting? Whoa there, put away that orange vest! This kind of hunting is all about locating the very best Dachshund breeder you can find. Because Dachshunds are popular, they're pretty easy to find — but a quality breeder is a different story. Unfortunately, for-profit breeders often churn out dogs with quantity in mind rather than quality, resulting in pets with health and/or temperament issues.

The good news is, great Dachshund breeders also abound, *if* you know where to look. A good Dachshund breeder is absolutely crazy for his or her beloved breed and is working in whatever way possible to ensure that Dachshunds get better and better with each new generation — in health, looks, and temperament. How do you know the good breeder from the not-so-good breeder? Well, that's what this chapter is all about. (If you're more interested in rescuing a Dachshund from a shelter or rescue group, skip to Chapter 5.)

The point of this chapter is to help you remember that just seeing an adorable Mini Dachshund for sale doesn't mean your search is over. You have some more work to do, and this work is important. It's time to track down the right Dachshund for *you* — and that hunt starts with the right breeder.

Finding the Right Breeder

So how do you find a breeder who loves Dachshunds and devotes his or her life to making Dachshunds stronger, healthier, and more beautiful? You do a little research, and you ask for help. Many local and national Dachshund clubs will be happy to provide you with referrals to breeders they've found acceptable. For instance, you can contact the Dachshund Club of America (DCA), which is a great resource for Dachshund information and of reputable member breeders who have signed a strict code of ethics about breeding practices. Check out its Web site at www.dachshund-dca.org and click on Breeders/Puppies, or you can go straight to its list of breeder referral coordinators by state at www.dachshund-dca.org/breederreferral.html. Also, check out www.dachshund-dca.org/clubs.html for a list of local branches of the national club. A branch in your area may be able to give you the most relevant information.

Another great way to find a breeder is by visiting a dog show (see Chapter 15). Dog shows bring many breeders to one place for your browsing convenience. Ask around and see what names you hear over and over. What kennel names have a great reputation? What breeder seems to be great in your area? Dog shows are full of people who probably have some pretty strong opinions about who the best breeders are. Be friendly and ask questions (but wait until the breeders or handlers are done showing and have a minute to relax). You can also ask breeders at a dog show any Dachshund questions you may have — from inquiring about the suggested price of a healthy pet to the best diet for a Miniature. But beware: You may get bitten by the bug and want to buy a champion and start showing!

In other words, you want to go where the Dachshund people go. You'll get the low-down.

You may think a "fancy" show breeder will charge a paw and a tail for a good Dachshund, but think again! Pet stores typically charge at least as much or more for their purebred dogs, and you won't be able to get much after-care advice, let alone see the parents or talk to the breeder about breeding priorities. And when you buy a dog from the newspaper or online, you may find a cheaper price, but how much support are you going to get? What kind of guarantee will you get? What happens if something is wrong with the dog? Will the breeder you find really know what he or she is doing? A hobby breeder who shows his or her dogs will definitely be your best investment and the most likely source of a healthy, happy Dachshund.

Visiting potential breeders

After you obtain some breeder names through your research, you can start talking to breeders and evaluating their breeding programs. Visit *several* kennels (even if you think you've found your dream Dachsie at the very first place you visit). Ask questions (see the following section for some possibilities). Look at the puppies, the parents, and the surroundings. Watch how the puppies interact with each other and how they behave toward you and the breeder. You can learn a lot about a breeder just by paying attention.

The following list presents a few red flags to watch for when visiting a breeder:

- The puppies shy away from the breeder.
- The adult dogs other than the mother don't seem approachable, or they act nervous.
- The surroundings are very dirty.
- The breeder avoids certain questions or refuses to let you see the parents of a litter.
- The breeder is eager to have you take home a Standard Dachshund puppy younger than 8 weeks or a Miniature Dachshund puppy younger than 12 weeks.
- The dogs look too thin or sickly, have bare spots in their coats, or have bloated bellies.

If you notice any of the red flags in the previous list, keep looking for better breeders. You may feel sorry for those poor puppies, but buying one just supports bad breeding, and you'll likely be in for a lot of expense and heartaches. The wait to find a really good breeder is worth it.

Some breeders aren't worth your time, no matter how cute the puppies are. If a breeder tells you one thing on the phone (or at a dog show or other meeting) but you find that the opposite is true when you visit; if the terms of a sale change when the breeder learns more about you (perhaps the dog suddenly becomes more expensive when the breeder sees your sports car, or the dog you want suddenly isn't available but a smaller, sicklier-looking pup is conveniently on sale); or if you get any kind of bad feeling about the situation, trust your intuition and move on. No matter how fetching and/or bargain-priced the puppies are, dealing with a disreputable or irresponsible breeder isn't worth it.

Good breeders, on the other hand, aren't out to make a profit. A "high" price on a Dachshund from a good breeder only seems high to someone on the outside. A good breeder probably just barely covers expenses, and many don't even do that. Plus, most breeders find that setting higher prices helps to screen out impulse purchases and people who aren't really committed to pet ownership.

Putting a breeder checklist to use

You need to ask a potential breeder plenty of questions, and a good breeder will ask you plenty of questions, too. But what do you ask in order to figure out whether he or she is breeding responsibly and producing healthy, happy, well-adjusted puppies? You don't have to be a pet detective. Just bring along this checklist to every kennel and dog show you visit, and don't be afraid to ask the breeders you meet every question. You can learn a lot from their answers *and* from what they don't — or won't — tell you. Here are some things to ask:

- ✔ **What do I need to know about Dachshunds in general and about your Dachshunds in particular?** You've probably done plenty of research by this point (or will if you continue with this book!), but you still want to know what the breeder has to tell you about the breed. Listen for a couple of things:

  - Does the breeder seem very knowledgeable about Dachshunds, or does he or she tell you only very general things you already know?

  - Does the breeder only tell you the good side of the breed, or does he or she let you know about the challenging aspects of Dachshund ownership?

  - Can the breeder give you a good idea about the specific dogs and lines of his or her kennel? What are the strengths and weaknesses of his or her particular dogs?

- ✔ **How long have you been breeding Dachshunds?** Find out how the breeder got started. If the breeder has been in it for decades, you've probably found somebody established and very knowledgeable. A breeder new to the game may also have great intentions and be producing great pups. But plenty of people try breeding and give it up quickly, so a breeder who has stood the test of time may be a better bet.

✔ **How often do you breed?** A breeder in it for 20 years who has bred only a handful of litters won't have "20 years of experience." On the other hand, a breeder in the business for only a few years who has already bred 100 litters probably is going for profit, not quality; chances are, the dogs he or she produces aren't kept in very good conditions. Your best bet: an experienced hobby breeder who breeds one or two litters every year or two.

✔ **What's your philosophy of dog breeding?** Asking this question gives you a little insight into what the breeder is all about. No breeder will say, "Oh, well, you know, I'm just in it for the cold, hard cash," But responses that sound ill-informed, vague, or don't have anything to do with health and temperament — or no response to a question at all — should raise red flags. Breeders who seem passionate about improving the health of the breed and enhancing the Dachshund's friendly and agreeable temperament — who say things like, "All my dogs would make great pets because, to me, *pet quality* means the highest possible quality" — are probably sources for excellent pets.

✔ **Have any of your dogs suffered from canine intervertebral disk disease? What are the chances my dog will get it?** Disk disease is a serious issue for Dachshunds, and you need to get the straight poop. (Also check out Chapter 17 for more on the issue.) If a breeder answers that yes, he or she has had dogs with disk disease, that's no reason to run. In fact, that means the breeder is being honest. Although some breeders are able to keep their lines largely free of this disease, the condition is so common in Dachshunds that most breeders who have been in the business for a long period of time have experienced it. Look for a breeder who's straightforward about disk disease. Honesty is much more important than waiting for a breeder to tell you, "In 35 years, none of my Dachshunds have ever had back problems." Chances are, if you hear that, you aren't getting the whole truth.

Breeders shouldn't breed Dachshunds that experience canine intervertebral disk disease. Sounds like a clear-cut rule. However, because disk problems typically don't manifest themselves until the average age of 4 years, and because no test can determine which dogs will suffer from it, Dachshunds are sometimes bred and then later develop back problems through no fault of the breeder.

✔ **May I call your veterinarian for a reference?** A breeder who won't give you the number of his or her vet either doesn't want you to know something or doesn't visit the vet very often. Both are bad signs. Better to have a breeder who takes puppies and dogs to the vet often than to have a breeder whose dogs are "so healthy they don't need a vet." All dogs need periodic, regular vet visits, and good breeders make sure they get them.

When you get the vet's contact information, call the vet and ask about the health and temperament of that breeder's dogs. The vet has no personal stake in whether the breeder sells a puppy, so assuming that the vet is a good one, you should get an unbiased review.

✔ **What kind of health guarantee do you offer?** Good breeders require that new owners take their puppies to the vet right away — usually within three to seven days, and more often within a day or two. If the veterinarian finds a serious health problem, the breeder should be willing to refund your money or replace the puppy. Of course, you may not want to give up your puppy, and you may be willing to do whatever it takes to get your puppy through whatever health crisis has arisen. But the breeder should make amends if you so desire. Get an agreement in writing.

✔ **What vaccinations does the puppy have already, and what will I need to do in terms of future health care?** The breeder should've given his or her puppies at least one set of standard vaccinations and should give you a schedule of vaccinations to be administered by your vet. Also, be sure to get the name and number of the breeder's vet so that your vet can call to find out what has been given so far.

Puppies need vaccinations, but overvaccinating isn't good for a puppy. If a 7- or 8-week-old puppy has already had three rounds of vaccines, that's too much; the breeder may be using vaccines to try to cover up poor health.

✔ **I plan to keep this puppy forever. If something comes up, however, that makes it impossible for me to keep the puppy in the future, will you take it back?** Not all breeders will do so, but many will because they care about their puppies finding and remaining in good homes. That doesn't mean you'll get a refund ten years later, and you shouldn't expect it. But most good breeders who truly love their Dachsies will want them back rather than have them end up in shelters or rescue programs.

Of course, you do plan to keep your puppy forever, don't you? A commitment on your part is as necessary as a good health guarantee. A breeder will be looking for signs that you'll be a responsible and committed puppy owner, not somebody looking for future opportunities to get rid of a canine inconvenience.

✔ **When can I take the puppy home?** Most good breeders won't let you take a puppy home until it's at least 8 weeks old; most Miniature breeders prefer to wait until at least 12 weeks. Those 6-week-old puppies in the pet store are simply too young, especially for a small dog. Between the 9th and 12th weeks, puppies learn to interact with their littermates; during this time, they build a healthy foundation for future interaction with other dogs. This development may even facilitate future socialization efforts on your part.

In addition to the benefits of sticking by their littermates, puppies get important nutritional benefits from nursing longer. Reserve your puppy, put down a deposit, and wait it out.

✔ **What sizes are your dogs?** Because Miniature Dachshunds are popular, some less-reputable breeders try to pass off tweenies, or small Standards, as Miniatures. Technically, a Miniature is a dog that weighs 11 pounds or less at 1 year of age. Because you're probably buying a puppy, you can't know for certain that your dog will grow up to be a true Miniature. However, experienced breeders can usually tell whether a puppy is going to be a true Miniature. (For more on dog sizes, see Chapter 3.)

The best way to tell that your puppy will be a true Miniature is to see *both* parents. Ask to have them weighed in front of you. If both are true Minis, chances are good that your puppy will be, too — especially if the puppy's pedigree has many champions. Champions in your puppy's pedigree means the line is probably breeding true, and your puppy will be more likely to look like its parents.

✔ **May I see some of your other dogs?** A breeder should be proud to show you his or her dogs. Look for good health and friendly temperament. The dogs should be approachable and easygoing. The breeder should be able to take any of the adult dogs out on a lead, and you should be able to go up to a dog and pet it without the dog displaying any growling, shying away, or nipping. These are serious signs of temperament problems in healthy adult dogs.

One important exception: A part of the breed standard says that the Dachshund should be bold to the point of brashness. This characteristic makes new mothers pretty protective, so if the mother of the litter you like doesn't seem to want you to get within six feet of her precious babies, don't be alarmed. That's just nature in action.

DACHSIE MOXIE

There's no dog like a show dog

Think you're buying a show Dachshund? Technically, if a breeder sells you a "show dog," he or she is guaranteeing that your dog won't have any disqualifying faults (see Chapters 2 and 15). But Dachshunds don't have many disqualifying faults. In fact, they have just one: The front legs shouldn't knuckle over. Now, a show dog with potential to win a championship is something else. If you want a show dog with winning potential, you need to do a little more research on what constitutes a winning Dachshund. Talk to your breeder and consider apprenticing with someone who's experienced with dog shows before choosing your potential champion.

TIP

Don't be too quick to ask about cost just yet. Just as you don't want to buy a puppy from someone breeding only for profit, a breeder doesn't want to sell to somebody just looking for the cheapest thing on four legs. When you determine that you're working with a good breeder, you can start talking dollars and cents. Dachshund prices can vary by geographical region, as well as by how closely a Dachshund pup fits the breed standard (see Chapter 2). Expect to pay between $400 and $800 for a well-bred pet.

Wait a minute . . . the breeder isn't through with you yet. Don't think that you'll be doing all the interviewing! A good breeder should screen you just as carefully as you screen him or her. Expect to be asked where you plan to keep your dog, why you want a dog, and if you can afford a dog. And get ready for a lecture on the responsibilities of pet ownership. A buyer who has done research and is open to instruction, and who truly seems to bond with a puppy, will look like a good prospect to a breeder.

Getting the Real Scoop on Contracts

Any lawyer would cringe if you buy an $800 dog without a contract; however, not all breeders use contracts. Breeders get a sense about buyers, and vice versa, and if everyone feels good about the purchase of a pet, both parties may feel a contract is an unnecessary formality. I admit that I've bought expensive things without a contract — I even leased a house without one (don't tell my lawyer). And perhaps you don't want to bother with the legal mumbo jumbo. But a lot of people don't make purchases or sell dogs without contracts in place, and that's sensible. However, contracts protect both you and the breeder and can simplify matters if any issues come up later — like a health issue, a bounced check, or any other dispute. Sure, contracts can be broken, but if they're legal and well-written, you have recourse if you suffer a loss.

The contract should state, in very specific terms, what will happen if something goes wrong and what kinds of matters the buyer or breeder must take responsibility for. For instance, the contract could state that if your dog is injured while in your care, the breeder isn't responsible; however, if the dog gets sick with something like parvovirus that she contracted under the care of the breeder, or if she has a serious genetic problem, the breeder is responsible.

The contract should also mention the following:

- ✔ **If something goes wrong, the responsible party should have a specified amount of time to correct the problem.** This setup prevents either you or the breeder from rushing to sue the moment something happens to someone's dissatisfaction.

- ✔ **What laws will apply.** If you and the breeder live in different states, the contract should specify which state has jurisdiction should a conflict arise.

- ✔ **What constitutes correction of the problem.** Will you get your money back? Will you get a replacement puppy? Will the choice be up to you? If you want to keep the dog and pay to have a genetic problem corrected or an illness treated, will the breeder help you with the costs?

In general, asking for a contract isn't a sign that you don't trust someone, and no good breeder should be offended if you ask for one. Most probably already have contracts they always use.

Picking the Best Puppy for You

When you pick a breeder, develop a relationship, and set the terms of the purchase from your chosen breeder, all you have left to do is pick a puppy. But how do you know which one to pick? Dachshund puppies are all so cute (see Figure 4-1). Is one as good as the next?

Yes and no. All the puppies up for sale in a well-bred litter probably will make great pets. In some cases, however, the temperament and tendencies of a particular puppy will turn out to be best suited to you. Who knows the litter best? The breeder, of course.

Figure 4-1: Which of these puppies is the pick of the litter?

The breeder can be an invaluable resource in helping you pick the puppy that will best match you and your situation. Good breeders get to know their puppies as they care for them, socialize them, and teach them the ropes of life in a human world. The breeder should know which puppies tend to be more boisterous, which are quieter, which love to fetch, which seem fond of cats, and which seem to adore kids. Let your breeder help you pick based on your needs, situation, and desires.

Of course, you may focus on one particular puppy and just know that she's the one. Or perhaps the puppy will choose you! You can't argue with chemistry. If you bond with a particular pup, and she seems healthy and well-bred and the breeder agrees that the match would be a good one, go for it. You've found your friend for life.

Wondering how to spot a healthy Dachshund puppy? Look for the following characteristics:

- ✔ A healthy coat with no bald patches
- ✔ Bright, shiny eyes that don't run
- ✔ Clean, white, sharp puppy teeth
- ✔ Clean ears that are free of parasites
- ✔ A clean rear end with no encrusted feces
- ✔ Free and easy movement with no limping
- ✔ A healthy display of energy and curiosity

Tempted by that shy or incredibly sleepy puppy — the one that's smaller than all the rest? You may be able to nurse the little one back to boisterous health, but excessive fatigue, lack of energy, extra-small size, or unusual shyness may be a sign that your puppy isn't thriving. You may be asking for heartbreak. Let the breeder handle that puppy and choose a healthy one instead.

Forming a Good Bond with a Dachsie Breeder

Finding a good breeder is like finding gold in the creek bed (okay, it's probably easier than that). Not only do you benefit right now, but you and your Dachshund benefit for the rest of your lives — if you play your cards right, invest in your breeder, and proceed wisely. When you find a good Dachshund breeder, forge a partnership. Good breeders should be happy to provide you with all the information you need, and most are excited to continue the relationship. If a problem comes up, the breeder can guide you. If your dog gets sick or develops a problem, the breeder can tell you what course of action to take. And most breeders just love getting holiday cards with photos so they can see how their little puppies have grown up!

I'm not saying that you should harass your breeder with constant questions. Breeders have lives — usually pretty busy ones. Because responsible dog breeding isn't a profit-making venture, most breeders are in it purely for the love of Dachshunds, so they have to hold regular jobs, too. They may have families, take their dogs to dog shows on weekends, and have a tough time getting a full night's rest when they have litters of puppies in their homes. Your breeder won't have time to talk to you on the phone every day, nursing you through your Dachshund's puppyhood trials and tribulations. That's why doing your research (like reading this book!) and becoming fully prepared for the responsibility of puppy ownership is so important.

But the breeder you choose *does* need to know about health problems that arise — especially genetic ones that could influence his or her breeding program. The breeder can help you out, and you can help out the breeder, too, by keeping in touch and sharing information about your Dachshund's health and behavior.

The following tips can help you maintain a good relationship with your Dachshund's breeder — ensuring that you, the breeder, and, most importantly, your Dachshund receive the maximum benefit of your commitment:

- ✔ **Don't call the breeder early in the morning or late at night.** That's just rude!

- ✔ **When you call, be polite, not demanding.** Express your awareness that you're taking up the breeder's time instead of taking the attitude that the breeder is there to serve you.

- ✔ **Don't mistake the breeder for your vet.** If the problem involves pain, bleeding, broken bones, or drastic changes in habits, appetite, activity level, or behavior, please call your vet first — and fast.

- ✔ **Don't assume that the breeder is at fault for a medical problem.** An accusatory tone puts a person on the defensive. Simply explain what's going on and get some feedback.

Make sure, *before* you buy, that you have in place a health guarantee that makes arrangements for what will happen in the event of a health problem. (See the section "Getting the Real Scoop on Contracts".)

- ✔ **Recognize that your breeder loved your puppy first and helped to bring it into the world.** The breeder is more family than business associate.

How Much Is That Dachsie in the Window?

I don't generally recommend buying a Dachshund from a pet store for many reasons:

- ✔ You usually can't see the puppy's parents.

- ✔ You can't visit the breeder's breeding facility.

- ✔ You can't ask the breeder questions.

- ✔ Most pet store employees don't know much about individual dog breeds.

- ✔ Pet store puppies often are taken away from their mothers and siblings earlier than most breeders and canine behaviorists recommend.

- ✔ The price to purchase from a pet store usually is significantly higher.

The problem with not being able to see the dog's parents, the breeding facility where it was born, or even the breeder is that you can't get a sense as to whether the adorable little Dachshund was socialized at all, raised in healthy conditions, or bred to minimize health problems (like disk disease). That Dachsie in the window may turn out to be a wonderful pet, but your odds for securing a pet with good health and temperament are better if you buy from a breeder.

However, if you simply can't resist that Dachshund puppy at the pet store (you're only human, after all), and you're willing to pay more money for a dog that comes with less background information, take a few very important precautions. You won't be able to tell everything about a dog from looking — not even a vet can do that. Health problems like disk disease may not become evident for several years. The following list presents some advice if you insist on buying a pet store puppy:

- **Try to get background information.** Your pet store puppy probably won't have parents on the premises, but the store should have a written record of the shots and wormings the puppy has already had. Don't expect to learn much about the puppy's temperament from the pet store, however. The puppy probably hasn't been in the store very long, and pet store employees usually aren't trained to determine things like temperament.

- **Give the puppy a once-over.** Is the coat clean and shiny? Are the puppy's eyes, ears, nose, and rectum clean? Does the puppy act happy and energetic? Red flags include small bald spots; "hot spots" (red, itchy places); dry, scaly patches; runny or crusty eyes or nose; dirty ears; a dirty rectum; and tired, slow, low-energy behavior. The puppy could be napping, of course, so come back later in the day to see if the puppy perks up and shows interest in you.

- **Get a guarantee in writing.** Most pet stores will guarantee their puppies for a certain amount of time, but that time period often is pretty short (a day or two or a week or two). Take the puppy to your vet immediately after purchase with the (written) understanding that, should the vet determine the puppy is in ill-health, you can bring it back for a full refund. If you know and accept exactly where the pet store's responsibility begins and ends in terms of a health guarantee, you won't run into misunderstandings later.

- **Make a commitment.** A pet store puppy, like any other puppy, may suffer from health problems later on. The dog will need plenty of socialization, attention, and training. Please make the commitment to care for your Dachshund and give it the training and love it deserves

Chapter 5

Rescue Me! Adopting a Dachshund

*I*n Chapter 4, I talk about purchasing your new dog from a breeder. As I state there, good breeders are great. But as you probably already know, buying a Dachshund puppy from a breeder isn't your only option. Many Dachshunds are waiting patiently for new homes in breed rescue programs, in animal shelters, and with families who can't keep them any longer. Many of these dogs are wonderful, devoted, well-trained family members who got the short end of the bone for one reason or another and no longer have a place to go. Common reasons why Dachshunds sometimes lose their homes are divorce, a death in the family, a move to a place that doesn't allow dogs, or an owner who simply can't handle the responsibility. This chapter points you in their direction.

On the other hand, some dogs are in rescue programs or shelters because their owners made mistakes in training and/or socialization, bought badly bred dogs, or just ignored their dogs until they became too much trouble. Sad as these scenarios may be, some of these dogs may not be reformable, and attempting to train and socialize any dog that grew up learning bad habits can be tough. Are you up to the task? This chapter helps you find out.

DACHSIE MOXIE

A rescue program's reason for being

According to the DCA's rescue program, Dachshund rescue is active around the country and was established

"... to aid Dachshund owners in the recovery of their animals when lost, strayed or stolen; to keep Dachshunds out of the hands of laboratories, animal dealers, puppy mills and similar enterprises, and to attempt to keep Dachshunds out of pounds and animal shelters. Sadly, Rescue is most used to place the hundreds of Dachshunds that have been abandoned each year and find homes that will provide the love and care these dogs deserve."

Help out a rescue program if you can; and if you can't, please don't make the problem worse by abandoning a dog you've promised to keep.

Making a Friend for Life

Adopting a Dachshund can be one of the most rewarding things you can ever do as a pet owner. People who've adopted often claim that their dogs seem eternally and exuberantly grateful throughout their entire lives. Will the dog know what you've done for him? Maybe not in so many words, but a dog who has lost his home and then finds one with you will probably be as devoted a dog as you'll find.

Of course, not every rescued or shelter dog comes pretrained, presocialized, and ready to accept a new home and owner without question. Some dogs were abused and/or neglected. Some weren't well-trained or socialized in the first place. Some may be sick or have health problems of some kind. Some were badly bred. Some, unfortunately, won't ever make good pets because they have too many strikes against them.

But many rescued Dachshunds turn out to be wonderful, loving pets. Some don't have any behavior issues at all, and others may need only a little extra TLC to regain that delightful Dachshund demeanor. If you feel like you need or want to provide a home for a Dachshund in need, that's wonderful. And even if you aren't sure, it doesn't hurt to look. Chances are, the Dachshund you'll find in the animal shelter or with a rescue group will make a great pet. Even if you "know" you want a Dachshund puppy from a great breeder, you may consider visiting an animal shelter and/or calling your local Dachshund rescue organization just to see what's out there. (You can find rescue information on the Dachshund Club of America Web site at www.dachshund-dca.org/rescue.html.)

Most rescued or shelter Dachshunds are a little older, and there are distinct advantages to adopting an older dog. Older dogs may already be housetrained, they may be used to kids and other pets, and they may even know a trick or two. Many of these dogs are friendly, sweet, and well-behaved, and they need only a loving home to make their lives — and your life — complete. Maybe you can provide one!

The Pros and Cons of Adopting a Dachsie

Before you run out and sign the papers to adopt a rescued or shelter Dachshund, put some serious thought into it. Sure, it's a wonderful thing to do. However, you don't want to get into a situation where you'll regret the adoption or, even worse, have to give the dog back. You should consider the pros and cons of adopting a Dachshund, weighing them against your situation and inclinations before making a commitment. The very last thing a rescued or shelter Dachshund needs is to think he has a new home and then end up back in rescue or in the shelter again. Adopting a dog means being very committed to keeping that dog until the end of his life. Someone has already broken that commitment at least once, which is why the Dachshund is waiting for a home.

Table 5-1 lists some pros and cons involved in adopting a rescued or shelter Dachshund. Look over the list again and again. Listen to your heart and to your head. You may feel awfully sorry for that Dachshund, but if what you really, really want is a puppy from a breeder, everyone will be better off if you follow your heart.

Table 5-1 The Pros and Cons of an Adopted Dachsie

The Pros	*The Cons*
He may already be housetrained.	He may have been improperly house trained, and older dogs make bigger messes.
He may already be accustomed to family life; he may love kids and understand your routine.	He may never have been socialized and may be frightened of — or even aggressive toward — children or strangers.
He may be eternally devoted to you for taking him in.	He may have suffered so much in the past that he's not capable of bonding with you.

(continued)

Table 5-1 *(continued)*

The Pros	The Cons
He may already be trained to obey basic commands.	He may be more difficult to train, and you may need to hire a professional trainer or canine behavioral consultant.
He may come with plenty of good habits already in place.	He may come with plenty of bad habits already in place.
He'll cost less than a dog from a breeder.	He may not be as well bred as a Dachshund from a breeder, and he may suffer from health, conformation, or temperament problems.
He may turn out to be healthy, well-behaved, and the best pet you could ever dream of!	Your experience with him may be a nightmare of massive vet bills and training traumas — unless you and the rescue group do a thorough job of screening him first (and sometimes even then).

You may be thinking that Table 5-1 leaves a lot up in the air. How can you tell which way a dog will be? Housetrained or not? Well-socialized or not? Kid lover or not? Healthy or not? Will your Dachsie be a lifelong family companion like the one in Figure 5-1?

Fortunately, rescue organizations and many animal shelters carefully screen the Dachshunds they're attempting to place, so they usually can tell you what they've observed about the Dachshunds' behavior, temperament, and health status. Take advantage of the people who know and ask a lot of questions. Do what you can to show them that they'll be placing the dog with someone who won't bring him right back in a couple of days.

Rescue worker phone etiquette

If you contact a Dachshund rescue organization, please be considerate. These people usually work out of their homes, so find out what time zone an organization is in and don't call early in the morning or late at night. Many rescue people will have an answering service that allows you to leave your number, but be advised that they'll call you back collect. Don't be offended. Remember, these people aren't getting paid, and if they had to pay for every returned phone call, their phone bills would get pretty hefty. Give them a break and accept all collect calls while you're trying to acquire a new family member.

Photo courtesy of Gail Painter.

Figure 5-1: Will your adopted Dachsie be a kid lover like this one?

Adopting through a Rescue Organization

Your best bet to find an available Dachshund for adoption is to contact a local or regional Dachshund rescue organization (see the upcoming sidebar for some tips). These organizations are manned by people who work long hours, usually for no pay, purely for the love of Dachshunds — to find a good home for every Dachshund they believe would make a good pet. The job is stressful and often frustrating. It can also be supremely rewarding, however, when a wayward dog finally finds the perfect place to live.

Rescue groups aren't like animal shelters, which have dedicated facilities and a paid staff (see the following section). Most rescue groups consist of one or just a handful of dedicated volunteers who take in abandoned dogs and try to find them homes — often with the help of volunteer foster "parents."

Adopting through a rescue group is similar to adopting through a shelter. Every group is a little different, but in most cases, you'll have to fill out a detailed application and answer a lot of personal questions. The rescue workers want to be sure they're sending off their dogs to committed and quality homes. In many cases, the rescue workers will require a home visit to see where you'll keep the Dachshund and what your home environment is like. Full of wild little kids? No fence? Other large, aggressive dogs? Or is it a Dachshund heaven?

Adoption usually isn't a quick process but it should be a thorough one. If a rescue group wants to give you a dog without any questions, you should ask some questions of your own to make sure you and this dog are a good fit and the group has screened the dog for health and behavior problems. Costs vary widely but usually are designed to simply cover the costs the rescue group has incurred to take in, house, heal, and train the dog.

When you hook up with a Dachshund rescue organization, you're likely to find a fantastic network of Dachshund lovers eager to help you help the displaced Dachshunds of the world. And the cause can be compelling. You may find yourself deciding to be a Dachshund foster home or otherwise involved in Dachshund rescue. There are worse ways to spend your free time!

You can find rescue coordinators by state through the Dachshund Club of America's Web site. Check out www.dachshund-ca.org/ Rescue.html or head to www.petfinder.com, a clearinghouse of shelter and rescue groups that allows you to search by your location and the breed/age/gender you prefer.

Some rescued Dachshunds have been abused or neglected and may need some patient, kind, and positive retraining and behavior modification (see the chapters of Part III for advice). If you're determined not to give up on your rescued Dachshund (and I hope you are), be prepared to exercise supreme patience and exhibit plenty of affection. Also, consider hiring a canine behavioral consultant, an animal behaviorist, and/or a private trainer. A professional has experience with dogs that have been mistreated and can provide you with a variety of personalized approaches to solving your dog's particular problems. Worth every penny, I say!

Working with Animal Shelters

Even if you don't have a Dachshund rescue program in or near your town (see the previous section), you probably have an animal shelter. The main difference between adopting from a rescue group and from an animal shelter is that the rescue group often specializes in a particular breed. They may be better at screening for problems, and they may have more time to give. Many animal shelters, however, do an amazing job at screening potential pets, and many even have obedience training programs to help make the animals more adoptable. It all depends on where you live and what's available to you, but check out both options: rescue groups and animal shelters.

Sometimes, animal shelters shuttle any purebreds off to rescue groups. In other cases, they may have purebred dogs, including Dachshunds, right there in the shelters. Your local shelter may take your name and contact you if a Dachshund comes in. But don't be surprised or offended if it doesn't; shelter workers, like rescue workers, often are overworked and underpaid. Your best bet is to visit the shelter often and keep looking. (If nothing else, frequent shelter visits will probably convince you to have your future Dachshund spayed or neutered.)

Some animal shelters are the spectacular culminations of the efforts of many people who are seriously committed to helping place the animals they receive and to educating the public. Others are barely scraping by on tiny budgets and have a hard time handling the load of animals they receive.

Whatever the case in your area, be aware that adopting a shelter dog often involves a lot of paperwork. You probably can't just walk into the shelter and get one. Many shelters check out living situations by calling landlords to ensure that they allow dogs, for example. It may seem like a pain, but just remember that all the questions, forms, and red tape are for the protection of the pets. The shelter wants to feel confident that you won't bring the dog right back in a few weeks or months.

Stick to the books: No dogs for college kids

If you're a college student, you may be frustrated to find out that your local animal shelter won't let you adopt a dog under any circumstances. Is that fair? I mean, you just know you'd be a fantastic dog owner. Actually, although many college students would make great and committed dog owners, students are notorious for abandoning their animals when they graduate. So many shelters have been burdened by huge influxes of pets come graduation time that this policy is in place to safeguard the well-being of the pets. Don't be offended. Be glad the shelter is working in the overall best interest of its animals. You can always adopt a pet after you're settled into your post-school life.

A Dachshund for life

Wherever you get your Dachshund, after you get it, it should be yours for life. Dachshunds live a long time — often 12 to 16 years — and you should plan to keep your new friend through thick and thin, for better or for worse, unless it's absolutely impossible to do so. Dachshunds (and all dogs, for that matter) are living, breathing, sentient beings that form a relationship with their owners, depend on a regular routine, and look to humans for guidance, care, and affection. They feel pain, loss, and neglect if they're hurt, abandoned, or abused. If you take on the responsibility of a dog, take it on for life. And if you absolutely must give up your dog because of circumstances beyond your control, at least see that it finds a new home where it can receive the proper amount of care and love — and won't be given up again.

Also, a shelter may not have the time to screen individual dogs for temperament and health. Buyer beware, in other words. You may get a great dog, or you may get a short-legged, long-bodied bundle of trouble. Best to do your research, trust your intuition, and be prepared for a lot of work, rehabilitation, and retraining (see the chapters of Part III). Then, if you get a great pet, you'll be happily surprised.

Adopting a shelter dog is a wonderful — even noble — thing to do. So many dogs desperately need good homes, and most of them won't ever find one. And the dog isn't the only one who benefits. Many people with shelter dogs are devoted to the point of fanaticism to their rescued pets.

Adopting a shelter dog is a serious commitment, so please don't take it lightly. Just because a dog doesn't cost $500 or $1,000 or more doesn't mean it isn't as deserving of love, good medical care, and your time. Be ready for a nervous, scared, confused pet that needs a lot of patience, attention, and consistent and positive training. Work with your new friend, and you may just discover that you have a diamond in the rough.

Part II

Starting Out on the Right Paw at Home

"Naaah – he's not that smart. Last time he took the SAT, he forgot to bring an extra pencil, came up short in the math section, and drooled all over the test booklet."

In this part . . .

In Part II, you find out how to prepare your home, your-self, and your family for a fun-filled life with a Dachshund. I tell you how to Dachshund-proof your home and family (including the kids), what things to buy, and what to expect when you bring home your energetic friend for the first time.

Chapter 6

Making Your Home Dachshund-Proof

*I*f you have small children or small siblings, you probably know all about childproofing the house. You cover electrical outlets, put childproof latches on the bottom cabinets, stow all the cleaners and household chemicals out of reach, and put those covers over the doorknobs so the little ones don't open the door and go wandering away.

But how much consideration have you given to puppy-proofing? A new puppy can get into a lot of trouble if the house isn't puppy-proofed, and Dachshunds in particular — who joyfully gnaw through or swallow just about anything they can get their teeth around and who are too short to jump safely from great heights — are particularly in need of a safe, secure, Dachs-proofed household.

How do you Dachs-proof your home? First, you read this chapter. Then you get busy and make a few changes before you let that puppy loose in the house. It only takes a moment for a puppy to get in trouble when you aren't watching, so just as with a baby, better safe than sorry. The extra effort you spend to prepare your home for your newest Dachsie resident is well worth it for everyone.

Considering a Dachs-Eye View of Home

The world looks a lot different to a Dachshund than it does to you. Can you imagine walking around with your eye level less than a foot above the ground? No? Try it. In fact, the best thing to do before you change one single thing about your household in preparation for your new puppy is to get down on your belly and look around each room in your house. (You may want to vacuum first. You'll be sliding around on the floor!)

Find a piece of paper and a pen or pencil; then get on down there. That's it, get right down to the floor. *All* the way down. You're still too tall if you're on your hands and knees. All the way down on your belly.

Now take a good look around: This is a Dachs-eye view of the world.

Try to think like a Dachshund puppy. Get excited, a little nervous, and very, very curious. From your Dachshund vantage point, what do you see that looks like fun? Ooh, a dangling miniblind cord! Could be perfect for a game of tug of war. Look at that bottle cap under the couch! Feeling the urge to ferret it out and give it a good crunch? What about that nice display of China figurines, almost within reach? Maybe if you jumped. . . .

Make a note of everything you see that could possibly cause trouble for a small dog. Stay down there until you're sure that you've exhausted the possibilities. Read on for some things to look for while you're surveying. Then, after you're done, you may just feel the urge to curl up and take a nap. See any comfy pillows? A Dachshund-friendly house should have at least a few.

The danger of choke chains

I don't generally recommend *choke collars* (one end slips through a loop on the other end so the collar tightens when pulled) because I don't think they're necessary when positive training methods are employed. Miniature Dachshunds in particular can be injured by a choke collar, but these collars can be dangerous for any Dachshund because of their small size and delicate spines. Plus, a choke collar could get caught on something with disastrous results. I wouldn't risk it! A better option is the Gentle Leader, or Halti Collar. These effective training devices give you more control over the dog without having to jerk your little one around.

Preparing for Demolition Dog

So you think your sweet little dog couldn't make *too* much of a mess? You'd be surprised. Do you really love your collection of antique teacups or crystal vases? Then either display them well above the level any Dachshund can reach or put them away for a while. Puppies are exuberant and curious, and they haven't yet learned what areas are off limits to them (see Figure 6-1). It's not the puppy's fault if he jumps onto that end table to see just what's up there and breaks something valuable. Imagine that you have a toddler in the house and pack away the fragile stuff accordingly.

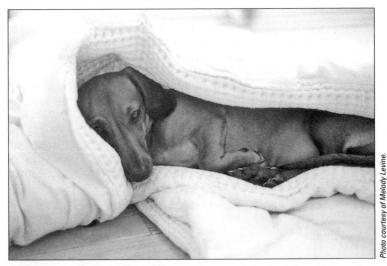

Photo courtesy of Melody Levine.

Figure 6-1: Dachshunds love to get into things, and that includes making a bed out of your favorite blanket.

Also, although a Dachshund is small, he has a pretty big mouth, and I don't just mean he barks a lot. He can also chew to the point of major destruction. *Really.* No two ways about it, Dachshunds love to chew. In fact, they not only love it, but they also consider it their dog-given right. Your Dachshund will consider anything that looks chewable to be his own personal property. So you thought that slipper was yours? Think again. As far as your new puppy is concerned, if he sees it and decides he wants to chew it, it's his.

The world is his chew toy

The best way to combat the loss of some of your more valuable pairs of shoes, not to mention your furniture, is to have a good supply of acceptable chew toys on hand. Stow them everywhere so one is always within reach. Look for sturdy chew toys without small parts that could break off. If you're consistent about enforcing the house rules, your new puppy will soon learn what is okay to chew and what isn't. Then, eventually, he'll develop enough self-control to stop himself from chewing that juicy-looking, brand-new sneaker.

Avoid giving your Dachshund cat toys, even if you have a Mini. Dachshunds are more enthusiastic chewers than cats and they have larger mouths and stronger jaws. Cat toys often have small pieces like bells, feathers, or felt that a Dachshund can easily swallow or choke on.

The best way to discourage this sort of destruction in the early stages is to offer a firm "No" when your Dachshund is in the process of chewing or clawing; then immediately redirect him to an acceptable but similar activity. For example, if your Dachsie is chewing your shoe, say "No!" and then take away the shoe, replacing it with a chew toy in his mouth. If he chews the chew toy, heap on the praise.

If you have a piece of furniture or other object that your Dachshund just won't leave alone, buy a bottle of chew-deterrent spray, like Bitter Apple brand spray, and follow the directions. This spray makes the object taste horrible, and your Dachshund will probably learn quickly to leave it alone. If this doesn't work, you may also try wrapping the area in aluminum foil or keeping a spray bottle filled with water on hand to deter the behavior. Or you can keep a can filled with pennies nearby to startle your Dachshund away from the forbidden area.

If you have a digger, you may want to consider purchasing a few carpet squares or remnants that are reserved for your Dachshund. He can dig and scratch on them to his heart's content. If he scratches and digs on your carpet or wall, move him immediately to his carpet — even help move his paws in a digging motion over it. If he gets it, praise him for all you're worth. He'll get the idea . . . eventually.

Choking hazards

Take a good look around your home for small objects on the floor or within reach that would fit in your Dachshund's mouth. Things like bottle caps, rubber bands, string or thread, loose screws, twist ties, small blocks or balls (such as cat toys), and even small wads of paper trash. All these things can be hazardous to your puppy. Small, hard objects can lodge in a dog's throat and block the air passages. String-like objects can actually cause internal damage.

If your puppy does choke on something, let him try to dislodge it himself. If your dog isn't breathing, whether unconscious or not, try to hook the object out with your finger, if he'll let you. Just don't force the object in farther. If that procedure doesn't work, you can try a movement similar to the Heimlich maneuver:

1. **Place your Dachshund up on all fours and then lift his front end slightly off the ground.**

2. **Put your fist (on a Standard) or thumb (on a Mini) on his upper abdomen just below his rib cage and then thrust upward.**

   Don't be too rough. You don't want to injure him. And keep doing this procedure a few times to try to get the object out.

3. **Do one of the following:**

   - If you can dislodge the object, take him straight to the vet after your dog can breathe. He may have internal injuries.

   - If you can't dislodge the object, rush your pet to the nearest vet or emergency pet care facility. If you can, take someone with you who can keep trying the modified Heimlich maneuver to dislodge the object en route.

If all this choking talk sounds scary to you, you're right to feel alarmed. The best thing to do is keep all choking hazards out of reach, especially if your puppy tends to try to chew on everything in sight. Some puppies are more inclined to chew than others, but chewing is definitely a Dachshund trait.

When you're looking for potential choking hazards, don't forget to look for strangling hazards, too. More cats than dogs are probably strangled in blind cords, but it can happen. Keep blind cords out of reach — especially if you have children. Keep *all* the little ones safe: human, canine, and feline. Small dogs can also get caught up in drapery sashes or miniblinds. Also remove any hook-like objects that are within reach but off the floor because they may possibly catch on your puppy's collar or leash.

Poisons

Want another thing to worry about with a chew-happy puppy?
Poisons. Even if you keep the drain cleaner and the bleach out of
reach, plenty of other household items and substances can poison
your puppy, from ibuprofen (like Advil) or aspirin tablets to rotten
food in your trashcan. Here are some common household poisons
that you should keep well out of reach from your puppy:

- ✔ **Cleaners of all types.** Some are more toxic than others, but
  who wants to wait and see which ones may be okay?

- ✔ **All human and pet medication.** Even if you're not sure that a
  specific medicine is toxic to pets, keep them all out of reach.
  Some medications, such as ibuprofen (Advil), are highly toxic
  to pets.

- ✔ **Pesticides of any type.** Even your pet's flea control product
  can be toxic if gobbled up. Don't let your puppy play with or
  chew any insect traps or bait, like rat, mouse, or roach traps.

- ✔ **Certain foods.** Dogs can be poisoned by chocolate, onions,
  grapes or raisins, and even sugarless gum. Even small
  amounts can be fatal.

- ✔ **Some houseplants.** They're poisonous to varying degrees.
  Keep your plants above Dachshund level.

- ✔ **Some miscellaneous items.** Many seemingly innocuous items
  can be extremely toxic to a dog, such as potpourri oil, coffee
  grounds, fabric softener sheets, dishwashing detergent, bat-
  teries, cigarettes, and alcohol.

While doing poison control, don't forget the yard. Keep your
puppy off the lawn if you've recently sprayed it with insecticides or
fertilizer. Keep all lawn and garden chemicals out of reach (not to
mention sharp objects). Keep your puppy out of the garage, too.
Gasoline, oil, and antifreeze can kill your puppy. Also, the following
common outdoor plants are poisonous to dogs:

- ✔ Azalea

- ✔ Oleander

- ✔ Castor bean

- ✔ Sago palm

- ✔ Yew plant

One tablespoon of antifreeze can kill a 20-pound dog, so imagine how little it would take to harm your Mini Dachshund. Antifreeze smells and tastes yummy to dogs. So Dachs-proof your garage and driveway in the winter by keeping antifreeze out of reach. Even leaking or spilled puddles on the driveway can mean death to your dog. (Note that you can now buy antifreeze that's advertised as safer for pets, but that doesn't mean you shouldn't still do every-thing you can to keep your pet away from it.)

If you know or suspect that your dog has been poisoned, call the National Animal Poison Control Center (NAPCC), a 24-hour emer-gency veterinary poison hotline. A $55 consultation fee may be applied to your credit card. Call 1-888-426-4435. Post this phone number on your refrigerator with your other emergency numbers. When you need the number, you'll need it fast. You can get more information at the NAPCC Web site, at www.napcc.aspca.org.

Compensating for Stairs

A big thing to consider when Dachs-proofing your home is how to make your stairs Dachshund-friendly. Stairs are hard on Dachshund backs (see Chapter 17), especially for the Minis because each step is a lot bigger to a 7-pound dog than to a 30-pound dog. If you have stairs in your home, that's no reason to give up your Dachshund dreams. But you do need to take a few precautions.

If you have the space and the resources, a ramp is great for Dachshunds. A ramp is most practical outside, where you can offer your dog an alternate route off the deck. The problem is that some Dachshunds ignore that carefully constructed ramp and take the stairs anyway. (Some gladly use the ramp, though. You just never know.)

You can install a gate so the ramp is the only way down for your pet, but now you're getting pretty fancy. Some gates, made for small children or pets, bolt onto walls or decks and have an easy-open swinging mechanism for the convenience of adults. This option is worth it if you can afford it, but it's not for everyone.

Inside is a different story. Most people don't have the space to build a ramp over half their staircase. The best solution is to install those pet gates (or baby gates) at the top and bottom of all stair-cases. The newer ones bolt to the wall and swing open so you don't have to take the whole gate off to go up and down. Most can be operated easily with one hand. Then, when your Dachsie has to go upstairs, you can pick him up and carry him. And when he's ready to go back down? Pick him up and carry him again.

Some people aren't willing to do this task, of course, and others argue that Dachshunds are built to be natural athletes and should be able to climb stairs. I won't argue. Some Dachsies race up and down the stairs all day long, every day, and never suffer from a back problem. Others may develop back problems, and you won't know whether or not it had anything to do with daily jaunts up and down your staircase.

Deciding whether or not your Dachsie is allowed to climb the stairs comes down to risk assessment. Going up and down stairs can be hard on those Dachshunds who'll probably have back problems anyway, and climbing the steps may trigger an incident. Other dogs, though, will be fine. You can play it safe but expend more effort, or you can expend a lot of effort to prevent something that may never happen. As long as you recognize that you're taking responsibility for your pet, you can make the decision.

Ledges and Couches and Beds, Oh My!

Some Dachshunds are impossible to keep off beds and couches, and when they decide to get down, they get down before you can stop them. Some people build little Dachshund ramps from their beds and couches so their Dachshunds can scamper easily down from high places. Others recognize that their pets are going to jump, and these folks just hope for the best. It's up to you to gauge your individual situation and determine what works for you and your pet, but it is possible to train a Dachshund to use a ramp.

Chapter 7

Dachs-Proofing Your Family

· ·

· ·

*K*eeping your home free of poisons and choking hazards is great (see Chapter 6), but it won't do much good if your toddler barrels across the room and sits squarely on your new puppy. Even an adult can unwittingly injure a Dachshund if he or she doesn't know how to hold one correctly. And that poor, scared little puppy will soon be at the mercy of your family.

Are they loud? Are they boisterous? Is your family life a little chaotic? All families are. But that doesn't mean you can't create a Dachshund oasis for your new puppy, especially when you first bring her home. Read on.

Giving Your Family Dachshund Lessons

After you secure your home environment (for details, see Chapter 6), it's time to Dachs-proof the occupants. Not everyone in your family automatically knows how to handle a Dachshund puppy, so a family meeting is in order. The topic of discussion? Life with a new Dachshund.

Make sure that everyone gets in on this meeting. Children especially need to know a few things about Dachshunds before you turn them loose on the poor, unsuspecting puppy. At the meeting, you can enumerate the nine no-no's of Dachshund ownership. The kids get an extra couple of tips, too.

Because of their unusually long bodies, Dachshunds must be picked up and held with good support on both ends at all times. Show your children (and adults, too) how to pick up a Dachshund before they try it on their own. Put one hand under the Dachshund's chest. Put the other hand under the Dachshund's rump. Lift slowly without twisting your dog and keep both ends fully supported. See Figure 7-1 for an example. Never lift a Dachshund by the front end only, allowing her back legs to swing around. This can injure her back.

The nine no-no's of Dachshund ownership

I won't go so far as to say that you need to require every member of your family to memorize and recite back to you the following list of Dachshund no-no's, but it won't hurt to post this list somewhere and make sure that everyone has read it at least once:

- ✔ **Don't overwhelm your Dachshund.** Dachshunds are relatively small dogs and can be easily scared or confused by lots of people, loud noises, and chaos. Give your Dachshund a place to go away from the family uproar. A kennel or crate is a perfect Dachshund haven.

- ✔ **Don't overfeed your Dachshund.** Dachshunds are prone to getting chubby, which wreaks havoc on their spines. Cool it on the treats and people food. Use pieces of kibble out of your Dachshund's daily food ration for treats and training, or vary her diet a bit with healthy people food like small pieces of raw carrots, broccoli, apples, and berries. Puppies love chasing a wayward, rolling blueberry around the kitchen!

  However, never give grapes, raisins, onions, or chocolate — these can be toxic to dogs (more on these and other hazards in Chapter 6).

- ✔ **Don't skimp on quality food.** Buy the best food you can find. Ask your vet for recommendations. Dog food quality is often directly related to dog food price, although you may occasionally hear otherwise. The more natural and the more meat, the better. I don't believe it hurts to add some healthy, fresh, whole human food to your pet's diet, either — up to about 30 percent of the meal and primarily meat — as long as you adjust kibble portion size accordingly. (See Chapter 8 for more on what to feed your Dachshund.)

- ✔ **Don't be a couch potato.** Dachshunds need exercise (just like you do), so don't neglect that daily walk. Some playtime in the fenced backyard is great for your Dachshund's health, too, and helps keep obesity at bay.

✔ **Don't ignore your Dachshund.** Dachsies thrive on human attention and affection, plus they look to you for guidance on good behavior. If you decide to bring a Dachshund into your life, decide to spend time training and simply being with your dog each day.

✔ **Don't let your Dachshund escape.** Dachshunds are proficient diggers and can be pretty clever escape artists. They also can't be trusted off leash near traffic, no matter how well trained you think they are. They are hounds and will follow a scent, oblivious to danger. You're in charge and must keep your Dachshund safely enclosed or on a leash. Otherwise, you could lose your friend.

✔ **Don't assume that your Dachshund can speak English or read your mind.** Your friend needs teaching so she can learn the house rules and proper behavior. That's your job as the human end of the Dachshund-human relationship. Figure out how to train your Dachshund and work on it every day. Puppy obedience classes are a great place to start. For more on training a Dachsie, check out Chapters 13 and 14.

✔ **Don't skip the vet visits.** All dogs need routine veterinary evaluations in addition to their vaccinations in the first year. As your Dachsie ages, these checkups become even more important. Keep your pet as healthy as possible by fully utilizing your vet's expertise to catch problems before they turn serious.

✔ **Don't ignore a yelp of pain or any sudden signs that your Dachshund is losing the use of her legs.** When an acute disc herniation occurs, time is of the essence. Waiting it out to see whether it goes away can mean paralysis for your dog. If you can't get her to a vet immediately, put her in her crate and *don't let her move.* (Movement can injure the spinal cord and cause permanent paralysis when the herniation could otherwise have been repaired.) Then get her to the vet or emergency-care facility ASAP. (For more on canine intervertebral disk disease and what to do if your Dachshund suffers from disc herniation, see Chapter 17.)

Your vet may have additional helpful tips for family members about life with a new Dachshund. Choosing a vet with Dachshund expertise is best. He will know from experience what to look for.

Dachs-proofing your kids

Kids love Dachshunds, and the feeling is mutual, but kids can sometimes get a little boisterous and rough with a small dog. If all children learned and demonstrated respect for their fellow creatures on this Earth, the world would be a kinder, gentler place. Do your part by Dachs-proofing your kids. What could result but family harmony?

Copy this list and give it to your kids. Read it or explain it to the younger ones. These are rules for your kids to live by:

✔ **Dogs love to play, but sometimes they need to be alone.** Everyone has their limits. After an exuberant playtime, give your dog some downtime in her den.

If a dog walks away from an approaching child, she's communicating that she doesn't want to be bothered. If the toddler keeps approaching and no parent intervenes, a bite is probably imminent. Listen to your Dachshund's body language!

✔ **Dogs need to have privacy when they eat and sleep.** No poking, prodding, or pulling a dog during dinner. Instinct may cause her to respond with a snap. Also, no rude awakenings, please. Dogs need to sleep a lot, and when they're sleeping, it's hands off.

✔ **No junk food.** Dogs need healthy food and may get sick if given candy, sweets, chips, or other unhealthy food. If your parents generally don't like you to eat something, or if they call it a *special treat,* don't give it to the dog. No, not even when Mom and Dad aren't looking. You wouldn't want your dog to get really sick just because of what you fed her.

✔ **Dachshunds — especially Minis and Dachshund puppies — aren't as tough as most kids.** They must be handled gently, not roughly. No tug of war for Dachshunds, either. The sharp back-and-forth movements can hurt their backs. Also, Dachshunds are small and short. Never drop them from your arms or from anything else. Hold a Dachshund only while sitting on the floor, and always support the Dachshund's back end when carrying her anywhere, even a short distance.

✔ **Never, ever pet any dog you don't know very well.** If you see a dog wandering around alone, leave her alone and tell a grownup. If you see someone walking a dog and think you'd like to pet her, always ask the owner first; then pet the dog slowly and talk softly. That's the way to make friends with a dog.

Kids can be a dog's best friend or a dog's worst enemy. Some kids are great with dogs and quickly become a puppy's primary trainer. Others, especially those under the age of 7 or 8, find it very difficult to handle a dog carefully and gently. Because Miniature Dachshunds are particularly small and can easily be injured as puppies, most vets and breeders don't recommend bringing a Mini into a household with children who aren't yet in the first or second grade.

Kid-proofing your Dachsie

Of course, when you mix up kids and dogs, the kids aren't the only ones with potential to do some damage. An irritated or injured Dachshund can snap at a small child (or even a large child), and a bite can break the skin.

When bringing a Dachshund into a home with children, introduce her to the kids one at a time. Have the kids approach slowly, pet gently, and talk softly. Eventually, your Dachshund will know everyone and feel comfortable. And remember to show your kids the proper way to hold a Dachshund. It's shown in Figure 7-1.

Figure 7-1: Hold the Dachshund close to your body and support her legs and underbelly.

Bringing a new baby into a home where a Dachshund is already firmly entrenched? Try this: A few days before you bring home the baby, bring home a receiving blanket with the baby's smell on it (don't wash it after the baby uses it) and let the Dachshund get to know the smell on the blanket. Then, when you bring the baby home, hold the baby and dog and let them check each other out.

It's also a good idea to keep a treat jar in the nursery. This will help your dog associate the new addition to the family with positive rewards. She'll welcome the crying of a newborn, even in the middle of the night, if it means a treat may be involved.

And don't forget to pay your Dachshund lots of attention. She'll be confused about the change in the family, and she'll wonder why you're suddenly so busy. Reassure her that she still has an important place in the family order, and maintain those training sessions, which double as bonding sessions during this potentially stressful time (see the chapters of Part III).

Dachs-proofing your other pets

Got cats? Dachshunds love them, especially Miniature Dachshunds (see Figure 7-2). Got other dogs? Dachshunds love them, too. However, introductions shouldn't be too sudden.

Photo courtesy of Alli and Pam Henley.

Figure 7-2: Most Dachshunds get along with cats just fine, with proper introductions.

One good way to introduce your new Dachshund and your other pets is to let each pet hang around in a room where the other pet has been for a while before letting them see each other. One vet I know suggests keeping them in separate rooms with a door between them so they can hear each other before they see each other. Curiosity may eventually get the better of any aggressive impulses.

Another suggestion is placing one of the pets in a large crate in the middle of the room while the other is free to roam around, and then switching roles. This can lead to a smoother introduction as each pet gets used to the presence of the other in a controlled way.

As with many dogs, unneutered males may not get along well with each other, and unspayed females may not, either. Best to have at least one (and I suggest *all*) of your pets altered (see Chapter 16).

Mastering Dachshund-Friendly Décor

Here's the really fun part. For many people, Dachshunds are more than pets. They're a way of life. Beyond Dachs-proofing your home, you can actually design your home around and for your Dachshund. Why not? If you've been in search of a decorating theme, this one's a lot of fun.

Making your home a Dachshund haven

Your home can be more than safe. It can be a Dachshund dream house. When you're Dachs-proofing your home, I recommend that you get down on your belly and look around for potential hazards (see Chapter 6). You can do the same thing to make your Dachsie's dream house — this time getting down there to look for what a Dachshund would like to see.

Low furniture, lots of cushions, a Dachshund-sized sofa, enclosed pet beds that give a sense of security (cat beds are good for Minis), and lots of blankets and quilts for burrowing all make Dachshunds feel at home. Who doesn't love a little luxury?

One of the great things about Dachshunds is that they don't have that typical doggy smell so characteristic of other hound breeds. In fact, Dachshunds usually appear exceptionally clean (unless you've just been tramping through the mud with yours). You might as well just give in and let her up on the sofa!

A feeding station kept scrupulously clean, a low doggy door for outdoor forays, a grooming center (especially for longhairs and wirehairs), and a dish of gourmet dog biscuits (for special occasions only) add the finishing touches to your Dachshund's haven.

Some of your décor can be just for you, even if your Dachshund doesn't appreciate it. Collecting Dachshund paraphernalia is fun (see the following section). For some reason, you can find more Dachshund-specific stuff out there than you can find for most other breeds. (Maybe it's their irresistible shape!) Dog-themed decorating items are abundantly available, from wallpaper with dog footprints to dog-printed bedding sets. If you're a dog person through and through (or if you're fast becoming one), why not show your true colors?

Dachshund paraphernalia: A collector's dream!

From framed Dachshund folk art to antique Dachshund-shaped boot scrapers, Dachshunds make for a great decorating theme and great collecting opportunities. Scan antique shops and flea markets for Dachshund items. Tell dealers what you're looking for, and they may be able to point you in the right direction. You can also purchase Dachshund paraphernalia on the Web. Check out the following Web sites:

- Distinctively Dachshund at www.disdox.com. This site has Basset Hound stuff, too.
- Dachshund Delights at www.doxidelight.com.
- Dachshund Treasures at www.dachshundtreasures.com.
- Dachshund Gifts at www.dachsundgifts.com.
- You can also find a lot of Dachshund stuff on general gift sites, collectibles sites, or dog merchandise sites. Or, you can search for Dachshund on www.ebay.com for hours of wiener-dog browsing. (Hey, it's more fun than playing solitaire.)

Chapter 8

Purchasing Your Dachshund Essentials

. . . .

In This Chapter

▶ Finding a den that's truly home sweet home

▶ Perusing the must-haves and why-nots of pet supplies

▶ Picking up grooming tools and toys

▶ Deciding what to feed your Dachshund

. . . .

*1*f you love shopping, this chapter is for you. And even if you don't, no need to despair. Many pet catalogs and Internet sites are at your service! This chapter is all about pet supplies — what you and your Dachshund need and what you don't necessarily *need* but think would be awfully fun to have. Every dog needs a few basics, and Dachshunds require a few special supplies. And then there are the luxuries. If you can afford them, go for it. If you prefer to keep your dog budget in check, your Dachshund won't mind. All she really wants is attention from you (along with exercise and a few good meals every day, of course).

You may be getting a little nervous. You've browsed over all the main topics in this chapter, and you're thinking, "How will I afford all this stuff?" You don't have to have everything on Day 1 (for more on the first day, see Chapter 9). Food and a den are all you really need at first. Grooming tools and toys should follow soon after, though. You can probably spread out your new dog purchases over a month or two, but do budget for them because your Dachshund is worth it. You've made a commitment to give her the best care, which doesn't mean ignoring her needs in order to save a few pennies. It means spending what's necessary to ensure her good health and happiness. You'd do the same for a child, wouldn't you?

Every Dog Needs a Den!

One of the most important pet supplies you'll buy — and *should* buy — before bringing your new Dachshund home is a crate. Personally, I don't like the word "crate." It sounds like something that should contain cartons of milk or oranges from Florida, not a living, breathing, beloved pet. It also conjures up images of cruel confinement, which is exactly what a lot of people imagine when they're told they ought to buy them.

Truth is, a "crate" will become your Dachshund's second best friend (after you, of course). Dogs are den animals, and they feel most secure when they have an enclosed, familiar place to retire to or to escape the fray of family life once in a while. So, I call crates *dens* instead, because as far as Dachshunds are concerned, that's exactly what they are. (Dens are also invaluable housetraining tools.)

Never leave a brand-new puppy in her den for more than two or three hours, even at night. Older puppies can last about four hours. If you work all day, someone should come home at lunch to give your pet a potty break. Even adult dogs, although they can last eight or nine hours in a den, prefer not to spend all day in confinement. If you're gone every day for nine or ten hours, consider hiring a dog walker or pet sitter to do the lunch duty.

Why dens are kind

Do you ever wish you could be magically transported to a luxurious bubble bath or steam room or peaceful meditation retreat, far from the shrieks of small children, ringing telephones, and malfunctioning appliances? Your Dachshund feels a little like that sometimes. Well, maybe not exactly. No one can say for certain how a dog feels (although some people are pretty sure they can tell, from time to time). But dogs do get overwhelmed, seem to suffer from stress, and, although social creatures, sometimes prefer to be alone. But your Dachshund won't take a bubble bath at will. Instead, when a dog is feeling overcome by commotion or simply needs some downtime, nothing feels better than retiring into the safety and comfort of the good ol' den.

Let your pet spend some time each day in her den, even when you're home, so that she learns that *den* doesn't equal *you going away.* She may dislike it at first, but after it becomes familiar, her den will surely be her favorite spot. Unless your dog is sick and needs your help, let the den truly be hers by never putting your hand in there. The less intrusive you are when it comes to your Dachshund's space, the more she'll feel secure in that space.

After you teach your Dachshund that her den is home sweet home (see Chapter 9 for more tips), you'll discover other ways the den can benefit both you and your Dachshund. For instance, the den will help your Dachshund learn to avoid accidents. Dogs don't like to soil where they sleep, so as long as you don't wait too long, your puppy usually will refrain from relieving herself until you take her outside. (Turn to Chapter 13 for more on housetraining.)

Also, if you have a little beggar under your table, your dog can spend time in her den when your family has dinner. It's a lot easier to keep the kids from slipping your Dachshund people food when you don't have a Dachshund in the kitchen, nosing around. Putting her in her den at dinnertime is kind to your pet, because it keeps her healthier and won't encourage bad begging habits.

Selecting your den

You can purchase a crate or kennel for your Dachshund at most pet stores or even at discount-type department stores. You can also find a huge variety of pet housing on the Internet, ranging in price from $15.00 or $20.00 to almost $100.00, depending on the brand, the design, and the store.

When purchasing a Dachshund den, look for a sturdy, well-ventilated plastic or metal crate with an easy-open door (easy for you to open, not your Dachshund). You want to find a size just big enough that your Dachshund can stand, sit, lie down, and turn around comfortably, but you don't want one so huge that she can relieve herself in one corner and sleep in another.

Because Dachshunds never get too big, get a crate that's big enough to house her as an adult. If it looks like too much space for your puppy, you can put a small box or toy or pillow in the den to fill up the extra space. Some crates come with dividers so you can "grow" the den as your puppy grows.

When you have a den picked out, fold up a blanket or buy a nice, soft cushion or pad for the bottom, and your Dachsie paradise is all set.

Plastic dens may not be particularly lovely pieces of furniture (although some brands look attractive), but to most Dachshunds, plastic dens feel more secure and safe on the inside than open-wire kennels, which don't resemble dens very closely. But wire kennels can work just fine if you drape a blanket over the top and three sides to give your pet a better sense of security. Also, avoid making your dog stand on a wire grate; the surface is uncomfortable, and puppies can snag their toes. Cover the bottom of the den with something soft — a cushion, pad, pillow, or folded blanket — and wash the material often.

A companion to dens: Dog beds for Dachsies

If you're talking aesthetics, dog beds (see Figure 8-1 for an example) are much nicer looking than crates and kennels. Some Dachshunds love them — especially the beds that are more enclosed. (Many Dachshunds, especially Minis, like those cushy, semi-enclosed cat beds.) If you want to (and can) get yours used to a bed, that's fine. You can buy some beautiful ones — even furniture-quality wooden beds sized just for small dogs.

Photo courtesy of John and Joyce Kane.

Figure 8-1: Some Dachshunds, like these longhairs, like to call dog beds home.

But even if your dog sleeps in a dog bed, she'll still appreciate and use a den. You'll appreciate it, too, when you suddenly need to confine your Dachshund for her own safety, when housetraining becomes a nightmare, or when you find that your Dachshund won't come out from under the kitchen chair because it's the closest thing to an enclosed den she can find.

Shop 'Til You Drop: A Pet Store Checklist

A den is a must. But what other supplies do you need to properly care for a Dachshund? In this section, I cover all the options — the must-haves and the why-nots. Take the following lists to the pet store (or log on to your favorite online pet store) and have fun!

Collecting the "must-haves"

Following is your list of pet supply staples. These items are pretty much non-negotiable. Your Dachshund needs them. You can spend a little or a lot on, say, a leash or a food bowl. You can even buy most of the supplies at garage sales or borrow them from friends who no longer have dogs. But you need to find the following items, one way or the other:

- ✔ **Food:** Buy as good a food as you can afford (see the later section "Kibble, Kibble, Everywhere . . ." for more about what to feed your Dachshund).

- ✔ **Leash (or *lead*):** Dachshunds must be kept on a leash when near traffic or in an unenclosed area. Keep your pet safe. You don't need to spend a lot. Four-foot lengths are good for new puppies. When your dog gets older, a 6-foot length is perfect. Choose leather or nylon, whichever you prefer.

- ✔ **Collar or harness:** A leash isn't much good without a color or harness. Harnesses are nice for Dachshunds because you won't risk pulling on your pet's neck. Don't leave a harness on all the time, though. It can rub away at your dog's coat. Collars give you a little more control, and some dogs seem to prefer them.

A collar for identification tags and a harness just for walks is the perfect combination!

- ✔ **Identification tags:** You probably already know that your short-legged hound dog shouldn't go wandering around the neighborhood, but just in case your little rascal digs out of your backyard or dashes through an open door and gets away from you, an identification tag can drastically improve your Dachsie's chances for a safe return home. Most pet stores have forms you can fill out to order ID tags, or you can look in magazines and pet catalogs.

Collars and ID tags can fall off, break off, or get lost. Or perhaps your Dachshund could escape on that one day you took off her collar, "just for a minute." For these reasons, a microchip or tattoo may be a better ID tool. Some animal shelters and rescue groups require that your dog have one of these (see Chapter 5). Microchips encoded with your dog's contact information are implanted under her skin, usually in her neck. Vets and shelters with scanners can scan found dogs to see if they contain chips. Tattoos identify your dog with a code on her ear, abdomen, or thigh. Anyone who finds your dog can contact a national database to find out where she belongs. Talk to your vet about the best identification method for your Dachshund.

✔ **Food and water bowls:** Any style bowl will do, as long as it's unbreakable and heavy enough so that your Dachshund doesn't keep knocking it over when she tries to eat. Weighted bowls, ceramic bowls, and metal bowls are good choices. Avoid plastic bowls, which can harbor bacteria and even lead to skin infections.

✔ **Shampoo:** Even if you don't use it very often (you don't need to bathe a smooth hair unless she gets really dirty), you should have shampoo on hand for those times when you need it. Use a shampoo made for pets, not for people. People shampoo is harsh and can irritate your pet's skin and eyes. (See Chapter 16 for more on grooming.)

✔ **Toothbrush and toothpaste:** It may seem silly to you, but brushing your dog's teeth is essential for her good health. Brushing keeps tartar buildup at bay (excessive tartar buildup must be removed by a vet, often under general anaesthetic, which is always a risk). Tooth decay and bacteria in your dog's mouth can lead to heart disease and other serious health problems — especially as your Dachshund ages.

Look for a toothbrush and toothpaste made just for dogs. People toothpaste isn't good for your Dachshund. A people toothbrush may work, but dog toothbrushes are longer with more compact, sturdier bristles, and they're angled in a way that makes brushing easier.

You can also buy pet toothbrushes that slip over your finger. For that matter, a gauze pad wrapped around your finger makes an effective toothbrush, and most dogs don't mind you rubbing their teeth this way — especially if you get them used to the process while they're puppies.

✔ **Nail clippers:** A dog with long nails risks a foot injury. Long nails on hard surfaces spread the footpads too far apart. They also make walking more difficult. Keep your dog's nails nicely trimmed with a pair of clippers. Ask your vet to show you how to clip (or have it done professionally once every four to eight weeks). Buy clippers made for dogs, not for humans. Human nail clippers can seriously injure your dog and probably aren't strong enough to cut your dog's nails anyway.

✔ **Brush and comb:** Your dog's specific grooming needs depend on what coat she has (see the section "Choosing Tools for the Well-Groomed Dachshund" later in this chapter), but a good natural bristle brush and a steel comb will work for all coat types.

✔ **Pet gate:** A pet gate is a must-have if you have rooms where your Dachshund isn't allowed or stairs you want to keep her from descending or climbing. Baby gates, pet gates — same thing.

Garage sales are good sources for buying gates, because people often sell their baby gates when their kids get older.

✔ **Toys:** Dachshunds (like girls) just want to have fun! (I can say that because I'm a girl.) A few toys are a must-have, even if they're homemade (see the section "Toys for Playtime!" later in this chapter).

✔ **Pet stain and odor remover:** Accidents happen, but if your dog smells a previous mistake on your carpet, accidents will happen again and again. Many pet products will truly remove the scent of a past indiscretion. Take advantage and make housetraining easier. Ask your local pet store employee to recommend a brand for your Dachshund.

Most Dachshund vets and breeders generally don't recommend vitamin supplements. Supplements can throw off the nutritional balance of your pet's diet. Unless your vet specifically prescribes something for your Dachshund, stick with the healthy, complete, nutritionally balanced food recommended by your vet, as well as occasional healthy treats. If your Dachshund has a health problem, a holistic vet may recommend supplements like glucosamine for joint health or probiotics for improved digestion.

Giving the "why-nots" a whirl

Beyond the must-haves are the "why-nots" — the pet supplies that are more luxury than necessity. If you want to spend the money, why not? Some of the items in the following list satisfy some pets more than others, and some are, admittedly, just for your own amusement and pleasure. But that's worth something, too!

✔ **Gourmet dog treats:** Fancy gourmet dog treats from dedicated dog bakeries are now widely available. If you live in a big city, you may live near a dog bakery. Here in Iowa, we have three different dog treat bakers at the local farmer's market! Browse around and pick out a few special treats for your Dachshund.

Don't overfeed your Dachsie, even if the treats are healthy. Many gourmet treats are all-natural and made of human-grade ingredients, but that isn't an excuse to let your Dachshund binge. A calorie is a calorie, no matter the source. One treat every day or so should be fine, but you may want to consider decreasing the kibble allowance on those days just slightly.

✔ **Puppy training pads:** Some people like to use pre-scented puppy pads that encourage a Dachshund to go on them rather than the carpet. Not every dog responds to these pads, but if the pads work for your puppy, they can help a lot with housetraining.

✔ **Retractable leash:** This is a very long leash that retracts into a plastic case with a handle. Retractable leashes are perfect for walks or hikes in parks, forests, or other natural areas where your Dachshund will love to go sniffing about. You can keep her safe while she explores.

A retractable leash isn't for everyday use, however, because it isn't good for teaching your dog to heel (see Chapter 14). And be sure to follow the directions when you retract so the leash doesn't whip around and hit you. Safety first!

Don't bring your Dachshund to the vet on a retractable leash. There are so many distractions at the vet's office, and many dogs wander too far from their owners and too close to others on this kind of leash.

✔ **Dog bed and other dog furniture:** Yes, companies make dog furniture. Little chairs, little beds, little fainting couches — all very lovely and impressive, and all pretty expensive. But what better way to make your home a Dachshund haven? Of course, if you drop a bundle on a fancy bedroom set for your Dachshund, be prepared. She may ignore it and prefer to curl up on the people couch instead. After all, that's where you sit!

✔ **Fancy clothing:** A Dachshund in clothes? Sure! Doggy fashion is big these days — from collars, bows, and sweaters to jackets, coats, and boots — and boutique-y pet stores are full of options. Dress your dog to match her unique personality. Behold Figure 8-2 for an example!

Photo courtesy of Vicky Cosgrove.

Figure 8-2: For some this is high fashion, and for others it's campy fun.

REMEMBER

If you live in a very cold climate, a few articles of clothing are actually more of a necessity than a luxury. Dog sweaters, jackets, or coats can keep your Dachshund warm on cold winter walks. Dog boots keep ice crystals and rock salt from getting between your Dachshund's footpads (they also protect your pet from sharp rocks and hot surfaces on summer hikes). The question is, can you get your dog to wear them? If yours won't, always wipe your Dachshund's paws with a warm cloth or even a baby wipe after winter walks. Even when it isn't snowing, rock salt and ice crystal residue can get between your dog's paws.

Choosing Tools for the Well-Groomed Dachshund

If you have a smooth Dachshund, you don't need much in the way of grooming tools. Longhairs and wirehairs require a little more — especially if you decide to do all the dog grooming yourself (see Chapter 3 for more on coat type). You can talk to your vet or a local groomer for tips on which grooming tools are best for your dog; for now, this section provides a short list of tools for you. (For more info on how to groom your Dachshund, see Chapter 16.)

Smooth grooming tools

Grooming a smooth Dachshund may be easy, but you still need a few tools of the trade:

- Natural-bristled brush

- Hound mitt — which has bristles sewn onto the palm — for pulling out shed hair

- Spray oil made for dog coats — if you want to make your Dachshund's coat look extra shiny (a common practice for show dogs)

  You can also use a little baby oil and your hands — but just a drop or two

- Moisturizing shampoo for smooths with dry skin

Longhaired grooming tools

Grooming a longhaired Dachshund is mostly a matter of keeping all those tiny little tangles from becoming great big mats. It takes a little skill and practice, but mostly it takes a commitment to regular grooming — preferably a comb-through every day.

Several books give good instructions on grooming longhaired Dachshunds for the show ring or for pet homes, but nothing beats watching someone who knows the ropes demonstrate for you. Your breeder may be the best person to show you; a professional dog groomer may also be willing to illustrate the basics. You can also talk to breeders at a dog show for tips and demonstrations.

Professionals may recommend additional tools, but here are the basic tools for grooming a longhair:

- Spray conditioner to use before brushing and combing

- Pin brush and/or a natural bristle brush

- Fine-toothed steel comb to work out all the tangles

- Straight scissors with blunt tips for trimming long paw hair and neatening the ends of the coat

- Mat splitter (hopefully you won't need it!)

- Shampoo with conditioner or crème rinse to keep tangles at bay

Wirehaired grooming tools

If you don't care about keeping your dog looking like a show dog, a wirehaired Dachsie can get by with an electric clipper shave whenever her wiry coat gets out of hand. If you want your dog to look ready for the show ring, however, you need a few other tools — including your thumb and forefinger, which you'll use periodically to pluck the longer hairs from your Dachshund's coat (it doesn't hurt her), or a stripping knife.

Just as with longhairs, you'll learn a lot by watching a pro demonstrate for you. (See Chapter 16 for more information about grooming the wirehaired Dachshund.) The list of wirehair grooming tools is short, but the grooming process is long:

- ✔ Natural bristle brush
- ✔ Steel comb
- ✔ Stripping knife (optional — you can also use your fingers)
- ✔ Scissors for neatening stray hairs
- ✔ Clippers with a variety of blades, including a #10

Toys for Playtime!

Dachshunds, like all dogs, need toys. Play is a puppy's work and the means by which she learns about the world. But not all toys are created equal. The following list presents the best ones you should buy (or make) for your Dachshund:

- ✔ Something very hard and appealing to chew on, like a hard rubber Kong toy. The Kongs are great. They have holes you can fill with dog treats or other tantalizing things; your Dachshund may work all day at trying to get the treat out of the Kong.
- ✔ Something with more "give" to chew on, like a Nylabone or Gummabone chew toy.
- ✔ Something soft, like a made-for-dogs fleece toy. Sure, your Dachshund probably will shred it and pull out all the stuffing, but she'll have a whole lot of fun doing it!

Be very careful with dolls or stuffed animals with plastic parts or eyes that can come off and pose a choking hazard.

- ✔ A ball or other object to chase, if your Dachshund likes to chase or retrieve.

Tug of war with a rope toy may sound like fun, but you should avoid playing this game with your Dachshund. The sharp back-and-forth movement can injure her back — even resulting in paralysis. Plus, some experts believe tug-of-war games can lead to possession aggression, which can become a major behavioral problem that's hard to correct. Stick to ball chasing.

Kibble, Kibble, Everywhere . . .

In the long run, dog food will turn out to be your most expensive pet supply, so you don't want to waste your money. But you do want to choose the best food that you can afford. Choosing the right food for your Dachshund may seem pretty tricky. So many brands! Should you choose a natural food? A meat-based or a grain-based food? And what about making your own dog food at home?

The publicity you hear and read about dog diets and pet food safety is indeed overwhelming, and eventually you'll have to make a decision. I can tell you what I've learned after several years of research and writing many articles on the subject — which I do in the following sections — but in the end, the choice is up to you because the experts don't always agree. The best you can do is find a food that satisfies all the following requirements:

- ✔ Your dog likes it.
- ✔ You can afford it.
- ✔ Your vet recommends it.
- ✔ It is nutritionally complete.

Which commercial food is best?

If you choose to feed your dog dry kibble — the easiest option — the number of choices is astounding. Corn-based, meat-based, hypoallergenic, natural, meat meal, fresh meat, by-products, no meat, human-grade ingredients — *how do you pick?* Well, your first job is to learn how to read the labels. The following list explains how:

- ✔ **Look for kibble that lists meat or meat meal as the first ingredient, and preferably also as the second and/or third ingredient.** Fresh meat and meat meal are both high-quality protein sources.

Meat by-products have protein and also things dogs in the wild may eat (organs, bone, skin, cartilage), but they also may contain ingredients that aren't good for your dog. You really don't know what you're getting, and many (but not all) vets discourage the use of food with by-products. Talk to your vet if this issue concerns you.

Some people are enthusiastic about vegetarian diets for dogs, but others believe this diet is unnatural and even unsafe for dogs. I haven't researched the subject enough to recommend it.

✔ **Avoid grain-based foods.** Although whole grains in moderation are probably just fine for your dog (some people don't think they are), highly processed grains or foods made mostly with grains may not contain adequate amounts of digestible protein. Some people also believe that grains cause skin allergies in many dogs.

✔ **Look for words you understand, like "blueberries" and "salmon oil" and "kelp."** Plenty of chemical names should give you pause. Although not all chemicals are bad for your dog (and many added vitamins sound like chemicals), it makes sense to me that dogs (and people, too) are designed to eat foods as close to their natural state as possible.

✔ **Look for a food that's naturally preserved with vitamins E and C rather than chemical preservatives.** The verdict is still out on the effects of chemical preservatives, but naturally preserved food is so widely available that I don't see any reason to take a chance.

✔ **If you find a food advertised as being "nutritionally complete," it must include a statement on the label that says it's appropriate for the maintenance and/or growth stages (in other words, for adult dogs and/or for puppies).** If your food of choice doesn't say that, it hasn't passed the test and isn't meant to be a dog's complete diet.

Even better is a statement that the food has been subjected to feeding trials by the dog food company and has been proven to be nutritionally adequate.

If you're feeling confused, here's some general advice: Find a good, quality kibble, naturally preserved, with meat listed first or second on the ingredient list, and that your dog likes. The higher priced foods probably are better and actually may be a bargain, because your Dachshund won't have to eat as much of them to get the same amount of nutrition. Plus, cheap foods tend to make for bulky, stinky poop. Premium foods make your Dachshund's waste much nicer to handle. When in doubt, ask your vet to recommend a food she prefers for her own dogs.

Popular beliefs about food variety

Perhaps you've heard that you should never switch your dog's food, or if you do, you should do so gradually. Perhaps you've also heard that your dog doesn't require any food but her own brand of kibble and that she should never be given anything else.

Not everyone agrees with this point of view. Dogs don't eat the same thing every day in the wild. And, personally, I find it hard to believe that the occasional addition of healthy people food — especially meat, because very few brands of kibble contain the proportion of meat nature intended for dogs to eat — will do any Dachshund harm. Sure, if you overdo the treats, you could encourage obesity; the trick is to keep the calories down and the nutritional density up. For example, avoid giving all the chicken skin or fat trimmings from your steak to your Dachshund; give him some of the meat instead. Regarding switching your dog's food gradually, yes, any change in diet should be done gradually. Dogs with sensitive systems are more likely to react adversely to dietary changes than normal, healthy dogs.

Most breeders and vets don't recommend canned food over kibble for several reasons. It's more expensive, it's less nutritionally dense, and some think it can promote tooth decay. But it does taste better, and some picky eaters prefer a spoonful of high-quality canned food mixed in with their kibble. As long as the types of food you give your Dachshund are high in quality, you'll be fine (especially if you brush your Dachshund's teeth every day).

Organic, raw, frozen . . . does it matter?

Lately, a lot of information is being passed around about organic diets, raw-food diets, and frozen prepared raw diets. Holistic pet food is trendy, but a lot of the hype comes from some pretty sensible ideas — namely that rather than chemicals, a dog's diet should contain food in a form as close as possible to the things a dog would eat in the wild. It may be worthwhile, although no studies have shown this yet.

The problem is, organic food is much more expensive, although people who choose organic foods for themselves and their families are often happy to pay the higher price.

Many people worry that raw-food diets — whether they're home-made or frozen prepared meals that you can buy in pet stores (they keep them in freezers) — put dogs at risk of food poisoning. Vets are deeply divided on this subject, so you should talk to your vet before you make a decision on this type of diet. Many Dachshunds with horrible skin allergies have improved dramatically on raw-food diets, but for others, it doesn't seem to make any difference — it could even make them sick. Only you and your vet can decide what's right for *your* Dachsie.

What about homemade diets?

Considering making your dog's food at home out of natural, healthy ingredients? Sounds appealing, yes, but it's time consuming. Of course, if you have one 6-pound Miniature Dachshund, you'll spend a lot less time making her food than if you have a house full of Standards.

The only problem with homemade diets is that if they aren't nutritionally complete, your dog can suffer. For example, a dog fed only meat will eventually experience severe health problems. More subtle nutritional deficiencies can happen, too, if your dog misses any essential nutrients.

Getting into the finer points of the homemade diet is beyond the scope of this book, but I can highly recommend a couple books on the subject that will tell you exactly what to do if you want to make your dog's food at home. These books are also filled with great general health information on dogs:

> *The Holistic Guide for a Healthy Dog,* by Wendy Volhard and Kerry Brown, DVM (Howell Book House)

> *Dr. Pitcairn's Complete Guide to Natural Health for Dogs and Cats,* by Richard H. Pitcairn, DVM, PhD, and Susan Hubble Pitcairn (Rodale Press, Inc.)

People food: The good, the bad, and the ugly

People food: Some of it is good, some of it is bad, and some of it is downright dangerous for your Dachshund. If it will help you to remember which is which, keep a copy of Table 8-1 on your refrigerator.

Table 8-1	The Scoop on People Food
Good People Food	**Bad People Food**
Baby carrots, broccoli florets	Hot dogs or any cured meat
Small pieces of green beans	Any candy (especially chocolate)
Fresh or frozen peas	Spoiled food of any kind
Plain yogurt	Sweetened yogurt
Low-fat cottage cheese	High-fat cheese
Berries	High-salt food
Small pieces of fruit	Grapes or raisins
Small amounts of olive, canola, or flaxseed oil	Butter or lard
Oatmeal, brown rice, and whole grains	White flour products
Large raw bones (if your vet approves)	Cooked bones (they can splinter)
Fresh, low-fat meat (minced)	High-fat meat

No matter how much your Dachsie begs, never give her a taste of that chocolate bar or chocolate chip cookie. Chocolate can cause dehydration and diarrhea that's difficult to treat and deadly if not caught in time. Dogs must also avoid onions, grapes, and raisins, which can all cause toxic reactions.

Chapter 9

The First Day: What to Do and What to Expect

*Y*ou have the den. You have the food. You have the chew toys. And now, much to your joy, you have the Dachshund. Yikes! Suddenly, the responsibility hits you: You have a dog. Now you get to take him home and begin your new life — your Dachshund-full life. And you feel like you aren't even sure how to make it home with that tiny, dependent puppy in your vehicle. Don't worry. This chapter talks you through your first day with your Dachsie, step by step. In a few short days, you'll be feeling like a pro.

The first few weeks with a new puppy can be pretty challenging, and you may sometimes wish you hadn't signed on for this job! But keep your eye on the prize. When you and your Dachshund finally work out the rules and understand each other, life will suddenly become sweet. You'll wonder what you ever worried about. "I have such a *good* dog," you'll tell your friends. But first, you have to get through the first day. The chapters of Part III dig deep into the topic of training, so head there after you get through the first day!

Taking the First Ride Home

Of course you want to cuddle your new puppy all the way home, but try to refrain. First of all, cute as he is and as much as you want to hold and cuddle him, he needs to be restrained safely in your car. You'd restrain your infant when bringing him home from the hospital, wouldn't you? Besides, in some states, the law says that you must.

Most states, however, don't require your dog to be restrained just yet. You can make it a family rule, though, and everyone will be safer if you do.

The two main types of pet restraints are harness seatbelts that attach to the car's seatbelts — with or without tethers that attach to the harness — and pet carriers with slots so car seatbelts can hold them securely in place. Pet carriers probably are best for brand-new puppies, because they may feel more secure to a nervous Dachshund. But either type is safe. (Pet carriers also are good for older Dachshunds that tend to chew destructively. Don't think they aren't capable of chewing up the seats while you're concentrating on the road!)

If you get in a traffic accident, you probably won't be able to hold on to your dog. He can be thrown around inside the vehicle, injuring or killing himself or other passengers. Plus, your dog can serve as a major distraction, possibly causing you to get in a traffic accident.

Nobody thinks they'll get into an accident, of course. Unfortunately, many people do. Knowing that, I can't think of a single argument not to buckle up your Dachsie — especially because dog seatbelts and pet carriers are so widely available and inexpensive.

According to a 2004 American Animal Hospital Association pet owner survey, 67 percent of pet owners say they travel with their pets, and 37 percent sometimes bring their pets to work with them. Buckle up, everyone!

Welcoming Your Dachshund Home

When you arrive safely at home, a real welcome is in order! Life has just changed dramatically for both your family and that little dog in your arms, so go ahead and make a bit of a fuss. You don't want to overwhelm your new dog, of course, but you do want to show him around, acquaint him with his new turf, and do what you can to let him know that he's in a loving and safe environment with your family. The following sections help you pull out the welcome wagon.

Puppies, like babies, are relatively simple creatures. They need sleep, food, water, love, and guidance. As long as you provide these five things on the first day (and for the rest of your puppy's life, although later his needs will expand), you're on the right track.

Giving the grand tour

First on your welcome-home list is the grand tour. This event is for you and your new pet, helping you to realize and acknowledge the changing nature of your family. Take your Dachshund from room to room and show him what is his. Your new Dachshund will want to see the Dachsie dining area, the sleeping quarters, the toys, the . . . hold on a minute! Aren't you forgetting something? That little guy probably has to piddle. Make your selected bathroom place your first stop.

First stop: Elimination station

Dogs like to eliminate in the same place all the time, if they can. If you provide your puppy with a spot in the yard just for this purpose and take him there as soon as you get home — even before you go inside the house — you'll set the groundwork for house-training success.

Pick a spot in the yard, put your Dachsie down, and let him sniff around and explore (keep that leash on if your yard isn't fenced). He may pick a different spot; unless it's the middle of your flower garden or some other objectionable place, let him choose. If he eliminates, praise him. If he doesn't, give it a few minutes. If he still doesn't eliminate, take him inside but don't put him down on the floor. Bring him back out 10 or 15 minutes later and try again. Keep this up until he does his duty. If you can keep him from having an accident indoors the first day, you've made great progress.

I explain *crate training,* or the method of using his den to teach your puppy how to control his bladder, in more detail in Chapter 13. For now, take your puppy outside to his elimination station frequently for the first few days — approximately every two hours — especially on day one. Soon, he'll learn what that special spot in the yard is for.

Some people prefer to paper-train their Dachshunds — take the dog to the newspaper or puppy-training pad indoors, rather than outside, when it's potty time. That's fine. On the first day, just pick a spot, spread out a newspaper, and take your Dachshund there first thing — and about every two hours after that. A scented puppy-training pad (see Chapter 8) may encourage elimination. Put it over the newspaper for added protection.

Your breeder may have used newspapers for the puppies to eliminate on, so even if you aren't paper-training your Dachshund in the house, don't line his den with newspapers. They may signal to your Dachshund that the den is his elimination station, and that's not what you want. Choose a comfy blanket or cushion for the crate.

Second stop: The Dachshund dining room

Next up is the dining area. Kitchens and bathrooms are good for puppy food and water bowls because, frankly, puppies aren't the neatest eaters. Set up a big water bowl before you pup gets home (though not too big — your puppy shouldn't have to strain to get a drink) and keep it full of clean water at all times.

After your puppy has eliminated in the yard, bring him in and feed him. When you get home, after the initial shock, your puppy will probably be hungry. Puppies need to eat more often than adult dogs, so if you have a puppy, feed him at least three times a day. (Make sure that you don't feed more than the daily amount recommended by your vet, including treats; see Chapter 8.)

A new dog has a lot on his plate, so to speak, so he may not be very hungry the first day. However, puppies, especially Minis, can't afford to go for a day or two without food. If your puppy refuses to eat for more than 12 hours or acts listless, tired, or very shy or scared, call your vet immediately. He could be sick and may require treatment.

Third stop: The rest of the home

After a nice meal, your Dachsie is probably ready to explore the rest of the house. You'll show him his sleeping quarters later, but for now, take him into all the rooms in which he'll be allowed. If he's a young puppy, you may want to limit him, initially, to just a room or two. Keep him on a leash if he seems nervous, and let him explore without interruptions from curious kids or other pets. Show him all the Dachshund-safe areas of the house, and don't forget to give him another bathroom break, about 15 or 20 minutes after his meal.

By now, your Dachshund may have figured out that there are some other interesting creatures around. Time for introductions!

Meeting the family

After your dog gets the lay of the land, it's time for him to meet the inhabitants. Introduce the members of your family one by one. Your Dachshund can become overwhelmed if everyone crowds around at once, so let each family member (especially kids) approach slowly and gently, speaking in quiet, soothing voices.

Some puppies are fine with a little chaos, but introducing your new member to the family one at a time gives him a chance to sniff each person's hand, check out each person's face, and enjoy a stroke or two. This approach may help your puppy learn who's who with a little more ease.

Don't pass your puppy around just yet. Let him sniff from the safety of your arms or the floor. Children, especially, should never hold a Dachshund while standing up because of the risk that they may drop him. Keep introductions on the down-low (in other words, with kids sitting on the floor).

Approaching the other pets

If you have another dog or cat or two, don't throw all your pets together right away. Confine your other pets before bringing your new Dachshund into the house. Put them in a room with something that has your new dog's smell on it — a blanket or mat from his den, maybe. Let your new Dachshund sniff around your house for at least an hour or so while the other pets are confined. After they've detected each other by scent, you can bring them face to face. Hold each pet for a while first to keep the situation controlled.

You may also let each pet have a turn inside a crate while the other sniffs the surroundings to see what's going on. Just don't let your hands off your new puppy during introductions.

Introducing new pets to resident pets can be tricky. Sometimes things go off without a hitch, but if somebody gets testy, you need to be there, immediately ready to separate the two.

Don't let a tense situation escalate. If either pet seems anxious, fearful, or aggressive, separate the two and continue to let them interact for very short sessions (just a few minutes) every few hours, with both pets firmly under the control of a responsible adult. Don't leave them together unsupervised until you're sure they're friendly toward each other.

What if my new Dachshund is an adult?

Adult Dachshunds entering new homes experience the same stress as new puppies. They may or may not be better trained than puppies. They don't know where they are or with whom they're about to share a life. They don't know where to eliminate, where to eat, or where to sleep. And they probably need to get used to a brand-new den. Follow the same instructions for a new Dachshund of any age; your new Dachshund will soon be a happy and well-adjusted member of your family, assuming that he was happy and well-adjusted before. (If not, you may have other issues to deal with; see Chapter 13.)

Don't forget to respect your original pet's space. Your dog or cat needs reassurance that the new puppy is an addition, not a replacement. Give your resident pet plenty of love, too!

Allowing for nap time

After the first potty break, the initial tour, snack, and introductions, your new Dachshund is probably exhausted. Time for a nap. This is your first opportunity to get your Dachshund used to his den. Put the den where you plan to keep it and let your puppy sniff around. Throw a few pieces of kibble inside and let him go in after them. Don't slam the door behind him; let him come in and out for a few minutes. If it's been awhile, take him outside to his special bathroom spot for another chance to eliminate. When you return, be sure the den is lined with a soft blanket, cushion, or mat and insert your Dachshund. Gently close the door.

You may hear whining. You may hear crying. You may hear frantic barking. Reassure your puppy in a gentle voice that everything is okay but that it's time for a nap. You can stay nearby for a bit if you don't make a fuss and you can ignore the whining. When you leave the room, be strong. Let him whine. He may not know he needs a break, but he does. Leave him there for at least 20 minutes — longer if he falls asleep.

When your Dachshund is inside his den, let him be inside. Don't talk to him or otherwise disturb him. Because a dog can't properly interact with you while in his den, talking to him can cause him anxiety, especially as he's getting used to his new situation.

When he wakes up, let him out immediately so he doesn't associate the den with too much unpleasantness at first. Take him directly outside to his special spot for a potty break and then come back in again for more fun and exploration.

Now you can play or try your first training session — something very simple, such as raising a piece of kibble above your puppy's head to make him sit as you say "Sit." (Chapter 14 has more on basic commands, including Sit.)

Surviving the First Night

The first night with a new Dachshund puppy, or any new dog, carries its share of burdens and joys. You go to bed, you get up, you take the puppy out, you go back to bed, you get up, you take the puppy out, you go back to bed, you get up . . . in between, who can sleep with that whining and crying? And who can get mad at puppies that don't seem to need sleep (see Figure 9-1)?

People with new babies don't sleep much either; fortunately, your puppy will probably learn to sleep through the night much sooner than a human infant. And if your Dachshund is older, he'll learn even more quickly because he's simply getting used to a new situation.

Photo courtesy of Judy Rosensteel.

Figure 9-1: Sleep? We don't need no stinking sleep!

You may spend the first night pulling out your hair, wondering what you've gotten yourself into. But don't call the breeder just yet to beg for her to take your puppy back. Approach the first night with optimism and a sense of duty, and you'll do right by your Dachshund. Taking your puppy out a couple of times during the first night is a labor of love and well worth the payoff in the end.

A few strategies can help you sail through that first night, and the nights to come, with ease. The following sections present these strategies.

The crying game

One of the hardest parts for dog lovers to endure is the whining. Your Dachshund will cry, moan, howl, plead, and beg on the first night. He wants to sleep with *you*. How can you resist? He sounds so pitiful, so pathetic, so lonely. If you were in that kennel, you'd want someone to take you out and cuddle you, too.

But you aren't in that kennel, and your Dachshund isn't a human. Dogs prefer to sleep in enclosed, den-like places. Yours simply hasn't grown accustomed to his den yet, and he won't if you don't give him the chance.

If the crying keeps you awake, you can always move your Dachshund to another room, although he'll probably be happier in the room with you. If the whining gets frantic, get up and take your puppy to his special spot in the yard or on the newspaper. Stay calm and reassuring, but don't make a big fuss; this will just reward your Dachshund for his whining.

Don't ever wake him up to take him out. He needs to learn to sleep through the night, so let sleeping dogs lie (as they say).

After your Dachshund is trained to sleep through the night without needing to go out, you have my permission to let him sleep under the covers with you, unless you really object to the idea. Truth is, under the covers is where most Dachshunds sleep — whether their humans originally intended things that way or not.

That doesn't mean you won't still use the den. Housetraining, naps during the day, confinement when you can't have your dog in the way, and trips to the vet all make the crate an invaluable resource. But at night, Dachshunds want to be near their humans and they love being underneath things, so when yours is sleeping through the night, you may just decide that the bed is okay. Besides, Dachshunds are insistent. They're persistent. They very likely *will* break you. And when winter comes, you'll be glad because there are few things in life cozier than a warm, snuggly Dachshund next to your cold feet on a frigid January morning.

But that day hasn't arrived yet. On the first night, you're still in the training stages. When enduring the whining, remember that you aren't being cruel; you're being kind. It just doesn't feel like it. And if you do give in and let him sleep with you because you just can't stand it, don't kick yourself. You aren't the first Dachshund puppy owner to cave!

In and out, in and out

In general, your puppy needs to go out every two to three hours during the night if he's about 8 weeks old — less often if he's older. That doesn't mean he won't *ask* to go out more often, however. He's lonely and scared, and he doesn't like being shut in that unfamiliar place. If whining can get you out of bed and him out of his crate, he'll keep doing it!

Maybe you'll get lucky. Some puppies sleep straight through the night or need to go out only once. If yours is more demanding, don't despair. Your puppy will soon learn, and in a few days, you'll be able to stretch the times between outings to four, six, and, hallelujah, eight hours. Most puppies learn in a week or two. Standards probably will sleep through the night before Minis, just because they have bigger bladders (see Chapter 3 for more differences).

 Adult dogs need to eliminate approximately four times per day, although some get by with fewer trips to the elimination station. Young puppies need to go more often, but almost always eliminate sometime within an hour after eating.

Good habits to get into

You can do a few things to help your Dachshund sleep through the night without the need to eliminate every hour:

- ✔ Unless your puppy seems unusually thirsty, limit water consumption after 7 p.m.
- ✔ Take your puppy outside to eliminate right before you put him down for the night.
- ✔ Take your puppy out first thing in the morning, at the same time every day. You can always go back to sleep on the

> weekends, but your puppy may not be able to hold it if you decide to sleep in.
>
> ✔ Check your puppy's bedding frequently in the early days. If he gets used to sleeping on wet bedding, he'll be more inclined to continue having accidents in his crate.

Keep reminding yourself that you're teaching your puppy to control his bladder and establish good habits. Then, after he's learned, you can relax the reins a bit. In fact, you may even be convinced to let your Dachshund sleep with you!

The Morning After: Starting a Routine

It's morning . . . already! The sun is up, and you've made it through the first night. Today is your first full day with your new friend. It's also the day for setting up the routine you'll live with most of the time.

Don't wait to incorporate your Dachsie into your routine. You don't have to make the first few weeks special for your Dachshund. If you can take time to be home more often, that's perfect, but don't center your entire day around your new dog. When things go back to normal, your dog won't understand the sudden change.

Dogs are creatures of habit, and they love routine. Let your new Dachshund know, from the very first full day, what the schedule will be. Everyone will get along more easily and happily that way, and your new dog will be glad to know what to expect. The following sections show you the way.

Setting up a family routine

Your new family routine should be a lot like your old family routine. You simply need to add a few steps here and there. If you're a list person, you can write your family's new schedule on a piece of paper; insert the following items where they make sense for your situation.

Young puppies need to go out for a bathroom break about every two hours during the day and every three to four hours at night, so you may need to add more potty breaks to this list (for more on housetraining, see Chapter 13).

✔ Take puppy out (first thing in the morning).

✔ Give puppy breakfast.

✔ Take puppy out (about 20 minutes after breakfast).

✔ Groom puppy.

✔ Train puppy.

✔ Pet puppy.

✔ Give puppy lunch.

✔ Take puppy out (about 20 minutes after lunch).

✔ Train puppy again.

✔ Take puppy for a walk.

✔ Give puppy dinner.

✔ Take puppy out (about 20 minutes after dinner).

✔ Pet puppy.

✔ Take puppy out (right before bed).

✔ Put puppy to bed.

✔ Take puppy out (when necessary in the middle of the night).

Yep, your day is more complicated than it was pre-Dachshund, and it will take a little more time. That may mean less time for television, talking on the phone, or whatever else you do with your leisure time, but that's the commitment you made when you decided to bring a dog into your life.

But keep this in mind: Incorporating your puppy's routine into your own is fun. Having a Dachshund around makes life better — just ask any devoted Dachshund owner. Your time spent will be well worth it.

Also, schedule in some quiet time a few times each day (preferably at about the same time) with your Dachshund. Pet and talk to him in a gentle voice without any demands or expectations. Tune out everything else and focus on your pet. You and your new friend will both come to anticipate these bonding sessions. Your Dachshund will grow to feel safe and secure in your presence, and you may experience some wonderful stress relief. Five minutes twice a day is plenty. It may well be the best ten minutes of your day!

Becoming creatures of habit

Because dogs respond well to schedules and routines, establishing a daily order is an important part of making your dog feel like his universe is secure and in order. In addition to establishing the routine, however, you need to make sure that all your tasks occur at approximately the same times each day.

Keeping a schedule isn't always easy, but it is important for your Dachshund, so try your best. Take him out at the same time each morning, feed him at the same times each day, and train, groom, walk, and pet him consistently — always in the same order, always at about the same time. (Okay, you can improvise some on the petting, but stick with the rest of it!) This kind of life is heaven for a dog and establishes a firm foundation that will make training much, much easier.

Grooming: Don't wait

You may be tempted to wait awhile before grooming your Dachshund — especially if you have a smooth (see Chapter 3). Isn't that too much to do on the first or second day?

Not at all. Grooming is a crucial part of your Dachshund's routine. It keeps your pet healthy, accustoms him to handling by you or anyone else (your vet most importantly), and alerts you to any lumps, bumps, bald spots, parasites, or other health problems before they become too serious.

Puppies don't need much grooming at first, but starting a grooming routine on the first day helps train your dog to accept and even enjoy grooming. Even if you plan to have your longhaired or wirehaired Dachsie professionally groomed, daily maintenance sessions with you are important for your dog's health and are great for stay-acquainted time. See Chapter 16 for more information on grooming your Dachshund.

Training on the first day

Your pup can learn good habits only through your instruction. Training is something that shouldn't wait. Why not begin training on the very first full day with your new Dachsie? Training should be fun for both you and your Dachshund. Positive reinforcement — praising the behavior you want rather than punishing the behavior you don't want — is a great way to teach your puppy the rules, and training sessions that use positive reinforcement are enjoyable for everyone. Check out the chapters of Part III for info on how to train your new Dachshund.

Remaining calm and patient

Dachshunds are adorable but stubborn little creatures, so cultivating the virtue of patience is a necessity for any new Dachshund owner hoping to establish a routine. Just when you think your pup will never learn, he does. (Or he just decides to give in and do what you want, probably because he figured out there's something good in it for *him!*)

Being impatient and getting irritated at your new pet doesn't help teach him how to behave. It only teaches your Dachshund how to fear you. If you feel yourself getting irritable, stop a training or grooming session immediately, or give your Dachshund a break in his den. If you think you can't stand to clean up one more accident, rethink your housetraining techniques. If you can't stand to clean up the chewed garbage one more time, move the garbage to a place where your puppy can't reach it. A lot of this is common sense if you step back and look at what's really going on.

Sure, puppy behavior can be frustrating, but in most cases, the behavior that really needs changing is yours. Your puppy isn't getting the message, and you need to reexamine your strategy.

 Most importantly, don't lose your temper and get angry with your dog. There's never a good reason to strike a dog. Hitting doesn't make sense to dogs; it only makes you appear dangerous and unpredictable. Manage your puppy's behavior in a way that will help improve the behavior to your liking. You're in charge. You can do it.

Calling On a Vet

Many breeders, rescue groups, shelters, and pet stores require a vet visit within the first day or two to activate the health contract. Whether or not this is required, a vet visit is a must for other reasons. A vet can do the following on your first visit with your new pet:

- ✔ Alert you to potential problems with your dog
- ✔ Instruct you on proper care
- ✔ Set up a schedule for first-year vaccinations
- ✔ Do basic maintenance that might be necessary, like de-worming and vaccinations
- ✔ Give you training tips and advice on behavior modification

Your vet is an invaluable resource in your dog's care, so take full advantage and visit often. And if your Dachshund has been under the care of another vet before he became yours, get that vet's contact information so your vet can get up to speed on what your Dachshund needs and what has already been done for him.

If you haven't found a good vet yet, ask your local rescue organization, animal shelter, or even local breeder for a recommendation to a Dachshund-familiar vet. Also talk to friends, especially fellow Dachshund owners, who use their vets for regular checkups. Although you can always vet-hop if you don't like the one you pick, your best bet — and the best situation for your pet — is to pick someone who receives rave reviews from experienced pet owners and who has a lot of experience with Dachshunds.

When you find a candidate, call ahead and ask for a tour of the veterinary hospital. This helps you determine if the staff is friendly, as they'll reflect the attitude of the doctors. A good hospital has nothing to hide and the staff will be proud to show you their hospital and equipment, and they should also be willing to explain their procedures and policies to you.

Find out if the hospital is a member of the AAHA (American Animal Hospital Association). These hospitals have voluntarily opened themselves up for inspection and must meet rigorous standards to be members. You can also find a hospital in your area at www.healthypet.com.

During your tour or initial visit, take the following good-vet checklist with you to make your evaluation and choice easier. Make several copies and fill out one for each vet you visit, if you visit more than one:

✔ Was it easy to make an appointment?

❑ Yes   ❑ No

✔ Was the person on the phone friendly and accommodating?

❑ Yes   ❑ No

✔ Is the vet's office easy to get to or too far away?

❑ Accessible   ❑ Inaccessible

✔ How do the prices compare with other vets in the area?

❑ Cheaper   ❑ On par   ❑ Expensive!

✔ Does the reception area look and smell clean? (A doggy smell is natural, but you shouldn't smell anything unpleasant.)

❑ Yes   ❑ No

✔ Is the office staff friendly and polite when you visit?

❏ Yes ❏ No

✔ Does your Dachshund seem interested when you visit, or does she seem nervous? (This isn't always a good indicator. Some dogs act nervous in new places, and your Dachshund may remember a previous vet's office where she received a vaccination shot.)

❏ Interested ❏ Nervous

✔ Do you have a good feeling about the vet? Is he friendly, open, and easy to talk to?

❏ Yes ❏ No

✔ Does the vet seem to have a genuine interest and love for animals?

❏ Yes ❏ No

✔ Does the vet seem to bond with you and your dog?

❏ Yes ❏ No

✔ Is the vet ready and willing to answer all your questions?

❏ Yes ❏ No

✔ Does the vet make you feel like he has plenty of time for you?

❏ Yes ❏ No

✔ Is the vet willing to give you references?

❏ Yes ❏ No

✔ Is the vet open and forthcoming about his training?

❏ Yes ❏ No

✔ Does the vet have any particular experience with Dachshunds?

❏ Yes ❏ No

✔ Do you have a good feeling about the whole experience after you leave?

❏ Yes ❏ No

Make some notes on the back of your checklist so that you remember specific things about each individual vet. It's easy to forget details when you've visited several. If the answers you give look favorable on the whole, congratulations — it looks like you've found a great vet for your Dachsie!

Part III
The Obedient Dachshund (Not an Oxymoron)

The 5th Wave By Rich Tennant

"We've had some behavior problems since getting 'Snowball.' But with patience, repetition and gentle discipline, I've been able to break Roger of most of them."

In this part . . .

Training: It's the key to having a healthy relationship with your Dachshund. After describing the Dachshund personality and helping you understand your role as a trainer, Part III shows you how to train your Dachshund around the house. You then receive some helpful advice on how to teach your Dachsie all the behaviors that any good dog should know. Finally, you find out all about dog shows and other fun competitions you can do with your Dachsie.

Chapter 10

Understanding the Defiant Dachshund

*Y*ou've heard it from this book (if you've read earlier chapters) and probably from many other places if you've been doing your Dachsie research: Dachshunds are notoriously stubborn. You may also have heard the words *defiant, willful, obstinate, head-strong,* and *intractable*. All true, yes, and appropriate in some Dachshunds more than in others.

But this trait is perfectly natural for a Dachshund; it's even part of her considerable charm. This chapter will help you understand why Dachshunds act the way they do in order to help you come to know and train yours better. So-called stubbornness is really a sign of Dachshund intelligence — of an independent thinker that's far more than an obedient automaton. Ask any Dachshund devotee about the Dachshund's stubborn streak, and you'll probably elicit a smile. Instead of angering those who love her, the stubborn Dachshund engenders affection, even pride, because the Dachshund's obstinate nature is anything but malicious. Your little pup is simply smart as a whip. (Feel free to brag about her!)

Looking for Signs of Intelligent Life

I've heard trainers, breeders, and behaviorists describe two types of intelligence in dogs:

- The kind of intelligence that makes a dog highly and easily trainable (Border Collies, Shelties, and Labrador Retrievers are this kind of intelligent, for example)
- The kind of intelligence that manifests itself as the ability to think without requiring direction from humans

Dachshunds tend to fall into the second category, so don't be fooled into thinking your stubborn, seemingly untrainable puppy is stupid. *Au contraire*. The problem may just be that your Dachshund is *too* smart.

Most dogs want to please the people they love, but not to the point of severe boredom through senseless repetition or through the performance of an activity that doesn't seem to have a point. Dachshunds revel in fun, but what's so fun about standing in the middle of the living room floor, being told to sit, stand, sit, stand, sit, stand, sit, stand? Keep your training sessions short, frequent, fun, and challenging. If you're bored, your Dachshund is probably bored, too. (For more training tips, head to Chapter 11 and keep going.)

Dachshunds may not be humans, but they aren't robots, computers, or animals that enjoy a life of servitude, either. They have many wants:

- They want to be with you.
- They want something interesting to do with their time.
- They want to enjoy their food, their sleep, and their playtime.
- They want to learn tricks and do what you ask, as long as it makes sense to their doggy minds.

So, the first thing to remember when approaching your Dachshund for your early training sessions is that training must be fun, must have rewards, and must be something you and your Dachshund do every day together —something you both anticipate and relish.

Most people are familiar with smooth Dachshunds, but there are two other coat types: longhairs, such as the Miniature Dachshund (above), and wirehairs (below).

A double-dappled Dachshund is a dappled Dachshund with patches of white.

Smooth Dachshunds are perfect for people who don't have the time or patience for grooming.

These wirehair pups demonstrate the Dachshund's lively, curious temperament.

Going on an errand? Take your Dachshund along.

This black-and-tan color combination is common in many dog breeds.

For a longhaired Dachshund, daily grooming is a must.

Dachshund puppies tend to chew, so provide them with plenty of chew toys.

Daily walks and even the occasional swim will keep your Dachshund healthy.

Though there's no denying a piebald Dachshund's beauty, they are disqualified from competition in every country except the United States.

Some red Dachshunds look almost brown, but Dachshund people still call these dogs "red."

Dachshunds love to be in the middle of everything.

Your Dachshund's daily routine should include plenty of socialization with people.

The Dachshund's compact legs serve as powerful excavators. Dachshunds can dig out anything and dig into or out of anywhere –

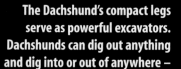

Cream Dachshunds can range from gold to almost white.

Dachshunds feel at home when they have blankets and quilts for burrowing

Why Dachshunds Are Independent Thinkers

Different dog breeds have been bred for different reasons. Some have been developed to be very in-tune to their humans' every need — working in close partnership to herd livestock or retrieve game, for example. Some have been developed to be strong, protective working dogs. And some have been developed to curl up and look pretty on the laps or in the sleeves of royalty.

Dachshunds (like most Hounds) have been developed to think for themselves (see Figure 10-1 for a Dachsie deep in thought). Traditionally, the best Dachshunds were the ones that could follow scents without constant supervision, that could go into badger dens and corner badgers on their own, and that could bark to alert their human companions that the prey was cornered. It was man and Dachshund against badger or rabbit or wild boar.

Photo courtesy of Gail Painter.

Figure 10-1: This Dachshund is a free (and deep) thinker.

DACHSIE MOXIE

Field trials: Independent thinking in action

Watching a Dachshund field trial is a great way to observe the Dachshund's independent nature in action. In Dachshund field trials, Dachshunds compete in pairs to follow the scent of a rabbit. (The rabbit isn't caught or killed; usually, it isn't even seen by the dogs.) When the dogs catch the scent, or *line,* of the rabbit, the handlers aren't allowed to intervene in any way to direct the Dachshunds. The dogs must trail the scent all on their own, followed by the watchful judges who determine which Dachshunds are most capable of following the trail. See Chapter 15 for more on these field trials.

In other words, Dachshunds — even the Minis — were made to perform reliably and intelligently without too much human intervention. Therefore, the best way to get through to a Dachshund so that she can learn your house rules and what you desire from her is to learn how to speak her language. The following sections dive deep into this topic.

Dachshunds Can't Obey What They Don't Understand

If only you could tell your Dachsie, "Listen here, Gertrude. When you feel the urge to eliminate, please let me know ahead of time and I'll let you outside." Or, "This is the deal, Otto. When I say 'Sit,' you plant your rump on the ground and stay there. And when I say 'Come,' you run right over here as fast as you can. If you do, I'll really like it a lot."

Sadly, dog training isn't that easy. But it isn't too hard, either. The first thing you have to realize is that your Dachshund doesn't speak English. Okay, sure, you know that. But have you really considered what it means? It means that your Dachshund isn't being defiant the first time you say "Sit" and she just stares at you with a look that says, "What planet are you from?" She just doesn't know what you're talking about. Her mother didn't tell her to Sit. How is she supposed to understand?

And, even if your Dachshund has learned "Come" in the living room, she may not understand that when she smells a juicy squirrel dashing through the park and runs madly after it and you shriek "Come!" hysterically that you expect the same response as you did in the living room. (And no matter how much you practice, your Dachshund may still chase that squirrel, so keep her leash on outside!)

Teaching your Dachshund what behavior you expect when you say certain words takes work and plenty of consistent practice. It also takes a certain degree of *showing* before the *telling* alone will work.

Never hold a grudge against your Dachshund. After a few seconds, your dog will have no idea what you're angry about. Dogs live in the present, and they only know that you're angry. If you decide to punish your pup for chewing your shoe by keeping her locked up for two hours or by ignoring her all day, your punishment will be ineffective and even destructive, because your Dachshund will learn to fear you or avoid you rather than listen to you.

Communicating with Your Dachshund

How do you talk Dachshund? First, you have to see the world from your Dachshund's point of view. Imagine that you're a Dachshund, scampering around about 8 inches off the ground. You've suddenly been uprooted from the home you knew, and here you are in a strange place with a strange creature who towers above you and keeps uttering strange, undecipherable sounds. The creature seems very nice, offering food and petting you. The voice sounds well-intentioned, and sometimes you get treats.

But sometimes the voice gets mad, irritated, and scary. Sometimes the creature appears dangerous, waving his or her arms wildly and yelling. Sometimes the yelling seems to be at you, but you can't imagine why. You want to do whatever will make the creature talk nicely, and you sure want some more of those treats. If only you knew what to do to elicit that behavior from your creature!

Oh well, you may as well go on exploring your new environment, relieving yourself when you have to and chewing on whatever you find that looks tempting. After all, this is what dogs do; you don't have any other instructions — at least none you can understand.

To get through to this uneducated and independent-minded little Dachshund, you have to be very specific in your rewards. The moment she does something good, praise her, pet her, even give her the occasional treat. When she's naughty, redirect her to the right activity (hand her a chew toy, move her to her outdoor bathroom, and so on) without making any fuss. Ignore her until she does the right thing again and then heap on the praise. *Now* she'll get the message.

Don't just praise your dog when she does something you ask her to. Also praise her when she does something well or right when you didn't ask. Constant positive reinforcement of good behavior is integral to developing a good relationship with your Dachshund. If you spend the whole day yelling "No!" and "Bad dog!" but never rewarding your Dachshund for the things she does right, she won't learn the self-confidence that's so important to a well-trained and happy pet. And she certainly won't learn what you want her to.

The following sections present more communication tips that will have you speaking Dachsie in no time. For more on the words you can teach your Dachshund, head to Chapter 14.

Accentuating the positive

Most people use a combination of training methods for their dogs, depending on the situation. Here are the most common methods of training:

- ✔ **Positive reinforcement** rewards desired behavior with something the dog wants, such as a treat or praise.

- ✔ **Negative reinforcement** rewards desired behavior by removing an unpleasant condition — like when you release a choke chain after your dog sits.

- ✔ **Punishment** discourages undesired behavior by inflicting something undesirable, such as a scolding.

- ✔ **Extinction** doesn't reinforce undesired behavior — like when you ignore your Dachshund when she jumps up on you.

Positive reinforcement used in conjunction with extinction is considered by many contemporary trainers to be the most effective, fast, and humane method of dog training. When your Dachshund does something you want her to do, reward her immediately and heap on the praise. When she does something she isn't supposed to do, don't reinforce the behavior. Completely ignore her. She'll hate that.

Of course, if she's doing something dangerous or damaging, you have to stop her immediately. Whisk her outside before she eliminates on your carpet or remove her jaws from your table leg. Accompany your removal with a firm "No!" But don't make a big deal about it. She won't understand, she'll get scared, and even if she does learn not to chew the table *in your presence* (because that's the only time she gets punished for it), she won't understand that she shouldn't *ever* chew on the table.

One of the most important things to remember when communicating with your Dachshund is consistency. If you praise your Dachshund for obeying your command one day and then ignore her for obeying your command the next day, she won't get it. If you refuse to let her on your bed one day and then let her on your bed the next day, she won't get that, either. Make the rules and stick to them. If you must change them, keep them changed. Dachshunds don't understand waffling.

Staying calm and upbeat

If you want to relate to your Dachshund, the most important thing you can do is stay positive. Getting angry when your Dachshund eats your loveseat or leaves a puddle on your antique quilt is understandable, but it won't do any good. Leave the room, get angry, get over it, come back, and resolve not to let it happen again, because (and you may not want to hear this) the whole thing was your fault anyway.

Dachshunds aren't malicious. They don't hold grudges. Your Dachshund isn't trying to wreck your stuff or disobey you. When she does something wrong (wrong according to your rules), it's only because she didn't understand that the behavior is unacceptable.

If you're always (or at least usually) calm, positive, upbeat, and happy when teaching your Dachshund the rules, as well as the fun things you and she can do together, she'll get your meaning much more quickly. Dachshunds are all about reward. What can they do to get one, and what can they do to get another one? It's that simple. Yelling isn't a reward. A slap on the rump isn't a reward. Rubbing her nose in an accident is most certainly not a reward. But a treat? A pat? A walk? An enthusiastic "What a good, sweet, darling little puppy dog you are!"? Now *those* are rewards that allow you to relate to a Dachshund.

Showing, telling, and reinforcing

Words make sense to a Dachshund only when they're linked with something you've first *shown* her how to do. For example, you can follow this three-step process:

1. Taking your Dachshund to her elimination station every hour or so the first day you have her is *showing* her.

Rewarding your good dog with new treats

Tired of the same old pieces of kibble for positive reinforcements? You can use many things to reward your Dachshund. Here are some ideas:

✔ Small pieces of lean meat, veggies, berries, a spoonful of plain yogurt or olive oil with dinner, pieces of whole-grain cereal (oat rings or wheat biscuits, for example), or bits of scrambled eggs will keep your Dachshund excited about training.

✔ A game of fetch or a run around the yard will energize your pup.

✔ An extra grooming session now and then will be appreciated (most Dachshunds love to be brushed).

✔ A walk with you is the *ultimate* reward for a job well done.

Some trainers don't believe in using food rewards, but Dachshunds are highly food-motivated, so as long as your rewards don't cause your Dachshund to become over-weight, using food rewards is a great way to train.

2. Associating this action with a word or phrase, such as "Go potty," is how showing leads to *telling*.

3. Praising her and/or offering her a bit of kibble when she does her duty is *positive reinforcement*.

Together, these actions result in a Dachshund that knows what you want and is glad to give it to you.

TIP

The most effective method, in my opinion, for showing, telling, and reinforcing what's expected of your Dachshund is *lure-and-reward training*. You use a lure, such as a piece of kibble or a treat, to guide your Dachshund into the desired position as you tell her the name of the position — Sit, Lie Down, Bow, or whatever. When she achieves the position, Dachsie gets the treat. Show, tell, and reinforce. Now that isn't a difficult communication.

Recognizing "Normal" Dachshund Behavior

Despite all the generalizations you hear about dogs and Dachshunds, the fact is, every Dachshund is different. Some are more stubborn than others. And some are jollier or bigger performers, or more retiring, or less likely to enjoy children, or more friendly toward strangers, and so on.

You can read every book on the planet about Dachshunds, dog behavior, and training, but until you get to know the personality of your Dachshund, you'll have only half the story. Putting any individual Dachshund in any individual home will result in a unique and special situation. The following sections give you some common Dachshund desires and behaviors and then explain how differences can occur.

A common Dachshund mentality

Most Dachshunds aren't complicated. (And neither are most people, really.) They share many characteristics, which I list here:

✔ They enjoy pleasurable activities. They require food, water, sleep, and affection. They absolutely love to go on walks, play outdoors, chase squirrels, chase balls (but not necessarily give them back to you), sleep under the bedcovers with you, and curl up on your lap to watch television. They'll do just about anything for your undivided attention.

✔ They don't enjoy being hungry, in pain, overly tired, uncomfortable, or frightened, and they absolutely hate it when you're displeased with them — especially if they don't know why. They don't want to be ignored. They want to be the center of your universe, and they sincerely believe they deserve to be.

✔ They don't know what "Sit" means until you show them. But they're smart, so after you show them, they'll understand. They don't know why you want them to do boring, repetitive things when they could be sniffing around or having lunch. But they'll do those things if the reward is big enough. They want to know *why* they shouldn't pull on the leash. So if you make it clear that pulling on the leash means no walk and that trotting politely by your side means a long walk, they'll be happy to oblige.

And that's about it. If only raising kids was that easy! (Actually, positive reinforcement works on kids, too, but that's a different book.) All you have to do is practice, practice, practice. Keep training fun, keep it happy, and keep it rewarding for *everyone* involved.

Nature versus nurture

Your Dachshund inherited certain traits and tendencies from her parents. She may be particularly smart or quick or laid-back. But nurture plays a big part, as well. Everything you do, everything you say, and the way you and your Dachshund live together shape her personality. Nurture affects her ability to learn, her desire to please you, and even her zest for life. Talk about a big responsibility!

However, even if you do everything the way you think (and I say) you should, your Dachshund may be particularly stubborn and hard, requiring sharper corrections (though never physical ones). Perhaps you have a sensitive fellow that practically faints with joy if you smile in his direction. You'll probably never need to raise your voice even slightly with this one, and you may never even need to use food as a positive reinforcement for training.

Maybe yours doesn't want to sleep in your bed at all. Maybe she already knows what you mean when you say "Come," and you hardly have to train her.

Maybe she pushes your limits to see how much she can get away with, even when she knows exactly what you want — just out of curiosity or tenacity or because she's particularly precocious.

All you can do is live and learn together, stay positive, and give yourself a timeout when you get angry (and you'll probably get angry from time to time). Keep at it. You and your Dachshund have a bond of mutual love, respect, and affection, even if you may not always like each other.

Some dogs seem to be completely untrainable. Well into the first year, though, their owners suddenly discover that these dogs are deaf — an affliction that happens sometimes with Dachshunds, most often in dogs with large areas of white. There are alternate methods for training deaf Dachshunds, which you can learn from a professional trainer with experience in this area. The following section digs deeper into the topic of health problems.

When training problems mean health problems

In some cases, training problems or certain unusual behaviors may indicate a health problem in your Dachsie. Apart from individual differences your dog shows, be on the lookout for any of the following behaviors and alert your veterinarian. Better to catch a health problem in the early stages than to ignore it until it becomes life-threatening.

Call your vet if your Dachshund

- ✔ Never obeys your commands when she can't see your face.

- ✔ Was housetrained but suddenly begins to have accidents inside the house regularly.

- ✔ Behaves aggressively for no good reason, especially if you've trained your Dachshund not to bite or if she has never exhibited aggressive behavior before.

- ✔ Suddenly becomes shy around people when she wasn't previously.

- ✔ Suddenly seems forgetful or confused, possibly bumping into furniture (more common in older dogs).

- ✔ Suddenly refuses to come, go on a walk, or move at all.

- ✔ Yelps when touched.

- ✔ Suddenly becomes destructive, fearful, or hysterical when left alone.

All these behaviors may seem to be training issues, but they could be signs of a serious health problem — possibly of an acute nature. Don't hesitate to call your vet. She's there to answer your questions and keep your Dachshund well.

The behaviorist is your ally

If your dog exhibits behavioral problems, seems untrainable despite your best efforts, or has any of the problems listed in the preceding section and your vet has ruled out a medical problem, consider contacting an animal behaviorist. No, it isn't like taking your pet in for psychotherapy. Dogs can suffer from very real and serious behavioral problems, and a behaviorist is trained to deal with these specific problems.

Don't be shy about calling a behaviorist. Plenty of people do, and plenty of people are very glad they did. Many dogs have been saved through simple behavior-modification techniques. Most dogs surrendered to animal shelters are there because of behavioral problems their owners couldn't or wouldn't handle. Don't let your Dachshund suffer this fate. Learn her language, train her, hire a professional when necessary, and immerse your dog in plenty of love. Now you're talking Dachshund.

An animal behaviorist may not have all the answers, but a good one may know just what to do when you've exhausted other avenues. Sometimes the most serious-seeming problem is really a simple matter.

Some dog trainers also call themselves canine behavioral consultants. These trainers may not have advanced degrees in animal behavior like a behaviorist, but they may have a lot of practical experience with behavior problems. A consultant could be a big help when you're trying to solve a training problem, depending on your situation, but behaviorists generally have more formal education. Only behaviorists can prescribe medication, such as a medicine that may be appropriate for separation anxiety or aggression.

Here are some resources to check out:

✔ To find an animal behaviorist, check out the Animal Behavior Society's public directory of certified animal behaviorists at www.animalbehavior.org/ABSAppliedBehavior/caab-directory.

✔ For a list of behavior consultants, check out the International Association of Animal Behavior Consultants (IAABC) at www.iaabc.org.

✔ For a list of trainers who specialize in behavior problems, check out the Association of Pet Dog Trainers's site at www.apdt.com and click on Dog Trainer Search.

Chapter 11

Taking Charge of Your Dachsie

. . . .

In This Chapter

▶ Understanding your Dachshund's inborn tendencies

▶ Recognizing natural Dachsie skills

▶ Discovering the power of Dachshund wiles

. . . .

Sometimes, despite your best efforts, you'll wonder who's training whom when you get to the end of a long day of Dachshund disobedience. Training a Dachshund is indeed a challenge, and it helps to keep reminding yourself who's the boss — as well as how to be the boss. Nobody ever said training a Dachshund was *easy* — but it certainly isn't impossible.

Your Dachshund won't mind being the boss, but he'd really prefer that you do the job — and believe me, your life will be a lot easier if you do. You don't want to spend your days subject to the capricious nature of this tiny tyrant. You must take charge, and this chapter shows you the reasons.

Knowing Your Dachshund's Instincts and Traits

The first step toward taking the reins in the dog-human relationship is to know your Dachshund. All Dachshunds have unique qualities and instincts. Knowing them and taking advantage of the characteristics of the breed will help you take and maintain control. (Chapters 1–3 also give you info so you can get familiar with the Dachshund.)

Each Dachsie persona in this section is probably a part of your Dachshund's overall personality. Some traits may sound more like your pet than others. Whichever types seem dominant in your dog, use those tendencies in your training and play sessions.

This is one of the advantages of owning a purebred dog. Although each Dachshund is different in some ways, they're all basically the same. Each characteristic in this section carries with it certain training challenges. (There are also certain games each Dachshund type enjoys, as well as certain organized competitive dog sports, if you want to pursue those things. Head to Chapter 15 for more.)

The hunter/tracker

Dachshunds were bred to hunt, to track scents, and to follow their quarry — with unwavering persistence and courage beyond their size — until the prize is won. What does this mean for your training?

- ✔ **Training challenge:** If your Dachshund detects a scent while you're working, training, playing, or walking together, it will take every ounce of doggie willpower for him not to dash off after it. Most of the time, he won't be able to resist. Your Dachshund is very likely to run away from you if you don't keep him on his leash in an open area. It isn't that he doesn't like you. He's just a hunter and tracker by nature, and you can't easily train out instinct.

- ✔ **Great games:** Dachshunds almost always enjoy games that mimic a hunting or tracking situation. Show your Dachsie a small ball, let him sniff it, and then throw it as far as you can (in a safe area). Watch him do his stuff. The tricky part is convincing him to give it back to you, but after he learns that returning the ball to you means another go-around, he'll probably be more than willing (in his own sweet time, that is).

- ✔ **An edge on the competition:** You can use your Dachshund's tracking ability for advanced training in competitive tracking, field trials, and earth dog or den trials. These organized sports really take advantage of the Dachshund's natural abilities, and Dachshunds love to have challenging work to do. Seeing a Dachshund in action, using his natural instincts, is truly inspiring. (For more on training your Dachshund for competition and getting involved in competitive dog sports, see Chapter 15.)

The digger

If you have a Dachshund and your backyard fence isn't buried at least a foot underground, you probably know all about the Dachshund's penchant for digging. Some Dachshunds dig more than others, but in general, they all love it — after they discover how fun it is. What does this mean for your training?

- ✔ **Training challenge:** Your Dachshund can behave in the most maddening ways: digging under your fence and running off, digging up your flower beds and vegetable gardens, and even attempting to dig through your carpeting and furniture. However, you have no excuse not to prepare. You can line the bottom of your fence with bricks or rocks or even pour a foundation under the fence. Grow your garden somewhere else or put a fence around it (dig a foot-deep trench and sink the fence into it). Sound like a lot of work? Sure, but it's all part of life with a Dachshund.

   If your Dachshund insists on digging in a specific area on your carpet or furniture, break out the Bitter Apple or another chew-deterrent spray and take action (consult your vet and follow the package directions). Be vigilant and prevent destructive digging before it gets too destructive. And don't get mad if your Dachshund digs. You can't argue with instinct, and he isn't doing it to make you mad. He just thinks it's really, really fun. You can relate to that, can't you?

   If your Dachshund loves to dig but you can't afford to pour a foundation under your fence, all is not lost. Line the base of your fence with cinderblocks to make digging more of a challenge, and then create a diversion. Build a sandbox in your yard as your Dachsie's very own digging playground, and train him to dig there by moving him to the box whenever he's in digging mode. Praise any digging attempts he makes in the box. You can even bury dog treats in the sand, just to inspire him. In extreme cases, your Dachshund may not be able to go in the backyard unsupervised, but a little extra vigilance is a small price to pay to keep your Dachshund safe.

- ✔ **Great games:** If you decide to build a sandbox just for Dachsie digging, you can play a game to help train him to use it. Show your Dachshund a toy. Let him sniff it and get him excited about it. Then go outside with him, bury the toy in the sandbox while he watches, and cover it up. Now ask your Dachshund to "find the toy!" Fun for all.

✔ **An edge on the competition:** Dachshunds are born for den and earth dog trials. If your Dachshund really likes to burrow under things (and what Dachshund doesn't?), you probably have a natural. Earth dog and den trials don't take much training. They're events that utilize a dog's natural instinct and aren't for exhibiting special skills developed by training (although the bury-the-toy-in-the-sandbox game probably will help to hone your Dachshund's natural instinct).

The athlete

Dachshunds may have delicate backs and may not appear particularly buff, but many are superior athletes (see Figure 11-1 for an example). Dachshunds are built to work, not to sit around looking pretty. Even Minis are designed to follow quarry into small dens. No lap dogs in Dachshund land (although they do love your lap). What does the Dachshund's natural athletic ability mean to your training?

Figure 11-1: This Dachsie looks like a natural athlete, no?

✔ **Training challenge:** Dachshunds like to move, exercise, and use their natural athletic ability, so if you're a sedentary person, you'll have to work to make sure that your Dachshund gets enough exercise. A Dachshund that doesn't get enough exercise is almost certain to cause trouble; he's got to get out all that energy somehow.

This natural athlete is game for training; he'll love active sessions with practice disguised as doggy sports. He'll also think you're really fun to hang around with.

Athletic as they are, Dachshunds probably shouldn't engage in certain activities too often. If a sport or activity involves running around sharp corners at high speed, shaking the neck (like in a boisterous game of tug of war), jumping down from high places, or racing up and down steep stairs, discourage your Dachshund from getting too rowdy. You want to keep his back in good shape.

✔ **Great games:** Dachshunds love to play. They're excellent runners, and some really enjoy jumping up to catch a ball (or grab your dinner off that low counter). Let your Dachshund refine his natural athletic abilities by playing active games. Throw a Frisbee and let him chase it. Set up an obstacle course and let him maneuver through it to find a favorite toy, ball, or food treat. And don't forget the all-important walk (see Chapter 14 for training tips). Your Dachshund loves to be on the move, and when your daily exercise is over, he'll be more than happy to relax, kick back, and allow you to pet him to sleep.

✔ **An edge on the competition:** Don't be fooled into thinking that your Dachshund can't compete in athletic activities, such as obedience and agility competitions, and in areas of competition reserved for Dachshunds, such as field and den trials. Dachshunds have achieved the highest obedience titles, which takes tremendous athletic ability. And although Dachshunds aren't typically thought of as the most agile breed, they can and do participate in agility competition as well — if jumps are adjusted for height. Your local dog club may have other events your Dachshund can participate in. If you think organized athletics would be fun, and your Dachshund enjoys that kind of thing, go for it.

The actor within

Your Dachsie is a real clown and is happiest when all eyes are on him. You may wonder whether anyone will pay attention to *you* again, because since you brought home your Dachshund, he's been the star of the household, and he likes it that way, thank you very much. You may even be tempted to call your little Dachshund a diva. What does this mean for your training?

✔ **Training challenge:** If you don't make training sessions fun, and if they aren't all about your Dachshund, forget it. What does a born performer want with tedium? With sharing the spotlight? Nothing. Take advantage of your Dachshund's showy side and make a big deal out of good behavior. The best way to discourage bad behavior is to completely ignore it. Your performer wants to be center stage and hates being ignored even more than being yelled at, so take advantage of this trait.

✔ **Great games:** If it pleases your little performer (and it probably will), teach him some really flashy tricks that are sure to elicit oohs, aahs, giggles, and applause from spectators. Tricks are sure to become a favorite part of your scene-stealing Dachsie's repertoire. Chapter 14 has all the details.

✔ **An edge on the competition:** Consider looking into a fun competitive activity called *canine freestyle* or *canine musical freestyle*. This competition involves a choreographed routine that includes both you and your Dachshund. Any dog can compete, but Dachshunds love to show off; if yours is good at obedience but you both like the idea of something flashier, freestyle may be right up your alley. Even if you're a little shy, your Dachshund can do most of the fancy footwork. For more on canine freestyle events, see Chapter 15.

Oh, Those Dachshund Wiles . . .

If you get a Dachshund, you're dealing with a hunter, a tracker, a digger, an athlete, and an actor destined for whatever stage you'll give him. The combination results in a unique set of what I like to call "Dachshund wiles."

Dachshund wiles are hard to define, yet exceedingly powerful. They make up the force that mysteriously compels you to hand over half of your hot dog to your devious little darling, even when you're still hungry. They keep you from answering the phone when your Dachshund is curled on your lap. They keep you from staying angry at your Dachshund for more than five seconds. And they somehow propel you, each and every night, to the very edge of your bed, reserving most of the space on your king-sized mattress for your 8-pound Miniature Dachshund.

A force to be reckoned with, indeed. And certainly a force to consider when training your Dachshund. What can you do in the face of such power? If you learn how your Dachshund uses his wiles, you'll learn how to put some of your own wiles into play.

How Dachsies manipulate

Dogs need certain things, like food, shelter, warmth, and companionship. They also desire certain things, like more food, more warmth, and a whole lotta companionship. Dogs don't like other things, like hunger, standing out in the rain, or being ignored. They're social animals, domesticated to enjoy the good life — and oh, how they love suppertime.

It only makes sense, then, that your Dachshund will do whatever he can to get more of what he wants and less of what he doesn't want. Any creature does this (even you). Some are simply more effective in their techniques than others. Your Dachshund will soon learn — all on his own — what behaviors encourage you to hand over the goods (treats, kind words, snuggles) and what behaviors cause you to go off the deep end or purposefully ignore him.

Are you a pushover? Your Dachshund will soon discover whether a cute expression accompanied by a slightly cocked head will melt your heart and cause you to toss another gourmet dog cookie in his direction. If you're not careful, he'll come to learn that barking, nipping, whining, or jumping results in treats and attention. (To a Dachshund, even negative attention like yelling is better than being ignored.)

Always remember to reward the good behavior, not the bad. In other words, turn the tables on your clever little pet. If he recognizes that begging only gets him ignored, but that lying quietly in the corner during dinner leads to you serving her dinner, then congratulations. You have the upper hand. When you make him realize that bad behavior results in nothing, and that good behavior — a well-behaved greeting when you arrive home, with an eager wagging tail but no jumping, for example — gets him plenty of praise, stroking, and kisses, you'll be manipulating him in the best way.

After your Dachshund is well-trained, you'll be able to bend the rules now and then. However, if you make it a habit to enforce rules only when you have the energy, you may as well forget the rules altogether. Your Dachshund won't understand inconsistent enforcement. He won't know how you'll react when he does something, so he won't even try to anticipate. He'll just do what he wants to do.

Why you must be in charge

If you don't decide from day one to be in charge of your Dachshund's behavior, he'll take you for a ride. You'll be a slave to his whims, his bad habits, and his begging, barking, chewing, housebreaking mishaps, and other behaviors that you never dreamed you'd have to endure. Remember back in those days when you used to say, "When I have a dog, he'll *never* do *that*"?

Raising a Dachshund is hard work. It takes vigilance, consistency, and a refusal on your part to give in. Of course, being consistent and firm, and steeling against those Dachshund wiles, is easier for some than for others. You'll be a step ahead of the game if you first figure out your personal training style, including your strengths and — more importantly — your weaknesses. Check out Chapter 12 to determine your personal training profile, and remember: Stay strong. Be consistent. *You* are in charge!

Chapter 12

Determining Your Trainer Profile

*E*very person has a unique nature and personality; attempting to practice any daily behavior that goes against your personality is probably futile. If you're crazy about chocolate, a diet of tofu and bean sprouts probably won't last for more than a day or two (just ask me — I know). You have to find a lifestyle that makes sense for your personal tastes and level of willpower.

Same thing with dog training. If you're a big sap, and one look at that cute little puppy is enough to drop you to your knees, a strict, regimented, authoritarian training style won't work for you. You'll probably end up with a Dachshund in your bed, and you'll probably spend plenty of money on fancy treats and expensive sweaters, feeling guilty all the while that you're doing something wrong. But you're not! You need to train according to your personal style.

Perhaps you love dogs and they're a big part of your life, but you feel that consistency and good behavior are paramount. You have no trouble making a set of rules and enforcing them. The dog is the dog and you are the master; your Dachshund can whine or bat her big, dark eyes at you all day, but you know that extra treats will make her chubby, and you have no intention of letting her jump on visitors or beg at the table. (You probably also have very well-behaved children — or you would.)

Part of the challenge of training a dog — especially a Dachshund — is recognizing that your personality and training style will impact your training effectiveness — and your Dachshund's personality. This chapter helps you determine your individual training style and develop a training strategy that's tailored to your strengths and weaknesses. You want to help your Dachshund, in your own personal way, to be the best Dachshund she can be. (For info on applying your style to Dachshund training, head to Chapters 13 and 14.)

Forming Your Personal Training Style

An analysis of your relationship with your Dachshund isn't complete without a little self-examination. For some people, training dogs is easy (perhaps for the owner of the star of Figure 12-1). Others can't seem to train the most willing and tractable of pets. What is it about human behavior that's sometimes so contrary to communicating effectively with animal behavior?

Photo courtesy of Adam Hare.

Figure 12-1: Are you the kind of trainer who can get a Dachsie to hold this pose?

Different people have different training styles. Play-based training or short drills, food rewards or praises and pats, learning tricks or unlearning bad habits — all are effective and possible as long as the training is consistent, loving, practiced daily, based on positive reinforcement rather than punishment, and fun for both you and your Dachshund. The following sections allow you to determine your training profile and form a training plan that will be effective and long-lasting.

Determining your training profile

You can be better prepared to train your Dachshund if you can identify your personal tendencies beforehand. Answer the following questions to determine your trainer profile. If some of the questions aren't relevant yet (for example, if you haven't brought your new puppy home yet), imagine how you think you'd react in the situation and then pick the answer that most closely matches your inclinations. Afterward, head to the following section to put your answers to use:

 1. **You just brought your new Dachshund puppy home with you, and you're introducing her to her new Dachshund den (see Chapter 9). She doesn't want to go inside. What do you do?**

    A. Throw in some treats, push her inside gently but firmly, and shut the door. She'll get used to it.

    B. Throw in some treats, offer some encouraging words, and then ignore her. If you aren't interesting to play with, the treats will seem more attractive and she'll go inside eventually.

    C. Think to yourself, "The crate looks so cold and uninviting. I can't possibly leave her in there all alone . . . that would be so *mean*."

 2. **You and your family are just sitting down to a nice family dinner. Where is your Dachshund?**

    A. In her crate. She won't even get a chance to learn how to beg in your house!

    B. Lying quietly nearby, on the kitchen floor. You're determined not to reinforce her begging by giving her table food, but you hate to have her miss out on the family dinnertime, because she *is* part of the family.

C. Under the table with her front paws on your lap, or staring winsomely at you and watching your fork with an eagle eye. She knows where to get the goods. Hey, is it really fair that you get to eat this good food and she has to be denied?

3. You give your Dachshund treats

A. During training when she fulfills a request.

B. To reinforce any good behavior.

C. Probably too often, but when she looks at the dog cookie jar with such longing, you can't resist. You want to make her happy.

4. Housebreaking has been

A. A breeze. You crate-trained your Dachshund, and she learned the ropes in a week. She never had an accident inside.

B. Fairly successful. You're still working on it, but she's getting the picture because you take her outside at the same times every single day. She still makes the occasional mistake, but you clean it up right away.

C. Um . . . To be honest, you just aren't comfortable with the crate because she whines so pitifully in there, and you can't seem to remember to take her out on a schedule. But that's okay, because you don't mind cleaning up the messes all that much.

5. Your training sessions are (or will be)

A. Strictly regimented. You hold them at the same time each day, and you have a planned schedule of what you'll cover in each session.

B. Daily, but they're pretty informal and fun.

C. Wait a minute . . . training? Isn't that sort of authoritarian? But come to think of it, you do ask your Dachshund to sit or stay or do whatever seems fun at the moment.

6. Your goals for your Dachshund are

A. To train her for competition — either in obedience, agility, field trials, or wherever her talents are (see Chapter 15).

B. To have a well-behaved family pet that knows and follows the house rules most of the time.

    C. To have a buddy and best friend. You aren't too concerned about whether she can do tricks. You just want her around for cuddling.

7. **Your vet tells you your Dachshund is overweight. What do you do?**

    A. Immediately restrict her food intake and increase the length of her walks.

    B. Cut back on the treats and begin measuring her kibble so that you don't overestimate. You also become more careful about walking her every day rather than skipping the walks when you don't feel like it.

    C. Buy lower-calorie treats and try to cut back on her food. But, when she acts like she's starving, you often give in and give her just a little bit more. After all, most people carry a few extra pounds, too. What harm could it do?

8. **Your Dachshund barks at everything — passersby on the street, trash blowing in the wind, and even at you when she wants something. How do you handle it?**

    A. You completely ignore her when she barks or put her in her den when she gets too loud — especially if she's outside disturbing the neighbors. No one should have to listen to such excessive noise.

    B. Recognize that Dachshunds bark but that excessive barking isn't tolerable. You keep the blinds shut on the front windows and ignore her when she barks at you. You make her come inside if she barks in the yard. Otherwise, you pay attention because she may be alerting you to something.

    C. You think to yourself, "Dachshunds bark. What about it?" You don't mind so much. Besides, if your friends don't like it, maybe they really aren't your friends at all!

9. **In your home, nighttime consists of**

    A. Peace and quiet, with your Dachshund curled up in her den, sleeping through the night (after the first few weeks).

    B. An occasional trip outside, but mostly your Dachshund sleeps nicely under the covers with you.

    C. Broken sleep. Every time your Dachshund makes a noise, you wake up and take her out or give her a toy to chew. You've even found yourself playing with her at 3 a.m. because she wants to play. You aren't getting much sleep, but you feel like your Dachshund needs the attention. You only hope she'll grow out of this stage and sleep through the night so you can, too.

10. **During the day when you're at work**

A. Your Dachshund stays in her den or in an enclosed, pet-proofed area (see Chapter 6). You either come home for lunch to let her out or hire a pet sitter or dog walker to cover the lunch hour.

B. Your Dachshund stays in the kitchen with a baby gate that keeps her out of the carpeted areas. Sometimes she chews things, but you're working on that bad habit. You come home for lunch as often as you can. When you don't, you usually have a mess to clean up.

C. Your Dachshund gets free reign of the house. You feel so guilty for leaving her that you think she deserves to shred the trash and have a few accidents. You can't blame her.

Letting your Dachshund puppy run free in the house when you're away from home can result in more than just property damage. Your Dachshund can be seriously injured or poisoned if she ingests certain types of trash or other foreign objects or substances. Dachshund-proof any room in which your pup will be left unsupervised for any length of time. Better yet, let her snooze in her den when you're away.

Developing a personalized training plan

After you answer the questions in the preceding section, you can check out where you stand to develop a personalized training plan. Tally your answers to determine whether you have mostly As, Bs, or Cs, and then read the applicable training-strategy discussion that follows. If you have an equal number of any two letters (or close to it), read both training-strategy discussions.

If you answer mostly As

You are (or will be) a highly disciplined, efficient, and consistent pet owner. You've probably always been a schedule person, and you encourage discipline and respectful behavior in everyone around you — spouse, children, and pets. For you, a dog is simply another family member that you expect to follow the rules and behave in an acceptable manner. If anyone can bring out the best in a Dachshund, it's you. Dachshunds crave consistency and want to know the rules.

Take advantage of your tendencies by keeping your Dachshund on a strict schedule, a healthy diet, and regimented training sessions. Systematic training is great, because you get a lot accomplished in the minimum amount of time.

Consider training your Dachshund for professional competition, if your dog has what it takes (see Chapters 2 and 15). *You* certainly do.

Your one challenge? Remembering to be *fun.* Consistency and schedules can get tedious if you don't maintain your sense of humor when others aren't quite as disciplined as you are. When your Dachshund slips up, gently nudge her back on track. Don't get angry or irritable when she doesn't measure up to your high standards. Instead, keep working with her (see Chapter 14 for troubleshooting tips). She'll get it, and if she can trust you to be kind and loving in your firmness, she'll do anything for you.

If you answer mostly Bs

You're the kind of dog owner most breeders are looking for. You know what your pet needs, and you do your best to give it to her. Sometimes you get busy, get off schedule, and bend the rules. You are human, after all. In general, though, you're a responsible and loving Dachshund companion who tries hard to teach your pet what it means to behave and have a fulfilling family life.

Your training sessions should be fun and full of play, which Dachshunds love. Your pet will respond quickly to your requests after she learns what you want.

Your biggest challenge? Keeping a schedule and remembering to train *every day.* Dogs thrive on consistency and regularity even more than humans do, so a routine is important for your dog — even if you can't always follow it. You'll do a great job, however; your Dachshund is lucky to have a pet owner as caring and responsible as you are!

If you answer mostly Cs

You're probably fully aware that you're not in charge of your Dachshund. She's in charge of you. You need to prepare for a life of servitude or change your ways. Don't be offended. I used to be in this category, and I know change is possible. Difficult, yes, but you don't have to alter your personality. For the sake of your Dachshund, you just have to summon up some inner strength and take charge. Sure, she's sweet. Sure, she's charming. Sure, she's just about the cutest little thing you've ever seen, and you love her to death. All the more reason to do what's best for her, which means not letting her run the show.

Dogs (like children) will challenge you at every turn, but they want nothing more than to know, without a doubt, what the rules are. They also want to know what to expect on a daily basis. Even if you can't manage a consistent and regular schedule for yourself (I can't, either), you can make a list of things you do each and every day for and with your Dachshund (see Chapter 9):

- ✔ Three meals (measure that kibble, please, or you'll overestimate)
- ✔ One grooming session
- ✔ One or two walks
- ✔ Two or three short training sessions

Do these things not happen at the same time each day? I know you're not superman (or superwoman), and that's okay. Better to do these important chores daily at whatever time works than not at all. You owe it to your pet, because she depends on you for structure. Plenty of love is great, but it isn't enough to make your Dachshund happy, healthy, and secure.

Many dogs are surrendered to animal shelters because their owners never bothered to fully housetrain them, and then they got tired of cleaning up after them. The next time you think crate-training or any other housetraining method is cruel, remember that surrendering your Dachshund to an animal shelter is much crueler. Do the kind thing and housetrain your Dachshund with consistency and vigilance (see Chapter 13). And remember: Dogs love their dens (or, they learn to love them)!

Attending Obedience Classes (For Your Dachshund and You)

Going to obedience classes when your puppy is about 3 months old creates a firm foundation for future training. It teaches both you and your Dachshund good habits and provides a structure to follow at home. Classes can help you communicate better with your pet, because a trained instructor teaches *you* how to train your Dachshund. Classes also help you feel more committed to your dog and invested in your dog's future behavior. Classes are fun and informative, and you get personalized attention to your dog's unique needs. Plus, your Dachsie learns how to meet and greet other dogs nicely.

Have some class: Avoid dumping at the shelter

According to a study published in 2000 in the Journal of Applied Animal Welfare Science, the pet owners who relinquished dogs to 12 U.S. animal shelters broke down into the following categories:

✔ 70 percent said their dogs had never been taught basic commands.

✔ Less than 6 percent said that they took their dogs to obedience class.

✔ Only 2 percent said they had their dogs trained by professional trainers.

And if you and your Dachshund love it, you can continue on with more advanced classes — possibly even training for professional competition (see Chapter 15).

No matter how good you think you are at training your Dachshund at home, obedience classes are a great experience for both you and your Dachshund. Every dog should experience them — as long as their owners can find good trainers. A seasoned dog trainer should give you ideas and strategies that hadn't occurred to you. He or she can help you deal with individual problems or tendencies of your own pet — something no book can do. Also, learning good behavior in a place other than your living room, and in the presence of other dogs, will help your Dachshund see that training applies every-where, not just at home.

But not all obedience classes are the same. You need to look for a teacher who advocates positive training methods rather than rough methods — such as the use of a choke chain. You certainly should avoid those who use leash jerks for corrections. Rough methods aren't necessary for training Dachshunds, in the opinion of many contemporary trainers. If used incorrectly or too harshly, they can injure your Dachshund's back.

To start the process of finding a good trainer, try the following sources:

✔ Ask your vet to recommend a good local trainer.

✔ Ask your dog's breeder, who may know just the right person.

✔ Ask friends with well-behaved dogs where they learned how to train their pets.

✔ Contact the Association of Pet Dog Trainers — an organization devoted to better dog training through education, and a great advocator of positive training methods. You can search for an APDT-certified trainer in your area at www.apdt.com (click on Dog Trainer Search) or you can give the organization a call at 1-800-PET-DOGS. Call Monday through Friday from 8:30 a.m. to 5:00 p.m. Eastern Standard Time.

After getting a referral, visit the instructor to gauge your interest. Ask the instructor running the obedience class to explain his or her personal philosophy of training. (If he or she is too busy to be interviewed, look elsewhere. Would your child's teacher refuse a parent-teacher conference?) What are his or her influences? What methods have proved most effective? Does he or she have any experience training Dachshunds? Also, ask for his or her references and *check them*. Sometimes, a recommendation or a warning from a previous customer tells you more than a trainer ever could.

If you hear terms like *lure-and-reward training, clicker training,* or *play training,* that's a good sign. But watch out for comments about choke collars, corrections, and discipline. Perhaps your Dachshund may occasionally *need* a raised voice, a stern look, or a timeout, but in obedience class, the training should be all about rewarding the good stuff. This is how Dachshunds learn best.

Lure-and-reward training is a method in which a lure, such as a treat or piece of kibble, is used to physically guide your dog into a position, such as a sit. *Clicker training* is a method in which a click from a plastic device (called a *clicker*) is associated with a food treat. Eventually, the click itself becomes rewarding to the dog and is used as a positive reinforcement for desired behavior. *Play training* is a method in which practice of certain commands is disguised as play.

Don't forget your intuition. If a trainer just seems wrong, for whatever reason, keep looking. If you feel good about a trainer and his or her methods make sense to you — they seem humane, kind, and in the best interest of the dogs — feel free to sign up.

Good luck and don't delay. Start training your Dachshund today!

Chapter 13

Teaching Your Dachshund the House Rules

*Y*ou've been worrying about training your new Dachshund, haven't you? What new dog owner doesn't? Bad behavior is a major cause of puppy and dog abandonment to animal shelters, and the saddest part is that the puppies and dogs aren't even to blame. They pay the price for their owners' lack of knowledge and commitment to preventing and dealing with behavior problems in the first place.

But that won't happen to your Dachshund, because you're fully prepared to teach him how to behave himself in a human world. Right? *Good.* In this chapter, I review all the training tips that you and your Dachshund can really sink your teeth into. Good luck, and may your Dachshund soon be the best-behaved dog on the block.

Housetraining 101

Admit it. Housetraining is your biggest worry. Nobody likes to mop up puppy pee and scoop up puppy poop. And maybe you've heard that Dachshunds are harder to train than some breeds. I'll admit it, it's true — they are. But they aren't as hard as some breeds, either.

The Mini Dachshund can be the most challenging Dachsie to train, but all Dachshunds have a stubborn streak. *You* get to go to the bathroom inside the house. Why shouldn't he? But even if you think he has a point with this Dachshund-centric argument, don't give in to stained carpets and a stinky house. You *can* housetrain your Dachshund.

Wouldn't it be great if your Dachshund never had a single accident in the house? It's possible. Difficult, but possible. Most importantly, if you do slip up (notice I say if *you* slip up, not your pup), don't give up hope. Clean up the mess, clean it well, and resolve to not let it happen again.

Few sights please a new dog owner like the sight of the little guy doing his duty in the proper location. Others may find this preoccupation slightly repulsive, but when your puppy squats or starts to poop in the right spot (outside, on the newspaper, or wherever you decide), don't be surprised if you suddenly begin to cheer out loud. And you should! (Just don't startle the puppy into stopping what he's doing.) Each successful bathroom venture puts you one step closer to housetraining success, and when you've housetrained a Dachshund, you know you've accomplished something major.

For some puppies and even adult dogs, housetraining is a long, protracted battle between dog and human, sometimes lasting for months. No one should have to put up with that — human or dog. And who wants to? You can eliminate elimination battles with a little knowledge and two to four weeks of extreme vigilance (maybe a little longer with a Mini Dachshund). The following sections show you the way. When your Dachshund is sleeping through the night and asking politely to be let out during the day, you know you have it made.

Understanding the elimination process

Puppies don't pee and poop at random. A very specific process happens inside them (and inside dogs and even humans of all ages) called the *gastrocolic reflex,* which is the internal mechanism that governs the elimination process. Eating triggers this reflex. The body makes room for new food by expelling the remains of old food in the colon. The result? Somewhere between 5 and 60 minutes after a puppy eats, he needs to poop. And after your puppy's tiny bladder fills up enough from drinking water, he'll need to pee also.

Every dog is different. Some puppies need to go out a lot, and others not so often. But the younger a puppy is, the more often he'll need to go. As he gets older, he'll learn to hold it longer. Your job is to know your dog's timetable.

You can figure out your puppy's timetable by taking him out every two hours during the first few weeks and watching him carefully. When you have it down, you've conquered a major housetraining hurdle. Take your puppy out on a regular schedule (see the next section), and always reward a successful bathroom effort with praise and the occasional treat; soon enough, your incorrigible little Dachshund will be fully housetrained — and sooner than you expected.

Your detailed guide to housetraining

Now that you have the basic principles down (after reading the previous section), you can discover how housetraining will work in your busy day. Take a look at these guidelines, or post them on your refrigerator (and for more reading, check out *Housetraining For Dummies,* by Susan McCullough [Wiley]).

If you decide to paper-train your Dachshund — or, like one senior owner I know, allow him to use the extra shower stall as his "litter-box" — the same guidelines apply, except that you whisk him off to his *inside* elimination station.

- ✔ **Before bringing your puppy inside the house for the very first time, take him to his elimination station while he's still attached to his leash and stay there until he does his duty.**

   If he won't eliminate, take him inside, put him in his den, close the door, and tell him in a gentle voice that you'll be back. Return in 15 minutes and try again. Don't take him anywhere else in the house until he has eliminated in his special spot.

- ✔ **Every two hours during the day for the first week, take him out to his special spot.**

   If he doesn't go, bring him in and put him in his den (nicely — don't get mad or none of this will work). Return every 20 to 30 minutes and try again until he goes. (***Note:*** Your puppy may have a stronger bladder, and you may find that you can take him out every three or four hours rather than every two. But start with two-hour intervals until you know your Dachshund's tendencies.)

   If you have to work all day and nobody will be home, have someone come by every few hours to let out your puppy. If you can't find a willing friend or family member, consider hiring a pet sitter. These professionals spend much of their days walking and playing with puppies and adult dogs for people who can't get home from work for long periods of time.

✔ **Within 30 minutes of a meal, take him outside until he goes.**

After you learn your puppy's e-time (see the section "Timing is everything"), you can alter this step to fit your puppy's needs.

✔ **For the first week, take your puppy out every four hours during the night.**

Set your alarm if you have to, but your Dachshund will probably wake you up. (If he's sleeping soundly, you can wait it out, but don't miss the opportunity when he wakes up.)

✔ **Always take your puppy out first thing in the morning, at the same time each morning, and immediately before bedtime, at the same time each evening.**

Sorry, that means on weekends, too! Continue this habit throughout your Dachshund's life. (You can always go back to bed after the bathroom break.)

✔ **Never, ever miss the sniff-and-circle routine.**

If you or someone else can't watch him, let your puppy rest in his crate where he'll be much less likely to have an accident.

For the first couple of weeks, be extra vigilant. It could happen any time, even when an elimination session isn't scheduled. After your Dachshund is housetrained, keep the concept in the back of your mind. Everyone forgets about letting the dog out every now and then. And note that after an extra-big meal, your Dachshund may need more outside time than usual.

✔ **For the first couple weeks, keep your Dachshund in uncarpeted areas whenever he's out of his den.**

Cleanup will be much easier, and the scent won't last like it will in carpet. (Purchase a reliable odor remover specifically designed for pet odors; see Chapter 8.)

✔ **If your Dachshund makes a mistake, remember that it's *your* fault, *not* your Dachshund's.**

Don't get mad. You can behave with urgency when whisking your Dachshund outside if you catch him in the act. You can say "No!" sternly and even sharply, which may interrupt him mid-accident so you can get him outside before he finishes. But don't yell at him (even if you're extremely irritated, which you very well may be), and for your dog's sake, don't hit him or rub his nose in his transgression (or, I should say, *your* transgression). He won't get it. He really won't. It will just make things worse, and he'll learn to fear you.

Dachshunds are fastidious, clean animals, and they lack the typical hound-dog odor. They don't want to eliminate in a manner that displeases you, and they don't want to mess up their living environments. They need only a little guidance from you to do what makes everyone happy. Be a patient, consistent, and loving housetrainer.

To help you keep track of when to take your Dachshund outside in the first week, make a copy of Table 13-1 (or make your own version) and circle the appropriate time of each successful elimination. The chart lists times in two-hour intervals throughout the day and four-hour intervals throughout the night, assuming that your Dachshund gets up at 7 a.m. and goes to bed at 11 p.m. Times are approximate. Modify them for your own schedule.

Table 13-1		**Daily Elimination Schedule**				
Monday	*Tuesday*	*Wednesday*	*Thursday*	*Friday*	*Saturday*	*Sunday*
7 a.m.	7 a.m.	7 a.m.	7 a.m.	7 a.m.	7 a.m.	7 a.m.
9 a.m.	9 a.m.	9 a.m.	9 a.m.	9 a.m.	9 a.m.	9 a.m.
11 a.m.	11 a.m.	11 a.m.	11 a.m.	11 a.m.	11 a.m.	11 a.m.
1 p.m.	1 p.m.	1 p.m.	1 p.m.	1 p.m.	1 p.m.	1 p.m.
3 p.m.	3 p.m.	3 p.m.	3 p.m.	3 p.m.	3 p.m.	3 p.m.
5 p.m.	5 p.m.	5 p.m.	5 p.m.	5 p.m.	5 p.m.	5 p.m.
7 p.m.	7 p.m.	7 p.m.	7 p.m.	7 p.m.	7 p.m.	7 p.m.
9 p.m.	9 p.m.	9 p.m.	9 p.m.	9 p.m.	9 p.m.	9 p.m.
11 p.m.	11 p.m.	11 p.m.	11 p.m.	11 p.m.	11 p.m.	11 p.m.
3 a.m.	3 a.m.	3 a.m.	3 a.m.	3 a.m.	3 a.m.	3 a.m.
7 a.m.	7 a.m.	7 a.m.	7 a.m.	7 a.m.	7 a.m.	7 a.m.

Common housetraining errors

Don't fall prey to these common housetraining mistakes and you'll have a big-boy puppy in no time:

- ✔ Missing your puppy's sniff-and-circle routine
- ✔ Leaving your puppy unattended before he's fully trained

✔ Not taking your puppy to the same place for elimination each and every time on his leash

✔ Allowing your puppy to eat or drink water after about 7 p.m.

If he's really thirsty, let him drink water but be sure to take him out again before bedtime.

✔ Not taking your puppy out immediately before you put him in his kennel for the night

✔ Letting your puppy sleep outside his crate for the first week

Biting, Gnawing, Chewing — Nixing All Toothy Indiscretions

Puppies bite, and if you didn't know it before you brought your Dachshund home, you surely know it by now (see Figure 13-1 for an example of a Dachsie that may be just waiting to gnaw on something!). Sometimes called *mouthing,* puppy biting is really just oral exploration. Great for puppies. Not so great for new shoes, chair legs, wall moldings, and the human fingers that are often the subjects of their inquiry.

Photo courtesy of Gail Painter.

Figure 13-1: Without training, he'll chew on you and everything you hold dear!

Some people think that puppy mouthing is cute and like to excuse it because it's a puppy's way of exploring the world. But you won't think the behavior is so cute when your puppy becomes an adult dog and is still shredding your possessions and nipping at people whenever they annoy him or he wants their attention. To a Dachshund, even a "Hey, cut that out!" is better than being ignored. The following sections inform you of all the necessary biting info and help you nip the nipping in the bud.

Don't let him chew on just anything!

Puppy teeth are sharp as needles. That's just one reason to discourage the mouthing of human flesh and other objects, but there are other reasons:

- ✔ Letting your puppy chew on your fingers teaches him that chewing is okay. You aren't doing your puppy any favors. Others won't be as indulgent as you, but your puppy won't know that. He'll only know that chewing fingers must be fine because you let him do it.

  The first important measure you must take to nip indiscriminate mouthing in the bud is to never allow your puppy to chew on your fingers. If he tries, don't let him. Keep your hands away from his mouth. If he accidentally gets a mouth full of fingers, quickly remove them and say "No!" If he never gets a chance to chew on you, he'll be less likely to give it a thought.

  If your puppy bites at your fingers, you can try placing your thumb under his tongue, holding his lower jaw gently but firmly, and saying "No teeth" for 10 to 20 seconds. This usually stops finger biting completely within one week.

- ✔ Because puppies love to chew everything, you must make it very clear which things are okay to chew and which are not. Your puppy must learn that a few select objects are chewable — and nothing else. This rule sets the stage for good oral behavior for the rest of your puppy's life. Never vary it.

  Objects your puppy shouldn't chew include furniture, shoes, toilet paper, string, as well as anything he could choke on, destroy, or that could injure him. Use your common sense. Prevention is best.

  However, you can't store your sofa away for the first year of your puppy's life. Same goes for the dining room chair, tables, and any other large piece of furniture your Dachshund takes a fancy to. If your dog insists on chewing these things, liberally apply some Bitter Apple or other chew-deterrent spray according to the instructions.

You can also give your puppy a quick, harmless squirt from a water bottle or shake a soda can with pennies in it to grab his attention. You can even employ the ultrasonic sound from an electronic device called Pet Agree. This gets a puppy's attention painlessly but effectively so you can redirect him from what he's doing. That's when you employ your secret weapon: a well-placed chew toy (see the following section).

If your Dachshund has never been a big chewer but suddenly becomes destructive or chews obsessively (including self-chewing), he may have a medical problem. Visit your vet and have him checked out. Skin problems, allergies, epilepsy, separation anxiety, or any number of other disorders may be the cause. Some dogs suffer from a condition, similar to obsessive-compulsive disorder in humans, that causes them to chew obsessively. Many conditions can be effectively treated by a veterinarian.

Whatever method you use to nip biting in the bud, you'll be developing something called bite inhibition in your young puppy's brain. He'll learn that he's not supposed to bite. If you never teach him, he'll never know this important bit of information about living with humans — and adult Dachshunds have *strong* jaws and *big* teeth.

Harnessing the power of a well-placed chew toy

Some Dachshunds chew on things more than others, and some Dachshunds aren't interested in any toy but their favorite. For the exuberant chewers, you can make use of a well-placed chew toy at every opportunity. Store safe, sturdy chew toys all over the house so that whenever your Dachshund gets too interested in chewing your fingers, toes, shoes, or furniture, you can immediately remove him with a firm "No" and then hand him an acceptable option. When he chews the toy instead, heap on the praise. "What a good dog!"

Your detailed guide to bite prevention

Ah, just what you've been waiting for. Here are the detailed guidelines to follow with your new dog in order to say good-bye to painful puppy bites and destructive chewing:

✔ **From the first moment you meet your new puppy, never, ever let him chew on you or anyone else.**

Pull your fingers away and say "No!" and then give him a chew toy. Praise him when he chews it.

✔ **From the first moment you meet your new puppy, never, ever let him chew on anything you don't want him to chew on when he becomes an adult.**

Apply some chew-deterrent spray according to the instructions and distribute chew toys around the house.

✔ **Keep chew toys in every room in which your puppy is allowed — plus one in his den and one in the car if he travels with you.**

Whenever he even thinks about chewing something forbidden, pop a chew toy in his mouth. He'll soon associate the chewing urge with a chew toy.

And if you catch him in the act, pull the old switcheroo: Remove him from the bad object and replace the void with the good chew toy.

✔ **Not sure how to anticipate when your puppy feels like chewing?** *Watch* **him.**

Some puppies start to chomp their jaws or lick their lips and look around.

✔ **Never fly off the handle because your puppy has chewed something forbidden.**

You either left an object out when you shouldn't have or weren't supervising his play. Guide him toward good behavior and don't reinforce bad behavior by making a big fuss.

Help! Dachsie's a demolition machine!

Some people complain that their Dachshunds destroy things when left alone. If you have a destructive chewer and must leave him alone, you need to keep him safely confined when you're away. Destructive dogs don't just wreck your stuff, they risk injuring themselves by choking, mouth and throat lacerations, intestinal obstruction, and even poisoning. Your Dachshund won't mind naps in his den, as long as you don't keep him in there for more than four or five hours without a break.

That's it. The tricky part is to be eternally consistent. Always enforce the rules. If you miss an enforcement opportunity, move on. Certainly don't punish your Dachshund; resolve never again to let him chew anything he shouldn't chew. I know, you're only human. But do your best — the more consistent you are, the faster your Dachsie will learn.

Convincing Your Little Barker to Quiet Down

If you have a Dachshund, you have a barker. Dachshunds bark for many reasons — some of them reasonable and some of them unreasonable. It isn't fair to get annoyed or angry at your Dachshund for occasional barking. He's been bred to bark for good reasons. But obsessive or unnecessary barking is something you can address and, in most cases, resolve. But how do you do it? The first step is to understand why your Dachsie is barking. The following sections take you there and beyond.

 Barking too much can be harmful for your Dachshund's health. If he barks obsessively, he puts himself under a lot of physical stress. Obsessive barking can also be a sign of a health problem or a sign that your Dachshund is particularly insecure or fearful (or just mind-numbingly bored). Barking also is harmful for you. At best, you'll find yourself continually irritated with your Dachshund. At worst, your neighbors won't be happy with you, and if you live in an apartment, you could be asked to leave or even be evicted if the noise becomes too bothersome.

Understanding why Dachshunds bark

Dachshunds bark more than some breeds because barking was part of the original Dachshund plan. When used in hunting, a Dachshund would corner its prey and then bark loudly and sharply to alert the hunter or farmer to come and finish the job. Sometimes, the Dachshund's bark had to be heard across great distances, or even from underground.

So, even if you don't hunt with your Dachshund, you'll still reap the, ahem, "benefits" of centuries of breeding. It isn't his fault, but it is something you should be prepared for.

Today, your Dachshund will bark for many reasons:

✔ Someone is invading his territory (his house, yard, human).

✔ Something resembles a threat, and he thinks you should be alerted.

✔ Something resembles prey (a squirrel, a cat, a piece of trash blowing down the street), and he wants to get it.

✔ He wants to get out of wherever you've put him (a pen, a den, a room with a gate or closed door, a yard with a fence).

✔ He wants your attention or wants you to return after you've left.

✔ He's really excited.

✔ He's suspicious or fearful of someone or something, such as a visitor or a noise (for example, a ringing phone or doorbell).

✔ He's bored or wants you to stop ignoring him *right now.*

Some of these reasons are justifiable — even desirable. If a stranger is invading your property, you want to know about it, and your Dachshund is just the guy to tell you. In such a case, you can determine who the invader is, and then you can show your Dachshund that the person is okay by letting in the visitor, or you can call the police. Praising your Dachshund for alerting you to the presence of trespassers (good or bad ones) is perfectly acceptable. "Thank you, good boy! Now you can be quiet." However, your Dachshund also needs to know when to stop.

Removing the cause of unwanted barking

Centuries of breeding aside, you shouldn't have to listen to unreasonable barking all day. You *can* stop barking by removing the cause. Doing so involves determining the cause first, of course (see the previous section).

But after you determine the cause of your dog's unreasonable barking, you don't want to encourage it. Heed the following tips:

✔ If your Dachshund barks at everything that moves outside the front window, you need only to keep him from looking out the front window. Draw the blinds or close the curtains, or keep your Dachshund in another room.

✔ If a squirrel is teasing your Dachshund in the backyard, bring your Dachshund inside.

✔ If the neighborhood kids are teasing your Dachshund through the fence, shame on them. Call their parents.

✔ If your Dachshund barks frantically whenever you leave him alone, begin keeping him in his den when you're away. Also practice keeping him in his den when you're home so that he knows his den is a safe place and doesn't always indicate your absence. Don't talk to your dog when he's in the den, though. This increases the likelihood of anxiety problems.

Talk to your vet or a trainer about strategies to address severe separation anxiety if this is a problem. Separation anxiety can be effectively treated by a professional, especially if caught early.

✔ If your Dachshund is really excited and barking up a storm, calm him down. A few happy barks uttered out of sheer joy when you and your Dachshund are playing together won't hurt anything, however.

✔ If your Dachshund is bored, give him something to do. Sometimes a five-minute, rousing game of fetch or a few favorite toys and a Kong stuffed with a couple of biscuits is all it takes (see Chapter 14 for more on the importance of play).

If your Dachshund is suspicious or fearful of particular noises, you can desensitize him to these sounds by exposing him to them over and over while keeping him safe and giving him treats. You want him to associate the sounds with rewards rather than fear. Desensitization turns a negative into a positive. Ask a behaviorist or trainer for tips on how to do this — especially if you're unsure about it or if your Dachshund seems severely traumatized by harmless sounds or objects. You don't want to make the problem worse.

After you eliminate all the causes you can and help your Dachshund resolve any irrational fears, your next step is to train your dog not to bark (see the following section).

Generally, I would never recommend having your dog *debarked* — a surgical procedure that alters your dog's vocal cords to lessen the volume of barking — unless the only alternative is to abandon the pet or face legal action. In fact, many vets now refuse to do this surgery because they believe it's cruel.

Also, shock collars and citrus spray collars are designed to discourage barking, but they punish a dog for behaving according to instinct. However, in severe cases of obsessive barking, these kinds of collars may be helpful, distracting the dog from his barking and giving you a chance to intervene and calm him down or redirect him. This is certainly preferable to debarking. Talk to your vet for more information if you have a severe case, but don't be too quick to use any of these solutions. Give training a fair chance first.

Manipulating your Dachshund's instincts

Training your dog not to bark requires an effort contrary to your human instinct. First, when he barks, you must show no emotion whatsoever except, perhaps, for a quiet disdain. Yelling and making a big fuss only reinforces his behavior, because he thinks you're barking along with him.

Basically, there are two major keys to training your Dachshund not to bark unreasonably:

✔ Remember that some barking is justified and desirable.

✔ Never, ever react to unreasonable or undesirable barking in any way except to dispassionately remove your Dachshund from the source of the barking when possible.

That isn't so hard to remember, is it?

Jumping: Not Joyous for Everyone

Dachshunds get so excited. They want so desperately to capture their humans' attention. They want to see what's going on, and that's hard to do when they live so close to the ground. You can almost hear them thinking: "How can I help but jump up? It's a fascinating, stimulating, and exhilarating world up there above my head!"

Don't buy it for a minute. Your Dachshund doesn't have to jump up on you or anybody else — ever. He can see just fine, and you, as his tall friend, have the responsibility of getting down to his level every so often. It's only fair if you don't want him to try to ascend to your level.

Fortunately, Dachshunds aren't very big, so they won't knock you down if they jump on you. Jumping is, nonetheless, bad manners, and your friends and neighbors may not think it's as cute as you do. Plus, jumping can put an unnecessary strain on your Dachshund's back. If you train your puppy not to jump from day one, everyone will be impressed with how well-mannered and restrained your little Dachshund is. Hop on to the following sections to find out how.

How you inadvertently encourage jumping

If your Dachshund jumps, he does it because you encourage it. Yes, you do. Encouraging jumping is all too easy. All it takes is a look, a smile, or any other sign of pleasure or attention that very first time your Dachshund applies his front paws to your lower legs.

Here's a scenario for you: You get home after a long afternoon. You can't wait to see your new puppy (it's been since lunch, after all — or longer if you have a dog walker or pet sitter). You open the door to his den, and he comes bounding joyfully toward you. Your face lights up as your puppy leaps up against your legs. How *cute!* You smile and say, "Good dog!" And you scoop your puppy into your arms. You're both in heaven.

You've just "told" your puppy that he gets a great big reward if he jumps up on you. Now he'll do it again and again and try it on others, and he'll keep doing it until he's full grown. If you suddenly get mad at him when he does it, he won't understand why. He'll think you're unpredictable and maybe a little bit scary. But he won't think, "Oh, I guess now I shouldn't jump up anymore."

Re-training your jumper

If you've already reacted with positive reinforcement to your jumping puppy, don't despair. It isn't too late to reteach your Dachshund that jumping isn't allowed. Even jumping adult Dachshunds can learn not to jump. Getting mad isn't the way to teach, however.

Every single time you come home or even into a room and your puppy runs to you and jumps up, you need to do something very difficult: Completely ignore him. Don't talk to him and don't look at him. Pretend he isn't even there. Wait it out. He'll be confused at first. He'll probably try to jump with even greater fervor. Eventually, though, he'll give up. Don't give up before he does.

When your puppy stops jumping on you, turn toward him and really pile on the praise. Get way down low so he can see your face. That's what he was trying to do, anyway. "Helloooo, puppy! Whatta good doggy! I missed you soooo much!" Pet him, offer him a treat — whatever will make him happy. You've just rewarded him for *not* jumping!

If, in the process of your praises, he jumps on you again, completely turn it off. Ignore him again. Don't look at him and don't speak. When he stops jumping on you again, praise him again, giving him all your attention.

Your puppy may not get it immediately, but after a few times, he'll get the gist. Dachshunds are smart puppies! After that point, never, ever reward him or pay any attention to him when he jumps on you. As soon as he stops, however, immediately turn your full attention on him with all the praise and petting you can muster.

You also can meet jumping with a blank expression and the word "Sit." When your dog sits, you can kneel down and praise him lavishly as he welcomes you home. (For more on training your Dachshund how to "Sit," see Chapter 14.)

If your puppy jumps on other people when they come to visit, have them do the same thing. Instruct visitors before they come inside about the plan. When your puppy quits jumping, a visitor can meet, greet, and pet him.

Teaching an Older Dog New Tricks

If you've adopted an adult Dachshund (see Chapter 5), he may already be housetrained, he may never bite or chew inappropriate things, he may not bark inappropriately, and he may know never to jump up on people. Or, more likely, he may need a little work on any or all of these areas.

Teaching an adult Dachshund is essentially the same as teaching a puppy. All the steps and methods that work for puppies work for adults, too. Some adults take longer to learn because they're changing old habits. Others learn much faster because they're more mature and have more life experience with humans than a pup. Maybe your adult dog used to be housetrained, got out of the habit, but will remember it quickly. Or maybe he's very eager to please you, so he tries extra hard to learn the rules.

In any case, don't assume that your adult Dachshund is untrainable. You know that line about not being able to teach an old dog new tricks? Forget it. Old dogs are perfectly capable of learning good house manners.

If your adult Dachshund seems to be having severe problems with behavior, first call your vet to rule out a medical problem. Then consider hiring a professional trainer and/or an animal behaviorist or canine behavioral consultant. Your adult Dachshund may have experienced abuse or neglect in the past, or perhaps he's never been trained in any way. A professional can help you address his issues and resolve them in the Dachshund's best interests. Do everything you can to help your adult dog adjust happily to his new home so you can live together in peace. (See Chapters 12 and 14 for more on this topic.)

Chapter 14

Putting Your Dachshund through Basic Training

In This Chapter

▶ Understanding the benefits and purpose of obedience classes

▶ Teaching your pup the good-dog basics

▶ Giving leash lessons

▶ Addressing your training problems

▶ Remembering the importance of fun

*A*fter you've conquered the house rules (see Chapter 13), you can move on to more fun training activities. Personally, *you* need a dog that's housetrained and doesn't bite or destroy things, but your *Dachshund* needs stuff to do — a purpose in life. A dog that can sit, roll over, speak, lie down, and heel on cue feels like she has important *work* and loves displaying the tricks that impress family, friends, and neighbors. (Applause doesn't hurt a Dachshund's ego, after all.)

But training isn't all about fun and games. It can also be a matter of life and death. If your untrained Dachshund slips out the front door between the legs of someone who isn't paying attention and then dashes for a squirrel across the street, all you can do is hope a car isn't coming. But, in the case of a well-trained Dachshund, you just may be able to get her to stop before she hits the street. Unfortunately, you may not be successful either way, because the instinct to give chase is strong in the Dachshund. But the better trained your Dachshund is, the greater her chances for survival.

Add to that the fact that most Dachshunds abandoned to shelters aren't trained and you have more than enough reasons to start teaching your Dachshund some basics today. This chapter is here to help.

Considering Obedience Classes

You may be fully committed to training your Dachshund at home. Good for you. But that doesn't mean you and your friend won't both benefit from a good obedience class. One of the biggest advantages to an obedience class is the socialization. Obedience classes expose your Dachshund to other dogs and humans so that your Dachsie learns more about the world. This is important for molding a stable and mature adult dog.

Socialization is the process of teaching an animal about the social world humans live in: what all kinds of other people and animals are about. This process helps puppies become well-adjusted and confident, less likely to be fearful or aggressive, and able to make smart decisions about which people and animals are friendly and which are threats. Knowledge is power, and that's exactly what socialization delivers to your Dachshund.

Obedience classes also teach your pup that you make the rules and that he must follow your lead no matter where you are. Classes give you some great new tips and tricks that you may not find in training books. Plus, I know how it feels to read something about training that makes perfect sense, only to start training and think, "Now, why isn't this working on *my* dog?" Professional teachers can address specific problems and see what you may be doing wrong.

Even if you register for nothing more than a puppy kindergarten or puppy socialization class, you'll be glad you did. You and your Dachshund both need training and a structure for your daily sessions.

Puppy kindergarten describes classes for young puppies or dogs that have never had any obedience training. These classes focus on socialization, and you may also learn how to teach your puppy some basic skills. You may even get help with housetraining and other new-puppy problems you may be experiencing.

Finding a teacher

If you find a teacher with a method you love whose style really works for you, you may find that you and your Dachshund can go up, up, up to the highest echelons of obedience competition. Or, if you're not into competition, you'll still have fun and learn *a lot.*

Finding a good teacher is important. Your veterinarian and/or breeder can probably recommend an obedience instructor or two. Also, ask other pet-owning friends which instructors they like and why. Some dog trainers will come to your house and help you with individual problems, which can work great for some Dachsies, but classes give you both the added benefit of interacting with new people and dogs.

Look for someone who teaches and uses positive training techniques (like praising good behavior) rather than negative techniques (like leash jerking). Also, look for someone you feel comfortable with and whose style you can relate to. Ask to watch a class, and talk to the trainer about his or her methods. Cost and location may also be factors for you, but don't settle on a teacher who doesn't make you feel comfortable just because the class is cheaper or closer.

Continuing your work at home

Obedience classes work best when you work every day with your Dachshund at home. Consider it homework. In fact, most obedience instructors really will give you homework assignments. When your teacher tells you to practice twice a day for 10 to 20 minutes, she means it. Otherwise, you'll find that obedience classes have little if any effect on your Dachshund's behavior. Beyond the essential element of a positive and fun approach, obedience training is all about two key concepts: consistency and persistency.

The ideal situation is holding two training sessions each day, but even one 5- or 10-minute session per day (adult dogs usually can't concentrate for much longer, and puppy sessions may be much shorter) goes a long way toward establishing a training ritual for you and your Dachshund. Make training just as important as brushing your teeth (and brushing your Dachshund's teeth!). Do it every day; you won't regret it.

But what do you *do* every day? A good obedience instructor will give you plenty of suggestions — maybe even a detailed format for your homework. The training she gives you may resemble some of the exercises in the following section. And if you haven't registered for your classes yet or you just want some variation, the puppy lessons in the following section are just what you need.

Important Lessons for You and Your Puppy

Training your Dachshund keeps her life interesting, keeps her safe, and keeps her out of the local shelters. This section covers some basic lessons and commands you can teach your Dachsie. Each lesson is simple, short, and fun — perfect for a puppy that's just learning the ropes or an adult dog that hasn't experienced a training session before.

For every lesson, be sure that you have a ready store of your dog's food (taken from her daily allowance) or very small treats so you can immediately reinforce good behavior.

No matter how consistent and persistent you are in your training sessions, if you don't make training fun for your Dachshund, you can forget the learning. A positive attitude, plenty of happy praise, and a sense of excitement are all essential elements to any Dachshund training session. If you have an old-fashioned notion of discipline, it's time to get modern. The old adage "No pain, no gain" doesn't serve you or your Dachshund well. The surest way to tell whether your Dachshund is having a blast is to consider whether *you're* having a blast. If the training is fun for you, it's probably fun for your Dachsie.

Getting a puppy's attention

Puppies are notoriously distractible. How on Earth are you going to teach your puppy to sit, let alone get her to pay attention to you long enough to hear you say the cue "Sit"? First, you teach your puppy when it's time to listen:

1. **Pick up your puppy and look her in the eye while saying her name.**

   Some puppies will look you in the eye immediately — even hold your gaze for a few seconds before twisting around to see what else is going on that may be of interest. Others will look anywhere but your eyes.

2. **Follow with one of these actions:**

   - **If she looks at you when you say her name, praise her and give her a treat.**

   - **If she won't look you in the eye, start making funny (nonthreatening) sounds.**

     Whistle, click your tongue, and say "Beep beep!" or "Toodleoodleoodle" or whatever other funny sound amuses you. (Remember, this should be fun for you, too.) *Note:* Don't use your puppy's name for this one yet. She probably hears it all the time, and you want to emit a new sound that will capture her attention.

As soon as she looks at you, smile happily, say "Good dog!" and give her a treat.

3. **Repeat Steps 1 and 2 a couple more times.**

4. **Try the exercise with the puppy on the floor and you sitting in front of her.**

   When she gives you her attention, be enthusiastic. Play with her joyfully, give her a treat, pet her gently — whatever she really loves.

   If, in Step 2, you had to go with the second option — making funny sounds — continue with the rest of these steps.

5. **After your Dachsie reliably turns her attention to you when you make your funny sound, add her name to the sound.**

   Do this, for example: "[*whistle*] Hans!" or "Beep beep, Hans!" Continue to reward your dog enthusiastically every time she gives you her attention.

6. **Repeat Steps 4 and 5 several times every day.**

7. **After several days, begin to drop the funny sound every other time. After a few more days, use only your Dachshund's name to grab her attention.**

   Continue to reward her whenever she gives you her full attention.

You can practice this lesson during walks, in the car, in the park, or wherever else you are with your Dachshund. Eventually, she'll learn that when you say her name, it's in her best interest to pay attention to you because something great is sure to happen.

Another way you can get a dog's attention is by showing her a treat and then holding it at arm's length to your side. The dog will stare at your hand and the treat. The instant she looks you in the eye, give her the treat. This will establish great eye contact and command; your Dachshund is listening. What will you tell her to do next?

You can, of course, name your dog whatever you like. Short names (or short nicknames of long names) that are fun and easy to say are most effective for training, however. Peter, Max, Trixie, and Sport make better choices than Bartholomew, Zachariah, Veronica, and Mary Margaret (although Bart, Zach, Vicky, and Meg would all work well).

Teaching "Come"

"Come" is the most essential cue in your Dachshund's repertoire. That doesn't mean she'll always obey it, though. You're doing pretty well if she *usually* obeys it. However, she must learn it because it can save her life someday.

The good news? It's easy to get most puppies to come. Puppies are curious, and they love people. If you squat down or lie down on the floor, open your arms wide, and look excited while calling for your puppy, she's bound to come, well, bounding over.

The older a puppy gets, however, and the more familiar *you* get, the less likely it is that you'll seem like the most interesting thing in the room. (Don't take it personally!) Your puppy may think, "Oh, yeah. That guy. But hey, I've never seen that new shoe over there before!" And when you get some serious competition, like a rabbit in the garden or a robin on the driveway, forget it.

So how do you teach your puppy that "Come!" means come and always means come, whether she feels like it or not? Habit, pure and simple. Dogs thrive on habit and routine. Practice the "Come" cue every day, again and again, whenever you get the chance. Always reward it. If you do it often enough, it will become second nature, and your Dachshund will come without even thinking about it. If your Dachshund sincerely believes that every time she comes to you, something great will happen, you've made yourself more interesting than that new shoe — at least for a few moments.

Here are the steps you must repeat for teaching the "Come" cue:

1. **Get down close to your Dachshund's eye level, about 5 or 6 feet away.**

2. **Open your arms wide and, with as much excitement and joy as you can muster, say "[*puppy's name*], Come!"**

   Wave a treat in the air, if necessary. If she comes without seeing the treat, give her one anyway to reward her.

3. **When she comes to you, heap on the praise.**

   Really heap it on — this is the big one. "Whatta good good good doggie! What a well-behaved perfect little puppy! She can come, yes she can!" Pet, kiss, play, and offer a treat — make it worth your Dachshund's while.

4. **Move back another 5 or 6 feet and try it again.**

If your puppy follows you before you've said "Come," say "Come" as she's following you. "Come, Spot! Whatta good Spot! Come! Thatta girl! Come, Spot!"

5. Do it again and again, until your Dachshund loses interest.

Probably five times is the most you'll get in at once. Work through the lesson again later. And again and again and again in the days after.

After your Dachshund understands "Sit" and "Wait" (see the following section), you can combine them with "Come." Have your Dachshund sit, tell her to wait, and then walk away. Then say "[*puppy's name*], Come!" Three cues for the price of one!

Here are two very important things to remember, so read up:

✔ **Never go for one day without practicing "Come" a few times.** Your goal is to have the sound of the word "Come" induce such a familiar and practiced response in your Dachshund that she obeys without even thinking about it.

✔ **If you use food rewards for only one cue, "Come" should be the one.** If you reward your Dachshund in a way that makes a big impression *every single time* she comes when you call her, she'll be more likely to obey you every single time you call her.

Teaching "Sit"

When your Dachshund has learned to pay attention to you when you address her (see the previous section), you can begin to add words to her name to signify different behaviors. But how do you get your Dachshund to know what you want her to do? Through the magic of lure-and-reward training.

Even before your Dachshund knows her name, you can lure her into a sit with a piece of kibble or a treat. You can even try the following lesson with puppies that you're visiting at the breeder's house to see which ones are most responsive to you:

1. Put your puppy in front of you — preferably up on a table so that you can be close to her eye level.

2. If she isn't standing, lift her up to a standing position.

3. Pick up a piece of kibble and hold it in front of her nose, as shown in Figure 14-1.

Put it just close enough for her to see and smell it but not close enough for her to grab it.

Figure 14-1: Let your Dachsie see and sniff the kibble before having her sit.

4. **When your puppy notices the treat, slowly raise the treat up in the air and slightly over your puppy's head.**

   How can she resist? She must try to follow it. But to do so, she has to raise her head, and to raise her head, she has to sit.

5. **As your Dachshund sits, say "Sit" in a relaxed and friendly manner and then immediately praise her.**

   "Good sit! Whatta good dog!"

6. **When she's fully seated, give her the treat without delay.**

   "Whatta good dog! Whatta good little Gretel!"

7. **Repeat Steps 1 through 6 once or twice, and then try the exercise on the floor.**

   Eventually, your puppy will associate the action with the word, but don't rush to get rid of the treat. Keep practicing for at least a couple of weeks, and if she doesn't get it, keep using the lure for a while longer.

8. **When she's very familiar with the Sit cue, practice holding the sit.**

In other words, after she's in the sit, don't give her the food immediately. Hold it over her head while you say "Wait" in a friendly and relaxed tone. Wait for two seconds to give her the treat.

9. **Gradually, over the course of several weeks, increase the time between the sit and the reward.**

Go from 2 seconds to 5, 10, 20, and 30 seconds, and then go for a minute. Vary the wait so she never knows how long it will be. Sit, wait, reward.

Later on down the road, when you want your Dachshund to sit for longer periods of time — say, while you get her dinner prepared or when you have to take a phone call — you can say "Sit, Wait" and then go about your business. When you give your pup a treat, you release her. You should also practice the extended stay by using "Down" rather than "Sit"; it will be more comfortable for your Dachshund. Find out how to teach "Down" later in this chapter.

For long sits, accompany the treat reward with a release cue, such as "Okay!" or "Go Play!" Eventually, you won't even need the treat. Your Dachshund will be happy to sit and wait for you. Of course, she'll always be happy to take a treat off your hands, too, so you needn't abandon the treat if you enjoy offering it occasionally. Keep her guessing to keep her paying attention!

Teaching "Stand"

The "Stand" cue is great for grooming sessions, for dog shows, or for pauses during walks when you want to chat with a neighbor. Follow the same steps that you use for teaching "Sit" (in the section "Teaching 'Sit'"), except that you lure your puppy into position in the following way:

1. **Put your puppy into a sitting position or have her sit by giving her the "Sit" cue.**

2. **After she's sitting, hold a piece of kibble in front of her nose until she notices it.**

3. **Pull the kibble in a straight line, parallel to the floor, away from her nose.**

To follow it, she'll have to stand up.

4. **As she stands, say "Stand" in a relaxed and friendly manner.**

5. **When she's fully standing, praise her and immediately give her the treat.**

   Heap on the praise. "Good stand! Whatta good Butch! Whatta good stand!"

6. **Add the "Wait" cue, as described in the "Sit" cue section, and then the release cue.**

   What a well-behaved Dachshund you have!

Teaching "Down"

The "Down" cue is good for getting your Dachshund under control. It's a more submissive position than the sit and can help to calm your Dachshund when she's getting overexuberant. Down also is an excellent position for extended waits. You can practice the long down when you watch television, have to work at your computer, when the family is having dinner, or when friends are visiting and are ready for adult conversation. (Life can't be about your Dachshund *all* the time!)

Teach the Down cue after your Dachshund has mastered Sit with the following steps:

1. **Tell your Dachshund to sit, reward her when she does, and then bring another piece of kibble into view.**

   Hold the new kibble just in front of your Dachshund's nose.

2. **When you have her attention, slowly lower the kibble to the floor in a diagonal line, away from your puppy's nose.**

   If she follows it with her nose but doesn't lie down, move it slightly away from her so that she has to lie down to reach it. If your Dachshund stands up to follow the kibble, moving out of the sit, take the treat away and start over with the "Sit" cue.

3. **As she goes down to follow the treat, say "Down" in a friendly and relaxed tone.**

4. **When she lies down, give her the treat and pile on the praise.**

   It may take a few tries for your Dachshund to figure out what you mean. Plus, some Dachsies just don't like to lie down. They'd rather be up and at 'em. But when she gets it, make lying down *super* rewarding; if you do, even the most active Dachsie will probably be willing to do it . . . on occasion.

It may help to train for "Down" when your Dachshund is tired — like after a walk or play session.

5. **When your Dachshund understands "Down" and reliably lies down on cue, add the Wait cue.**

   Gradually extend the time between the down and the reward — the same procedure you use for the long sit (see "Teaching 'Sit'" for details).

   You can add a release cue (like "Okay!") after a long down and practice it often. Whenever you plan to be in one place for more than five minutes, practice the long down.

You can practice the long down during pauses on your daily walk, but don't make your Dachshund lie down on hot pavement. Let her practice the "Down" cue on the grass.

Mastering the Leash

This section's set of cues are for when you and your Dachshund are walking together — you on one end of the leash and your Dachshund on the other. You may ask "Just who's walking who?" as your Dachsie drags you down the sidewalk. The daily Dachshund walk can be an immensely enjoyable experience, provided that your Dachshund is well-behaved. If not, it can become an irritating and trying task that you'll probably soon abandon.

Lure-and-reward training doesn't work with leash lessons because they involve behaviors or actions that you can't really lure your Dachshund into. However, a few simple, alternative strategies will make your Dachshund's walk all it should be.

See every walk with your Dachshund as a training opportunity. Practice the following lessons each and every time you and your puppy venture outside.

A collar is more likely to strain and even injure your Dachshund's neck than a harness that fits around her shoulders and torso. A harness can give you more control over your puppy and may be more comfortable for your Dachshund. Check your local pet stores, online pet supply companies, and mail-order pet supply catalogs for available harnesses. (See Chapter 8 for more on leashes, collars, and harnesses.)

Teaching "Walk"

Few things are more irritating than a dog that continuously pulls on her leash throughout an entire walk, and few things are more humiliating than being dragged around the block by a 9-pound wiener dog. Teach your Dachshund how to *heel* — walk nicely beside you without pulling — by positively reinforcing heeling behavior. Soon, your walks will be a joy. Just follow these steps:

1. **Put on your Dachshund's harness (or collar, if you choose) and leash and then take her outside.**

2. **Stand next to your Dachshund with the leash in your right hand and the Dachshund to your left.**

   The leash should hang loosely in front of you. Stand still. Don't talk to or look at your Dachshund. She'll probably pull a little, wander around a little, and sniff a little. Eventually, she'll get bored. (If she doesn't, move to a more boring location — say, the middle of a wide cement driveway.)

3. **When she quits moving around and stands or sits next to you, look down happily and say "[*puppy name*], Walk" and begin walking.**

   "Oh, joy!" your Dachshund thinks. "A walk! Hooray!" Off she dashes.

4. **The moment — no, the *instant* — you feel the tension on that leash tighten, stop.**

   Stand perfectly still. Don't look at or talk to your Dachshund. Don't even say "No." Just stop.

   But this isn't what your Dachshund expected. She thought you were going for a walk. What gives? "C'MON!" she's thinking. Don't budge. Finally, your Dachshund will give up and come back to you.

5. **When she comes back to you, praise her and begin walking.**

   "Good dog! Let's walk!" "Hooray!" She'll lunge ahead again.

6. **When she lunges ahead again, stop again.**

   Remain dead still. Now your Dachshund may be getting pretty frustrated, but let her figure this one out. When she stays by your side, you move, and the two of you get to walk. Yippee! But when she pulls and lunges on the leash, you stop. No walk. Boring!

7. **Keep at this stop-and-go routine until she gets it.**

If she doesn't get it today, she'll get it soon. Every time she stays at your side, say "Walk" and then walk. That's the big reward — one of the biggest in your Dachshund's mind.

Here are a few more "Walk" tips:

✔ **Never move when your Dachshund pulls on the leash, no matter how old and experienced she gets.** Never make an exception. Even when she's 10 years old, stop. Ignore her and don't move until she's back at your side in a mannerly way. As long as she stays at your side, the two of you can stroll as long as you like. But if you give a Dachshund an inch, she'll drag you a mile.

✔ **After your Dachshund has learned to stay by your side on walks, you can throw in a few curves — literally.** Walk in an arc to the right and to the left, walk backward, walk in a circle, walk in a zigzag. See how well she can learn to tune in to your movements — even anticipate them. If, at any time, she makes a wrong move or puts any tension in that leash, always stop.

When your Dachshund has figured out the game, the "Walk" cue can become great fun — kind of like a challenging guessing game (and Dachsies love a challenge). It can also serve as an excellent foundation for more advanced obedience work, including the fun and creative freestyle competition (for more on freestyle, see Chapter 15).

✔ **After your Dachshund has mastered the "Walk" cue, you can pick up the pace and change the cue to "Run."** But don't run too fast or for very long with your Dachshund. Because their legs are so short, Dachshunds have to work twice as hard as other dogs to keep up with you.

Teaching "Wait"

If you've been working on the long sit and long down, which I cover earlier in this chapter, your Dachshund is probably already familiar with the cue "Wait." You can use this cue on your walks, too — at crosswalks or when you stop to chat with a neighbor. Positively reinforce your Dachshund when she waits patiently at your side in a sit or a down.

Practice "Wait" on a walk only after your Dachshund has mastered "Walk":

1. **While on your daily walk, whenever you approach a crosswalk or any other stopping point, say "[*puppy name*], Wait" and then stop walking.**

If your Dachshund keeps moving, stand completely still and ignore her, just like you do when teaching the "Walk" cue in the previous section.

2. **As soon as she figures out that you've stopped and comes to wait at your side, tell her to sit or lie down.**

3. **When she sits or lies down, praise her and offer her a treat.**

4. **When you're ready to move again, give the "Walk" cue and start walking as before. (You can throw in a "Stand" first if you want to.)**

Practice "Wait" a few times on every walk, in conjunction with "Sit" or "Down" each time. Your neighbors will be so impressed!

Troubleshooting 101: Conquering Training Problems

It's easy to read about dog training. It sounds so simple, so obvious, and so effortless. Then you sit down and try it, and it doesn't always go the way the book says.

Often, the problem is that you aren't in the right mood. Or you just don't have the energy to enforce certain rules consistently. Or you don't train as regularly as you should, so your Dachshund forgets. Following are a few common training problems and how to address them.

If you're really having problems, go to obedience class or just give your trainer a call (see the earlier section "Considering Obedience Classes"). Many trainers will even come to your house to conduct training sessions for your dog and for you, too! You'll soon be back on track.

✔ **Your Dachshund won't listen.** Don't be impatient with training. Go back to Lesson #1 — getting your dog's attention. If you don't have your Dachshund's attention, you can't get anything else done. Don't proceed until she learns that when she hears her name, something fun and good will come from your direction. Move up slowly from there.

You can *always* go back to square one. And remember, your Dachshund won't listen to anything you have to say if you say it like you're extremely annoyed or bored. But if you have something fun to say? Something great? Something so exciting that no Dachshund would ever want to miss out on it? Now you're talking. (And your Dachshund is listening!)

✔ **Your Dachshund won't follow the lure.** Impatience on your part may be the culprit. You hold the treat in front of your Dachshund and raise it up. Your Dachshund looks up, sits halfway, and then stands. Do you say, "Close enough!" and give her the treat? Sitting halfway isn't close enough, however, and you've just rewarded your Dachshund for doing something incorrectly. Don't give her a treat, not even once, unless she does something the way she's supposed to. If she doesn't get it on the first few tries, try again tomorrow. And the next day. Some Dachshunds are slower to learn, but yours really does want that treat, so keep trying until she understands.

Another reason for not following the lure could be that your Dachshund just isn't very hungry right now. It may help to train her before her meal, when she's hungrier; the treat will be a more interesting motivation then.

✔ **Your Dachshund has a very short attention span.** Of course she does, especially if she's a puppy. Have you ever met a human toddler? You get the point. Don't worry if your training sessions are effective for no longer than a couple minutes at first. A few tries at "Come," a play break, and one or two "Sits" makes for a perfectly respectable training session for a young puppy.

✔ **Your Dachshund refuses to come.** Try training in an area with fewer distractions. You have to be the most exciting thing around for "Come" to work. If your backyard has many other yards, dogs, and wildlife in view, forget it. You can practice "Come" in the bathroom (put the trash away) or other relatively empty room, with no other people or pets around. Also, try training before a meal when your Dachshund may be hungrier or just after a nap when your Dachshund may be more alert and well-rested.

If you're really having a hard time with this cue, don't use the word "Come" unless your puppy is on a leash so you can slowly and gently pull him toward you. Then give him a treat. This tactic will keep your puppy from getting confused about what exactly you mean by Come.

✔ **Kibble treats aren't good enough.** Different Dachshunds are food-motivated to varying degrees. If pieces of your Dachshund's regular kibble just aren't motivation enough, try healthy, homemade or store-bought treats broken into small bits. Or try small pieces of healthy people food, like baby carrots, blueberries, oat cereal circles, or, for the Dachshund that needs an extra push, very small slivers of cooked poultry or meat (avoid processed meat like hot dogs and lunchmeat) or low-fat shredded cheese.

✔ **You keep getting angry.** Puppies can be so frustrating. If you can't keep your cool, though, training simply won't work. Anger will only hurt your relationship with your Dachshund. Try training at a different time of day, when you'll be in a better mood. Also, maybe your training sessions are too long. Start with sessions that are only a couple minutes long. How irritated can you get in two minutes? If you're still having problems, you may need to get to the root of your irritation. If something else is bothering you, don't take out your human troubles on your innocent, if rambunctious, little Dachshund.

Keep working, keep trying, and never lose your sense of humor. Most training traumas can be resolved if you stay creative and ask for professional help when you need it.

Recognizing the Importance of Play

I can't emphasize enough how important it is for you to keep training sessions cleverly disguised as play. Whatever you do with your Dachshund should be fun. If you get bored, your Dachshund is probably getting bored. If you get angry, your Dachshund is probably getting frightened or at least thinking she'd like to put some distance between herself and that big grumpy human.

Although Dachshunds can be stubborn, the way around their hardheadedness isn't through intimidation or violence. Manipulate with charm and teach with joy, and you'll soon convince your Dachshund that doing what you say is what she wants more than anything else. With a little patience and a sense of humor, you can do it. And your Dachshund can't wait for you to try!

Chapter 15

Advanced Training and Competing for Fun

*W*ow! It turns out that your Dachshund is great at this training stuff (see Chapter 14). He loves to learn new tricks, and the two of you have great chemistry when it comes to training sessions and obedience. Maybe you have a champion in the making. If you want something else to do in your spare time that includes your Dachshund, why not consider a little friendly competition?

The more you explore dog competitions, the more you may be surprised at how endless your options are. You can travel the dog show circuit, compete in traditional obedience competition — or its new, easier version called *Rally* — and participate in field trials, agility trials, and earthdog tests. Other fun events include canine freestyle, tracking, and just plain showing off in front of your friends! And for the truly well-rounded Dachshund (and I don't mean chubby), a versatility award is perhaps the ultimate accomplishment.

But how do you get from interested dog-human team to champion dog-human team? First, you train. This chapter takes you through the process and outlines the many competitive and fun options you have.

Preparing for Competition

If a particular dog sport or area of competition interests you, the first thing you can do to prepare is to attend some events where the sport or competition is featured. Your local all-breed dog club or your regional breed club probably will have information about the event(s) that interests you. Make a call. You also can look on the American Kennel Club Web site for dog events near you. Search simultaneously by area of interest and by state at www.akc.org/events/search.

When you watch your competition of choice, you'll probably come up with a lot of questions about how it works. You can check out the section about your area of interest in this chapter and do some research online by looking at the Web sites of clubs that sponsor the event — like the AKC, the UKC, or clubs specifically dedicated to your sport of choice. You also can look for books devoted to your area of interest, which will tell you how to get started.

Depending on where you live, you may also be able to take a class that will help you and your Dachshund train for events. Because agility is so popular right now, a lot of local trainers offer agility training classes. You can search for classes that focus on conformation shows, obedience competition, and training for the Canine Good Citizen test.

A basic obedience background is essential for any canine sport, so be sure your dog at least knows the basics (see Chapter 14). One good place to start? Taking the Canine Good Citizen test. See the following section for details.

Taking the Canine Good Citizen Test

The *Canine Good Citizen test* is an exam that proves a dog has basic good manners and can act like a good citizen in public. The purpose of the test is to encourage all dog owners to teach their pets good manners and proper behavior. If every dog possessed the skills necessary to pass this test, surely the vast numbers of dogs abandoned to animal shelters would decrease, as would the cases of dog-related injuries. Any breed and any mixed breed of dog may take the test and earn the award. Unlike many other types of canine competitions where purebred status is a must, the Canine Good Citizen test is an equal-opportunity test — even if your Dachsie has a little, say, Schnauzer blood or Beagle blood or something else.

You can train your Dachshund for the CGC test at home (although training in a class may be easier). Knowledgeable members of local dog clubs, 4-H clubs, or other clubs that promote the well being of our canine friends usually administer the test. It involves ten individual tests, each determining how well your Dachshund can perform according to basic good manners:

✔ **Accepting a friendly stranger.** Your Dachshund must remain quiet and well behaved when a friendly but unknown person approaches, speaks to you, and shakes your hand. While you and the stranger talk pleasantly, your Dachshund must stay next to you and not show any sign of guarding you, of shyness, or of moving toward the stranger (barking and jumping up on the person are no-nos).

✔ **Sitting politely for petting.** In this test, your Dachshund must sit at your side while someone he doesn't know approaches and pets him on the head and body. The stranger must then walk behind and around you and your Dachshund. Your Dachshund must not act shy, aggressive, or resentful toward the stranger. Again, no barking and jumping! (Don't stop reading yet; your Dachsie really can do this!)

✔ **Accepting grooming.** The purpose of this test is to show that your Dachshund can be safely and easily examined and handled by a stranger, such as a vet, groomer, or friend. The evaluator combs or brushes your Dachshund and gently examines his ears and each front foot. Your Dachshund must accept such handling without acting shy or aggressive.

✔ **Controlling your dog for a walk on a loose leash.** You must demonstrate your control over your Dachshund for this test. Walk with him on either side of you on a loose leash — meaning no pulling on the leash for either of you. During your walk, you must make one left turn, one right turn, one about turn (which is turning around and going back the way you came), one stop during the middle of the test, and another stop at the end. Your Dachshund must stay in a good heel and may either sit or stand during the stops.

✔ **Walking through a crowd.** Your Dachshund must demonstrate his self control in a public place for this test. You and your Dachshund must walk around and by at least three people, during which time your Dachshund may display interest but not excitement, shyness, or resentment. You may direct, encourage, and/or praise your Dachshund during this test, but he must not pull on the leash and must remain at your side.

✔ **Sit and Down on cue while staying in place.** This test determines your Dachshund's knowledge of basic commands. Ask your Dachshund to sit and to lie down. You may make each command more than once and may use more than one word. (You can include your Dachshund's name in the command, for example, or add words of encouragement.) Next, you must ask him to stay, after which you walk down a 20-foot line away from him. During this walk, he must stay in place, although he can change position (move from lying down to sitting, for example).

✔ **Coming when called.** Your Dachshund must demonstrate his understanding of "Come" (see Chapter 14). In this test, you must walk 10 feet from your Dachshund, with or without saying "Stay." Turn to face your Dachshund and call him to you. He must come when called.

✔ **Reacting properly to another dog.** For this test, your Dachshund must demonstrate his good manners around another dog. No, really, stop laughing! I'm serious. With your Dachshund on a leash, you must approach another handler with another dog on a leash, standing approximately 10 yards away. You and the other handler must stop, shake hands, talk pleasantly, and then continue past each other for 5 yards. Both dogs should show casual interest in each other but shouldn't leave their respective handlers' sides and shouldn't act shy or aggressive (or bark, roughhouse, or growl).

✔ **Handling distractions.** Distractions are a part of life, and in this test, your Dachshund demonstrates how confidently he can handle them. The evaluator sets up some common distractions, such as a book being dropped to the floor or a jogger running by. Your Dachshund must show some natural curiosity in, and may even appear startled by, the distraction. But he must not act aggressive or fearful, try to run away, or bark at the distraction.

✔ **Staying calm during supervised separation.** The last test determines how well your Dachshund can behave when you aren't around to influence him. The evaluator says something to the effect of "Would you like me to watch your dog?" and you agree. Hand the leash to the evaluator and walk out of sight. The evaluator holds your Dachshund's leash for 3 minutes. Your Dachshund needn't maintain a Sit or Down position, but he shouldn't bark excessively, whine and cry, howl, pace, or act very nervous. Slight agitation is acceptable, because your Dachshund really has no idea where you went, and he loves you so!

During the CGC test, you have one chance at each test. If you fail, better luck next time. You can attempt the test again at a later date. Just keep practicing! Some of the sections are harder for Dachshunds than others, but many Dachshunds have earned their Canine Good Citizen awards, and yours can, too. It's a wonderful and significant accomplishment, and the training will make your Dachsie a better companion. Stick with your daily training sessions, and remember: Patience is a virtue. After your Dachshund has his CGC, why not aim even higher?

Showing Your Dachshund: Isn't She Lovely!

Maybe you think you have the most beautiful Dachshund you've ever seen (like the owner of the one in Figure 15-1). You may be right! If your Dachshund is very close to the breed standard (see Chapter 2) — especially if he has champions in his pedigree — he may do well in and sincerely enjoy a conformation dog show.

A *conformation dog show* is a dog show in which a trained judge analyzes each dog's conformation to determine which dog most closely matches the written breed standard. The dog the judge deems closest to perfection should be the winner.

Show dogs can't be spayed or neutered. The basic purpose of dog shows is to evaluate breeding stock. The best breeding specimens earn a championship, meaning they can put "Ch" before their registered names as a title. If your Dachshund is spayed or neutered, he can't compete in conformation shows unless they're informal (and non-title-earning) fun matches.

If you still want to pursue this exciting but extremely competitive sport, your dog must be registered with a purebred dog registry like the American Kennel Club (AKC) or the United Kennel Club (UKC). You can find out more information about AKC conformation shows at www.akc.org/events/conformation/index.cfm. For more about UKC conformation shows, head to www.ukcdogs.com/conformation.htm.

Photo courtesy of Gail Painter.

Figure 15-1: Maybe your lovely Dachshund could be a show dog.

Shining in Obedience Competitions: Surprise 'em All!

Maybe beauty contests aren't your kind of thing. Or perhaps your Dachshund doesn't particularly like to sit still and look pretty. But if he has a particular knack for basic obedience cues and you're great at teaching them (see Chapter 14), obedience competition or the less-competitive sport called Rally may be for you. In Rally, dogs and their handlers (that's you) compete on a course designed by the judge. The judge tells you where to start, and you and your Dachshund move along at your own speed through 10 to 20 stations. Each station has instructions about what you have to do to move on — such as stopping and sitting, doing a U-turn in a particular direction, weaving around cones or posts, having the dog stay while you walk around him in a circle, even jumping over hurdles. You can talk to your dog all you want to try to motivate him to do the right thing. It's fun!

At a Rally trial, your dog has the potential to win honors for first, second, third, fourth, and qualifying prizes, and he can also earn titles: Rally Novice (RN), Rally Advanced (RA), Rally Excellent (RE), Rally Advanced Excellent (RAE), and more. For more information on the requirements for earning titles and all the rules and regulations for Rally, look to www.akc.org/events/rally/index.cfm.

The point of more formal obedience trials is to show that your Dachshund has learned how to be a well-mannered and useful companion. But he must prove it in a much more competitive and rigorous way than in either the Canine Good Citizen test or a Rally trial. Advanced obedience work includes tests of tracking ability — a Dachshund specialty. (These tests are hard work, so both you and your Dachshund should be in good shape.)

To attain an obedience title, your Dachshund must earn over half the points in each specified exercise under three different judges at licensed or member obedience trials. The titles you can earn in obedience competition are as follows:

- ✔ Companion Dog (CD)
- ✔ Companion Dog Excellent (CDX)
- ✔ Utility Dog (UD)
- ✔ Utility Dog Excellent (UDX)
- ✔ Obedience Trial Champion (OTCh.)
- ✔ Tracking Dog (TD)
- ✔ Tracking Dog Excellent (TDX)
- ✔ Variable Surface Tracker (VST)
- ✔ Champion Tracker (CT)

To discover more about AKC obedience rules and for more information on how to get started, look to www.akc.org/events/obedience/index.cfm. For information on obedience through the UKC, head to www.ukcdogs.com/obedience.htm.

I also recommend that you attend an AKC- or UKC-sanctioned obedience competition to see how it works, or attend less-formal obedience events sponsored by your local dog club.

Spayed or neutered dogs may participate in both Rally and obedience trials if they're registered with the appropriate organization. Some less-formal obedience events by local clubs may not require any registration. However, puppies less than 6 months of age, females in heat, and lame, deaf, or blind dogs may not compete. Dogs that attack other dogs or appear dangerous or overly aggressive will be disqualified.

Canine Freestyle for Dramatic Dachshunds

If your Dachshund is better at funny tricks and garnering appreciative applause than executing commands with extreme precision, and if you're a music lover with a relative amount of natural grace, the two of you may love to compete in *canine freestyle* — a wonderful event that combines obedience moves with choreography. You pick the song, you make up the moves, and then you and your Dachshund perform for the crowd . . . and maybe even earn titles!

You should attend a few events to see what it's all about. You also can find out more from the Canine Freestyle Federation (www.canine-freestyle.org) and the World Canine Freestyle Organization, Inc. (www.wordcaninefreestyle.org). Because you have the *music* in you!

Competing in Field Trials: A Dachshund's Destiny

Dachshunds are one of only a handful of breeds eligible to participate in field trials. The purpose of *field trials* is to give breeds designed for field work the opportunity to exercise their natural abilities — their penchant for hunting, following a scent, and cornering vermin.

Dachshund field trials are different from field trials for other dogs, like retrievers. Dachshunds are best at tracking small game through dense brush and alerting hunters to the location of the game. In a Dachsie field trial, you reenact this scenario under controlled conditions (no wildlife gets hurt). Dachshund field trials are based on Brace Beagle field trials, in which a pair, or *brace,* of dogs track a rabbit.

Field trials usually are held in a fenced area so the Dachshunds can't escape or become lost. Some field trials divide the male and female Dachshund competitions; others don't. The following list explains how the contest begins and ends:

1. A Field Marshall calls each brace to attention.

2. Volunteer brush beaters scare up a rabbit, and whoever sees the rabbit first shouts, "Tally Ho!"

3. After the rabbit has been spotted and has scurried away, the Dachshunds are brought to the place where the rabbit was spotted.

4. Each handler encourages his or her Dachshund to find the *line,* or scent, of the rabbit.

5. As soon as the Dachshund catches the scent, the handler releases the Dachshund; he or she must then stop giving instructions but may follow the dog — behind the judges only.

6. When the judges have seen enough to judge the Dachshund's ability to follow the scent with persistence and enthusiasm, they ask the handler to pick up the dog.

The ultimate goal of field trials, beyond having a great time, is to earn enough points for the title *Field Champion (FC)*. Versatile Dachshunds that attain this title and are Champions of Record in conformation are considered *dual champions*. These same Dachshunds that also earn an obedience championship are considered *triple champions*. (See the section at the end of this chapter for more on versatility.)

If you're interested, you should visit a field trial or two to see what it's all about. Ask the people running their Dachshunds how you can train your Dachshund for competition. Usually, you'll meet friendly people and get plenty of great advice. To find a field trial in your area and to discover more about AKC field trials, check out this site: www.akc.org/events/field_trials/dachshunds/index.cfm. You also can call your local dog club for more info.

Tracking tests for sniff-happy hounds

If your Dachshund loves to follow a scent (and what Dachshund doesn't?), consider tracking. *Tracking* is a fun, addictive, outdoorsy sport, a sort of competitive form of canine search and rescue. Your Dachshund can earn tracking titles, and you'll have fun watching him use his natural nasal abilities. For more information on AKC-sponsored tracking events, check out www.akc.org/events/tracking/index.cfm.

Competing in Agility Trials: Poetry in Motion

Agility is hot these days because everyone loves to watch it. Who can resist dogs jumping through hoops, running over teeter-totters, and tunneling through chutes all on one fast-paced obstacle course? The dogs can't resist it, either. If your Dachshund is athletic and you think he'd enjoy agility, consider training him for agility work. Many local trainers offer agility classes because it's just so *fun*.

Agility helps both you and your Dachshund stay in great shape. It's also the perfect outlet for your little performer. Any dog may participate in an agility trial, whether or not it's registered or spayed/neutered.

Some Dachshund owners may be nervous about training their Dachshunds to do agility because of the jumping. Luckily, jumps are adjusted for the height of the dog, so a healthy, athletic Dachshund at his ideal weight should have no problem with the jumps. However, if your Dachshund has had back problems before, or you believe that he's at risk for disk disease (see Chapter 17), stick to obedience or another less stressful activity.

Dogs can earn a number of titles in agility competition, each more difficult to achieve than the one before:

- Novice Agility (NA)
- Open Agility (OA)
- Agility Excellent (AX)
- Master Agility Excellent (MX)
- Master Agility Champion (MACH)

The obstacle course in an agility trial varies depending on the level of competition, but all levels include contact obstacles with certain areas a dog must touch when going through. Dogs must achieve the obstacle course in a set amount of time (also depending on the level of competition) and must successfully maneuver on, in, over, or through each obstacle. The following list details some of the obstacles used in agility events:

- **The A-frame:** Your Dachshund must go up one panel of the A-frame and go down the other panel after touching the contact zone, in whatever direction the judge orders.

✔ **The dog walk:** Your Dachshund must go up one ramp, cross a center section, and go down the other ramp after touching both contact zones, in whatever order the judge specifies.

✔ **The seesaw:** Your Dachshund must ascend a plank, cause it to seesaw the other way, and then descend, waiting on the opposite side to touch the ground before getting off — after touching the contact zone, of course.

✔ **The pause table:** Your Dachshund must jump onto a table, pause for five seconds in a Sit or Down position (according to what the judge decrees), and then dismount.

✔ **The open tunnel:** A flexible tube must be positioned so that your Dachshund can't see the end of the tunnel when he enters. He must go in one end of the tunnel (the one the judge indicates), go through the tunnel, and come out the other side.

✔ **The closed tunnel:** This tunnel has a rigid entrance connected to a soft chute. Your Dachshund must enter the tunnel and exit through the chute.

✔ **The weave poles:** Your Dachshund must go between the first two poles from right to left, move from left to right between the next poles, move from right to left between the next poles, and so on.

✔ **The single bar jumps:** Your Dachshund must jump over a set of bars without knocking off the top one, in the direction the judge specifies.

✔ **The panel jump:** Your Dachshund must jump over a top board without knocking it off, in the direction the judge specifies.

✔ **Other single jumps:** Courses can include other types of single jumps for your Dachshund to jump over.

✔ **The double bar jump:** Your Dachshund must jump over two top bars without knocking off either one, in whatever direction the judge specifies.

✔ **The triple bar jump:** Your Dachshund must jump over three bars of gradually increasing heights without knocking off any, in whatever direction the judge specifies.

✔ **The tire jump (or circle jump):** Your Dachshund must jump through a tire opening in the direction the judge specifies.

✔ **The window jump:** Your Dachshund must jump through a window opening in the direction the judge specifies.

✔ **The broad jump:** Your Dachshund must jump over a series of obstacles of varying heights without touching them. He must enter between marker poles placed near the front and exit between marker poles placed near the back.

Agility is so much fun that it may become an every-weekend activity for you and your Dachshund. Why not? Your Dachshund would rather spend his weekends playing with you than doing just about anything else. To find out more about AKC-sponsored agility events, look to the following site: www.akc.org/events/agility/index.cfm. To find out more about UKC-sponsored agility events, check out www.ukcdogs.com/Agility.htm. You also can call your local dog club for agility information.

Competing in Earthdog Tests: Born to Burrow

Bottom line: Dachshunds love to dig. But you already know that. If yours is a digger extraordinaire, he may have the right stuff for earthdog tests or den trials. Most Dachshunds do. Earthdog tests are a lot of fun, and any AKC-registered Dachshund (or Terrier) 6 months of age or older may participate, including spayed and neutered dogs. Den trials are similar but sponsored by the American Working Terrier Association (AWTA), or a local group. Many Dachshunds need minimal training to excel in this sport — it's in your Dachsie's genes.

In an earthdog test, a den is set up by digging a trench and tunnel, placing a 9-inch x 9-inch wood liner in the trench, and covering it with earth. The tunnel and trench have certain twists and turns, as required by the level of competition, and at the end of the tunnel are bars separating a caged rat from the dog (don't worry, the rat doesn't get hurt). The tunnel can be opened at the end so you can lift your Dachshund out when he's finished. Tunnels for the higher levels of competition have false exits, false entrances, and false scented dens.

To start the competition, your Dachshund is released and must enter the specially constructed tunnel, following it through to the end where the rat is caged. He must bark or scratch at the cage, or *work the quarry,* for a specified amount of time.

Beginners can start out with the *Introduction to Quarry* test (not required for more advanced levels of competition). This test requires that your dog get to the rat within two minutes and work the quarry continuously for at least 30 seconds. This test can help you determine whether your Dachshund is a natural at earthdog tests.

More advanced levels of competition and titles are as follows:

- ✔ **Junior Earthdog (JE):** For this test, you must release your Dachshund 10 feet from the den entrance. He has 30 seconds to reach the rat from the time he's released, and then he must work the quarry, staying within 12 inches of it, continuously for 30 seconds. Tunnels for this level of competition are 30 feet long with three 90-degree turns.

- ✔ **Senior Earthdog (SE):** For this test, you must release your Dachshund 20 feet from the den entrance. He has 90 seconds to reach the quarry from the time he's released, and he must work the quarry continuously for 90 seconds. Tunnels for this level of competition are 30 feet long with three 90-degree turns, but they also include a 7-foot false exit and a false den consisting of a 4-foot side tunnel with no exit and a heavily scented bedding area with no rat.

- ✔ **Master Earthdog (ME):** For this test, two dogs work together. You must release your dog a specified distance from the real den entrance. However, the den entrance is blocked, and a false den entrance is available, so part of the test is to see if your dog can find the real den entrance and bark to be let in. Dogs that bark at the false den don't qualify for this title. The first dog to reach the real den is temporarily removed so the second dog can have a chance to find it, too.

  The first dog is then allowed in the tunnel and must reach the quarry within 90 seconds and work the quarry for 90 seconds. While the dog is working the quarry, the judge simulates digging sounds on the top of the den with a piece of wood for 30 seconds; the dog shouldn't be distracted by this noise. The first dog is then removed, and the second dog is given his turn.

  The tunnel for this test is the same as the tunnel for the Senior test except for the blocked entrance. A 20-foot scent line leads to the entrance, and the false entrance is placed somewhere along the scent line. Also, within the tunnel is an 18-inch section that narrows to a 6-inch passageway, and the tunnel contains a suspended PVC pipe obstacle, 6 inches in diameter, with 9 inches on each side of the pipe's center line.

To find out more about AKC-sponsored earthdog events, look to www.akc.org/events/earthdog/index.cfm. To get the scoop on AWTA Den Trials, head to www.dirt-dog.com/awta/index.cfm. You also can call your local dog club to see if you can discover more about other nearby opportunities.

Becoming a Versatile Dachshund

Dachshund breeders, like many other breeders, are becoming increasingly insistent that Dachshunds be beautiful and healthy, show stoppers and athletes, and always able to perform the functions for which they were originally bred. In an attempt to encourage versatility rather than overspecialization, the Dachshund Club of America has established a versatility program that awards a Versatility Certificate (VC) to Dachshunds that distinguish themselves in several areas.

To earn a VC, a Dachshund must have 18 or more VC points obtained from a conformation show and at least three of the following five groups:

- ✔ Field trials
- ✔ Obedience (including the Canine Good Citizen award, which is a requirement for a VC certificate and equals one point)
- ✔ Rally
- ✔ Agility
- ✔ Earthdog or den trials
- ✔ Tracking

Depending on the titles or points earned in each group, a Dachshund earns varying numbers of VC points. A triple champion (championships in conformation, field trials, and obedience) automatically qualifies for a VC.

A Versatility Certificate is a great accomplishment. It encourages well-rounded Dachshunds, and the hope is that breeders will avoid breeding just for looks, field abilities, or obedience skill. The more wide-ranging a dog's abilities, the healthier and stronger he tends to be. Plus, a Dachshund with a variety of important jobs is a busy, happy, challenged Dachshund.

For a fantastic publication from the Dachshund Club of America that features information about the VC and training for all the different areas, check out www.dachshund-dca.org/Media/ VersatilityCert.-2007.pdf. (You have to be able to read a .pdf file on your computer, but free software allows this.)

Part IV

Helping Your Dachshund Stay Healthy

Apparently what happens is they try to push a tree over. When they find out they can't, they go running off in frustration.

In this part . . .

*I*n Part IV, you find out what it takes to keep your Dachshund happy and healthy, including finding the vet that will provide the best care. I describe in detail the back problems that many Dachshunds develop and show you some preventative measures. I also discuss some other health problems Dachshunds could develop. Finally, I address the health needs of older dogs and how you can enjoy your Dachsie's golden years.

Chapter 16

Healthy Dachshund 101

*Y*our Dachshund is the very picture of health. You find it difficult to imagine that your bouncing bundle of energy could ever get sick or injured. However, it's precisely when animals (and people) are at their healthiest that preventive measures are most effective. To keep your Dachshund puppy or dog in glowing health, from the tip of her nose all the way to the tip of her tail (and that's quite a haul, as dogs go!), read this chapter. Here, you find out how to follow a few basic preventive health measures.

Beyond prevention, the most important thing to take away from this chapter is this: Pay attention! The people who know your Dachshund best are you, your family, and your vet. Always remain vigilant for signs that something isn't right. Changes in behavior, appetite, sleeping habits, water consumption, or movement may be signs of a health problem. Bumps, lumps, dry patches, bare patches, and other irregularities you detect during your daily grooming examination may also signal a problem. Never hesitate to ask your vet about your Dachshund's condition. The sooner you catch a problem, the easier it will be to resolve.

Keeping Your Puppy (Or Older Dachsie) Healthy

Puppies are vulnerable. They look it when first born, too, but after they fill out a little and commandeer entire households, bending each helpless human to their will, they may not seem so helpless.

But regardless of how sturdy and authoritative they look and seem, Dachshund puppies can easily fall prey to a number of serious, even life-threatening, diseases. While nursing, they receive immunities from their mothers, but after weaning, this immune protection drops off quickly. Until they develop their own immune systems, they're particularly susceptible to the most serious contagious diseases.

Puppies can also develop nasty parasite problems, suffer from a lack of good grooming, and fall victim to ruptured disks in their back (although disk problems are more common a few years down the road; see Chapter 17). How do you keep your puppy healthy? By taking a few simple measures, which I outline in the following sections.

Vaccinations

Vaccinations protect your puppy from canine parvovirus, distemper, hepatitis, leptospirosis, and rabies, as well as diseases that may be more prevalent in your area (such as coronavirus and Lyme disease). One of the most important things you can do to keep your puppy healthy is to get her vaccinated first at 5 to 6 weeks of age. If you buy your Dachshund from a breeder (see Chapter 4), she should've had the first one or two vaccinations done already. Continue to vaccinate your puppy according to the regular schedule suggested by your veterinarian. Different vets will recommend certain vaccinations at certain stages, so talk to your vet about when your puppy needs which vaccines.

Canine parvovirus is a highly contagious viral disease that comes in a diarrheal form and a cardiac form. If not treated, it's usually fatal — especially for puppies. *Distemper* is another highly contagious and often fatal viral disease that causes severe neurological damage in its advanced stages. *Hepatitis* is a highly contagious virus that begins with a fever and can end in coma and death. *Leptospirosis* is a bacterial disease that can cause death or severe kidney, liver, and digestive tract damage. It can also be transmitted to humans, along with rabies.

A debate is ongoing about vaccinations. Many people claim that pets are overvaccinated and that some of the vaccines from the first year last longer than vets previously thought. That could be. Others claim that serious diseases can result from vaccinations. That may also be true, especially with vaccinations of older dogs. But for puppies, that first year's vaccination schedule is *crucial.* You can talk to your vet about how often your dog needs booster shots after the first year, and you can work out a schedule of less-frequent vaccinations later, but please don't neglect these initial vaccinations.

The one vaccine required by law is the rabies vaccine, so even if you're anti-vaccine, you're required to have proof of this one. You must show this proof to license your dog, board her in a kennel, and sometimes even to get veterinary care. Nobody wants to risk rabies, so be diligent about the rabies vaccine. Many places, like boarding kennels, doggy daycare, and even dog parks, require proof of other vaccinations, too. Unless your dog has a serious health problem and your vet advises against the vaccines, there really is no reason to ignore the first year of vaccinations.

That's not to say that vaccinations don't involve risk. In rare cases, animals react adversely to vaccinations. The most serious reaction, an anaphylactic reaction, usually occurs in the first 15 to 60 minutes. This can lead to sudden cardiac arrest, so keep a close eye on your puppy for the first hour after a vaccination. Other less-severe reactions can happen later, from general fatigue, discomfort, and loss of appetite to a local infection at the site of the vaccination. The chances your Dachshund will have a reaction are extremely slim, though, and most vets agree that the benefits of vaccination far outweigh the risks. But always watch your Dachshund carefully for a week or so after vaccines. If your Dachshund changes her behavior or gets ill in any way following a vaccination, call your vet immediately.

Some people suggest that puppies should never be around other dogs until all vaccinations are complete. But what about puppy obedience classes? If you bring your puppy to obedience classes at 3 or 4 months of age, be sure to choose a class that requires all puppy owners to show proof of vaccination. You should be okay. Better to have a well-trained puppy and take the very small risk that something may get passed around. Not training or socializing your puppy is a bigger risk because you'll be more likely to give your Dachshund away when she gets to be too much trouble. Besides, your Dachshund will already have a few rounds of vaccinations under her belt, and she's already working on building up her natural immunity — now she can build up her good manners!

Sterilization: Spaying or neutering your Dachshund

Do you want to become a Dachshund breeder? Are you ready to devote most of your waking hours to the intense and often heartbreaking efforts of breeding, whelping, and raising, as well as studying to improve the health and temperament of Dachshunds? Are you ready to barely break even when you sell the puppies, to take back any puppy for any reason, to remain committed to every dog out of litter after litter, and to watch puppies fail to thrive and die in your arms?

If not, *please* sterilize your Dachshund. We are in the midst of a crisis in this country. Pet overpopulation is out of control, and the number of animals euthanized each year is staggering and saddening.

According to Spay USA (www.spayusa.org), every day 10,000 humans are born in the United States. In the same time frame, 70,000 puppies and kittens are born.

The fact is, Dachshunds like to run, dig, and escape. Even under the best of conditions, your Dachshund could get free. If a female does, she could easily come home pregnant. If a male does, he could easily impregnate the neighbor's champion Shih Tzu. You could end up with a litter of unwanted puppies on your hands — how will you find homes for them? At worst, your neighbor could take you to court.

Sterilization doesn't cost much. In fact, many humane societies offer vouchers to make the procedure even cheaper; give your local society a call. Sterilization also is very safe for dogs. There's a slight risk to any dog that undergoes general anesthesia, but almost all dogs come out of it just fine. Sterilization can even improve the behavior of dogs, and health benefits come with early sterilization (such as a reduced incidence of mammary tumors and fewer prostate problems).

I can't think of any reason why you wouldn't want to sterilize your Dachshund, unless you specifically bought a specimen to serve as the foundation of a breeding program. In this case, you've made the full-fledged commitment to be the best breeder you can be. But that is the subject of another book.

Pest control

No matter where you live, and no matter how often you keep your Dachshund inside, your pup probably will have some contact with some kind of pest. Fleas are everywhere, for instance, and in the southern states and parts of California, fleas have established a comfortable and prolific year-round existence.

Ticks are everywhere, too, in the wooded areas of most states. Lyme disease — a serious and sometimes fatal disease spread by the deer tick — has been detected in 47 of 50 states. People can catch it, too, and become seriously debilitated by it. Many puppies, no matter how well they're bred, are born with intestinal worms, and Dachshunds can easily pick up worms at any time during their lives. Mites that infect the ears or the skin abound, causing mange and other painful skin problems. Heartworms, dastardly critters, can kill your Dachshund by taking up residence in her blood vessels, lungs, or heart after transmission from a single mosquito bite.

In other words, pest control is something every pet owner must deal with. Pests come in many forms, and none of them are any fun. But each of them can be dealt with easily, as long as you practice a little prevention and address any pest problem as soon as you detect it:

✔ **Fleas:** Fleas are uncomfortable for your Dachshund and can cause complications ranging from severe allergic reactions to tapeworms. You probably won't be too fond of fleas jumping on and off your arms and legs either, and if your Dachshund isn't close by, the fleas will be happy to bite you. In rare cases, fleas can even infect humans with bubonic plague. Yikes!

Flea solutions: Prevention is the best solution. Apply a spot-on adulticide flea treatment (ask your vet for a recommendation) every month during flea season. A few drops between your dog's shoulder blades will kill the fleas that land on your Dachshund, even before they have a chance to bite (see Figure 16-1). You can also treat your dog with an oral insect-growth-regulator treatment once a month all year round. Any flea that does bite your dog won't be able to hatch any eggs, and the flea reproduction cycle will be halted before it can start. Leading parasitologists are recommending the oral protein Lufenuron as the core to flea control with topical to kill adult fleas if you see them, due to the inevitable resistance fleas are developing to topical agents.

Ask your vet which flea products are best for your Dachshund. And don't forget a thorough vacuuming around the house, along with washing your dog's bedding in hot water — if you see any fleas. This combined approach should take care of the problem pretty quickly.

✔ **Ticks:** Ticks can pass on severe diseases. The notorious Lyme disease is just one of many. Ticks are always dangerous when you walk with your Dachshund in wooded areas. They range in size, but sometimes the very smallest, barely visible ticks are the most dangerous.

Tick solutions: Please don't try to burn off ticks or yank them out carelessly with your bare hands. You could injure your dog or cause an infection if tick parts get left under the skin; you could even infect yourself if the tick bursts and the blood gets on you. Instead, use a spot-on product made to kill ticks if you go out in tick-infested areas with your Dachshund. If your Dachshund does get a tick and you find it during your daily grooming session, pull it straight out slowly with tweezers or with your fingers (wear rubber gloves or use a tissue). If your Dachshund shows signs of listlessness, fatigue, and loss of appetite, Lyme disease could be the culprit. See your vet right away.

✔ **Worms:** Roundworms, tapeworms, hookworms, and whip- worms can cause a variety of symptoms, ranging from diarrhea and vomiting to weight loss, severe fatigue, pneumonia, and even death. If you aren't thinking "Yuck!" at the very thought of worms, read on. Roundworms look like thin spaghetti, curled in your dog's feces. Tapeworms look like ¼- to ½-inch wiggly segments in your dog's poop or on the skin or hair around the rectum. Hookworms penetrate your Dachshund's skin, and the eggs can be detected under a microscope in your Dachshund's feces. Whipworms look like 1-inch threads.

Figure 16-1: A few drops of treatment between the shoulder blades should keep fleas away.

Worm solutions: Have every new puppy you adopt dewormed, usually a few times. In many cases, good breeders have this done for new pet owners. Have your vet check fecal samples a few times because worms can shed eggs intermittently, so a negative sample doesn't always mean your puppy doesn't have intestinal worms. To prevent reinfection, always keep your yard free of dog feces, and keep your Dachshund from sniffing poop from other dogs on walks. Many worms are transmitted when your Dachshund eats, or even sniffs, the feces of another dog (including your own dogs). A fence will help to keep stray dogs and their remains out of your yard. Once or twice a year throughout your Dachshund's life, continue to have your vet do a fecal examination to check for the ongoing presence or arrival of worms.

✔ **Mites:** Mites cause severe itching and a variety of unpleasant and unattractive skin conditions — sometimes referred to collectively as *mange*. Some mites infect your Dachshund's ears; others live in her skin. Suspect ear mites if your Dachshund shakes her head a lot and scratches at her ears. Dark earwax is another sign.

Scabies is a skin condition caused by a mite, and humans can get it, too. Scabies itches and often results in hair loss. *Chiggers* are tiny, red mites that live in wooded areas and burrow under your dog's skin, causing itching and redness. Other types of mites cause puppy dandruff, mild itching, and hair loss, and some live in the hair follicles and infects them.

Mite solutions: See your vet to acquire various types of creams, drops, dips, or shampoos, depending on the type of mite he finds. And don't wait. Your Dachshund won't enjoy being bald and itchy.

✔ **Heartworms:** Heartworms are transmitted from mosquitoes and, if left untreated, will kill your Dachshund. They travel to your dog's heart and mature there, reaching lengths of up to 12 inches. A dog with heartworms can be treated (the treatment isn't cheap), but if the heartworms are too advanced, it may be too late.

Heartworm solutions: First and foremost, prevent, prevent, prevent. Give your Dachshund a heartworm pill on schedule every single month, all year round — or always during mosquito season — for her entire life. Even if your Dachshund doesn't go outside for very long, she can still get a mosquito bite. In fact, indoor-only Dachshunds have contracted heartworm from mosquitoes that got in the house. Also, avoid mosquito-infested areas whenever possible; use a product designed to repel mosquitoes on dogs when you must. (Don't use your human bug spray on your dog, however.)

Heartworm pills are great for preventing heartworms, but if your Dachshund already has heartworms, a heartworm pill could be fatal. Always have your Dachshund tested for heartworms *before* beginning heartworm pills. Most vets recommend a yearly test just before mosquito season. Never neglect this yearly test because an extra year or two carrying around a heartworm population could make a big difference in how treatable the problem will be.

Practicing Good Grooming

Keeping your Dachshund well-groomed is an important part of maintaining her overall health, for the following reasons:

- A healthy, mat-free coat makes examination of the skin easier and doesn't harbor pests, dirt, or bacteria.

- Tartar-free and plaque-free teeth aren't susceptible to gum disease. Brushing also prevents more serious conditions like heart disease, which can result from bacteria in your dog's mouth traveling to her heart.

- Short, clipped nails keep your Dachshund's feet healthy and correctly positioned on the ground. They also keep your Dachshund from sliding on slick surfaces, which could possibly injure her back.

- Clean ears are less likely to harbor mites and develop infections. Regular ear examinations help you detect the presence of such conditions if they occur.

- Emptied anal sacs don't become impacted or infected.

Grooming can become part of a daily or weekly routine, and it's a good idea to start grooming your puppy the very first day you bring him home. Your grooming session will differ depending on your dog's age and coat, but a regular grooming routine will usually go something like this:

1. **Tell your Dachshund "It's grooming time" and bring him to the grooming spot.**

   Good choices are the bathroom countertop, the back porch, or a table in a room that can stand a little Dachshund hair.

2. **Gently massage your Dachshund from head to toe, feeling for any lumps, bumps, or irregularities.**

If you do this task every day, you'll catch any changes as soon as they occur. And don't forget to examine your Dachshund's coat and skin for changes.

3. **Pick up each foot and wiggle each toe, feel the footpads, and then gently examine and rub each ear.**

   These typically are sensitive areas, and if your Dachshund is used to having them touched, he'll be much easier for your vet to handle.

4. **If your Dachshund's nails need clipping, clip them.**

   Regularly clipping off the tips of your dog's nails shouldn't be a problem after your puppy gets used to it. On your very first vet visit, ask your vet to show you how to clip your Dachshund's nails so you can do it yourself. It doesn't hurt as long as you don't cut down too far.

   Your vet can show you how to avoid cutting the *quick,* or the small vein in your dog's nail. When nails are clipped frequently (about once every two to four weeks — less often if your dog walks on cement frequently), the quick retracts somewhat and you don't have to worry as much about cutting it. If you're lax in your clipping duties, though, the quick tends to extend closer to the tip of the nail. If you do clip the quick, your dog may yelp, and you'll have to stop the bleeding. Keep a product on hand for that purpose (many are available in pet stores).

5. **Brush your dog's coat with a soft-bristled dog brush. Add a once-over with a steel comb for longhaired and wirehaired Dachshunds**

   Check for any sign of parasites as you brush, and work out any tangles with the comb.

6. **Brush your dog's teeth.**

7. **Apply a pest-control product if it's time (see the section on controlling pests in this chapter).**

8. **Praise your pup for behaving so well!**

All dogs have anal sacs on either side of the anus, and these sacs are probably responsible for scent identification between dogs, along with uses in courtship and/or marking territory. The anal sacs fill up with a thick, extremely smelly liquid that's usually drained when dogs excrete feces.

However, some "lucky" breeds — including many of the small breeds and the beloved Dachshund — tend to develop impacted anal sacs. Have you seen your Dachshund dragging her rear end around on your carpet? That's your first clue.

Your vet can drain the anal sacs, as can your groomer (if you ask really nicely). Depending on how often your Dachshund's sacs get impacted, this procedure should be done every six to eight weeks. Having someone else do it can get expensive if you're on a tight budget, though, so you *can* do it yourself — although I don't recommend it if you're squeamish. If the anal sacs become impacted often or abscessed more than once, a vet can surgically remove them.

Getting Regular Exercise: Move It or Lose It!

Every living thing with muscles needs to exercise. Exercise helps keep your Dachshund young, strong, and slim. Couch potato Dachshunds may be more prone to disk problems (see Chapter 17), less able to fight off disease, and generally less healthy than their more athletic counterparts.

How much should your Dachshund weigh? That depends on her size (Standard or Miniature), muscle mass, and other factors. In general, however, you can tell whether your Dachshund is too fat by checking periodically (your daily grooming session is the perfect opportunity) for the following:

- ✔ **Look at your Dachshund from the side.** Do you see a nice tuck where her tummy is, or does her tummy hang down? If it hangs down, she's too fat. If her belly looks overly bloated, she could have worms, so check with your vet before putting her on a diet.

- ✔ **Look at your Dachshund from the top (see Figure 16-2).** She should look more like a squash than a sausage. Her body should get narrower between the back of the rib cage and the hips. A too-sharp narrowing, however, could signal that your Dachshund is underweight.

- ✔ **Feel your Dachshund's ribs.** Can you feel the individual ribs under a thin but slightly padded layer of skin? Just right. If you can't find any sign of ribs, however, your Dachshund is too fat. If the ribs are very visible without even touching them, your Dachshund may be too thin.

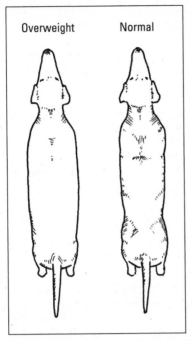

Overweight   Normal

Figure 16-2: An overweight Dachshund looks more like a jumbo frank than a regular wiener.

> ✔ **Feel your Dachshund's ribs.** Can you feel the individual ribs under a thin but slightly padded layer of skin? Just right. If you can't find any sign of ribs, however, your Dachshund is too fat. If the ribs are very visible without even touching them, your Dachshund may be too thin.

Exercise is crucial for overweight Dachshunds. However, if your Dachshund is overweight, don't begin a rigorous exercise program right away. That extra weight puts a strain on her back, as well as on all her muscles. She needs to build up strength before she can do too much, just like an out-of-shape human. Start with slow, short walks and watch for signs of excessive fatigue, such as heavy panting or sitting down and refusing to move. (You can bet a Dachshund will make her wishes clear!)

If you suspect that your Dachshund is over- or underweight, also check with your vet to rule out a health problem (such as a thyroid or digestive issue) and formulate a plan of action. A new diet, new feeding habits, or simply a decrease in treats and table scraps will probably be the prescription (see Chapter 8). Certainly, the second part of the prescription — especially if your Dachshund is overweight — will be an increase in her level of exercise.

But what if you have trouble getting off the couch yourself? How are you supposed to get your Dachshund to exercise? Following are some tips:

- ✔ **A daily walk is good for you and your Dachshund.** It doesn't have to be fast. Remember, your Dachshund's legs are a lot shorter than yours, so she gets far more steps per block than you do. It doesn't have to be long, either. A spin around the block in the morning and, ideally, in the evening is all it takes.

- ✔ **Going on an errand?** Walking down to the neighbor's house to borrow a cup of sugar or a power saw? Taking the kids to the park? Take your Dachshund along. The more opportunities she gets to move — even for short periods at a time — the better.

- ✔ **If you have a fenced-in yard, let your Dachshund spend time out there each day to romp around.** Go out with her and throw balls, play chase, and work on tricks. If you just let her out, she probably won't get enough exercise on her own (unless you have other dogs she can play with).

   If you don't have a fenced-in yard, look into installing a fence. Dachshunds adore being outside without a leash, but it just isn't safe without a fence.

   Dachshunds dig, so bury that fence a foot or so into the ground, if possible. If not, stay outside with your Dachshund or keep a close eye on her.

Training is hard, physical work for your Dachshund. Two or three daily training sessions, without fail, serve as an excellent form of exercise. See the chapters of Part III for much more on this topic.

Meditating on Holistic Health Care

When searching for the perfect vet, chances are you've encountered or at least heard about one or more holistic veterinarians in your area. The movement toward more holistic and natural health care is big right now — and nowhere more so than in the world of animal companions.

Holistic veterinarians may practice any or all of a number of different holistic healing techniques (most specialize in one or two), including homeopathy, herbalism, flower essences, acupuncture, acupressure, pet massage of all types, nutritional therapy, even chiropractic treatment, to name some of the more common methods.

Homeopathy works on the principle of *like treats like* — treating symptoms by using very diluted substances that normally cause those symptoms to put the system back into balance. *Herbalism* is the use of herbs as medicine to balance the system. *Flower essences* treat the emotional energies. *Acupuncture* is the application of needles to certain energy centers of the body to release blockages, and *acupressure* is the application of pressure to those energy centers. *Pet massage* helps loosen tight muscles and connective tissue. *Nutritional therapy* involves improved diet and supplements to help prevent and heal disease. *Chiropractic treatment* aligns the spinal column and joints to free blocked energy.

Should you use a holistic veterinarian for your Dachshund? Some Dachshund owners swear by holistic vets and would never take their pets to a regular vet again. Others wouldn't consider a holistic healer for their Dachshunds. The decision is up to you and should be based on your own personal inclinations and feelings about the matter. If you use a holistic health practitioner yourself and you think the methods make sense, your pet may benefit similarly. If you don't like the idea for yourself, you won't feel comfortable about taking your Dachshund to someone who works in a more holistic mode.

Some of the strongest proponents and strongest detractors of holistic health are among those whose Dachshunds have fallen prey to canine intervertebral disk disease (see Chapter 17). Testimonials abound about Dachshunds that regained the use of their legs through holistic techniques after full paralysis. Others argue that only mainstream medicine should handle such a severe, acute medical event. Again, the choice is up to you. Go with your gut feeling and do what feels right.

The approach I recommend generally is a combination of the two approaches, often called *complementary health care.* More and more vets recommend this approach as well. Holistic healing is great for preventive medicine, to keep the system healthy and balanced. It can also be, in my experience, highly effective for chronic conditions, such as arthritis, degenerative joint diseases, and diabetes, for which mainstream medicine has no cure. I know people who swear by pet acupuncture or herbalism, for example, and sincerely believe it provided pain relief and a return of function for pets that the mainstream medical establishment said couldn't be helped.

For acute conditions, serious injuries, and dangerous illnesses, however, I would be more likely to choose the *allopathic,* or mainstream, conventional vet. Mainstream medicine in this country is best in emergency situations and for curing life-threatening conditions through surgery and other procedures requiring extensive skill and training. However, the more vets learn, and the more they combine their efforts, the more the lines blur. Someday there may be no difference at all, and every vet may use all available methods for the greater good of pet health.

Chapter 17

Handling Dachshund Health Problems

In This Chapter

▶ Understanding why your Dachsie may have back problems

▶ Recognizing and addressing disk disease

▶ Debating paralysis and quality of life

▶ Reviewing other common Dachsie health issues

*I*n general, your Dachshund will probably stay pretty healthy throughout most of his life. But every dog can fall prey to an occasional health problem. In this book, I talk a lot about the fallible Dachshund back. Maybe you have a Dachshund that's already suffering from disk disease, or maybe you're a little nervous that he could experience back trouble. You are right to worry a little, if worrying will encourage you to take some precautionary measures. Dachshunds do tend to have back problems, and prevention is your best course of action.

Dachsies also tend to experience a few other health problems. Yours probably won't, but you'll know what to look for, just in case, after reading this chapter. Here, I discuss everything from back troubles to paralysis to conditions and disorders your Dachshund may have to deal with.

Why Good Backs Go Bad

The title "Why Good Backs Go Bad" is a bit of a misnomer, because many Dachshunds don't have good backs to start with. Dachshunds are a *chondrodystrophic* breed (along with a handful of other breeds, like Pekingese, Cocker Spaniels, and Basset Hounds). Any dog — or any human, for that matter — could experience disk disease, but because of the way they're built and because of the nature of their backbones, Dachshunds are particularly susceptible to canine intervertebral disk disease (sometimes called IVDD or CIDD).

Canine intervertebral disk disease is a serious problem in Dachshunds and other chondrodystrophic dogs. Dachshunds have a disproportionate skeletal structure. They're unusually short and unusually long, so their backs take on an unusual strain. In addition, their spinal disks are more prone to rupture and degeneration than other breeds. The weakest part of the disks typically is the side nearest the spinal cord. One sudden move, one sharp turn around a corner, or one leap off a bed is sometimes all it takes to cause a disk to rupture and leak — or, in severe cases, burst out of its covering, putting pressure on and injuring the delicate spinal cord.

Approximately one in four Dachshunds experiences a disk problem — most between the ages of 3 and 7, with 4 being the most common age of onset. The following sections dig deeper into Dachsie back issues and present some strategies for prevention.

Understanding your chondrodystrophic canine

Your Dachshund's spinal column is made up of small bones called *vertebrae* that surround and protect the spinal cord (see Figure 17-1). His spinal column consists of four primary sections: the cervical spine, or neck area; the thoracic spine, or chest area; the lumbar spine, or lower-back area; and the sacral spine, or pelvic area.

The spinal cord is the information highway of the body, sending messages from the body to the brain about what's going on in the environment and from the brain back to the body telling the body what to do in response to the environment. In other words, the spinal cord is the link between what you think and what you do. Without it, you can hear a car coming but you can't jump out of the way. You can burn your hand but can't remove it from the heat source. You can see something you want but can't go get it.

Fortunately, spinal columns are very good protectors most of the time. In addition to the hard, bony vertebrae, fibrous, fluid-filled cushions in between each vertebra protect the spinal cord. These cushions are called *disks*. How do they do their job? They help the spine move more easily. They also reduce shock to the spine and spinal cord by absorbing the various jolts, jerks, twists, and turns all living beings must occasionally experience.

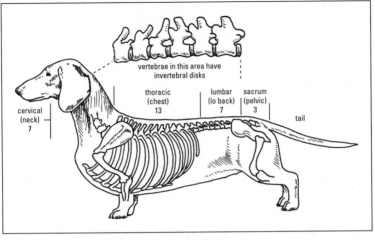

vertebrae in this area have
invertebral disks

thoracic
(chest)
13

lumbar
(lo back)
7

sacrum
(pelvic)
3

cervical
(neck)
7

tail

Figure 17-1: The spinal column of a Dachshund.

In some instances, however, a jolt gets through to the spinal cord and injures it or causes a vertebra or disk to break or rupture. A ruptured disk is what happens in CIDD, and as soon as it happens, every second counts. In Dachshunds, the lower spine, or lumbar region, is the most susceptible to back injury. In fact, five single disks are responsible for 99 percent of ruptures in Dachshunds.

Spinal cords can't take much pressure. A ruptured disk that presses on the cord can quickly cause lasting damage. If the spinal cord can't receive blood, oxygen, and glucose, it will eventually die. And if the spinal cord dies, information can't move from the brain to the body or back again.

If a disk *herniates,* or bulges out from between the vertebrae, the severity is classified into Type I and Type II:

- ✔ In a **Type I herniation,** the disk tears and the inner matter, called the *nucleus,* leaks out. This type of herniation is most common in chondrodystrophic breeds such as Dachshunds, and it's a medical emergency. The leaking nuclear material can put damaging pressure on the spinal cord, and if the damage is too severe, your Dachshund may become permanently paralyzed. Emergency surgery — preferably within the first 12 hours after the injury (and up to 24 hours after) — often is successful in restoring function, although it doesn't come with a guarantee.

- ✔ **Type II herniation** is less severe. The disk develops small tears that allow small amounts of nuclear material to escape, causing the disk to bulge and press on the spinal cord. This herniation can develop gradually and may be less obvious until it becomes severe. It's common in degenerating disks and can lead to gradual paralysis. Type II can also be treated surgically, but some people prefer to keep their pets confined so the disk can heal itself. Type II ruptures typically manifest as back pain and respond well to medical therapy and cage rest, but they eventually recur.

Type II herniations can be dangerous for several reasons, however. Too much bulging can cut off nutrients to the spinal column, causing it to die a slow but permanent death. Also, the Dachshund's body could interpret leaking nuclear material as a foreign invader. In some dogs, the immune system will attack, causing further damage to the spinal cord.

Preventing disk injury

Can you prevent CIDD in your Dachshund? Maybe. Some dogs will probably get it no matter what. Others may have a tendency to get it but won't. Still others may have no tendency at all, so the first and best method of prevention is to find a Dachshund that isn't prone to CIDD.

The problem is, no one can tell for sure which Dachshunds are prone and which ones will stay clear. Scientists do know that CIDD is genetic, however, so a great prevention method is to purchase a Dachshund with little or no CIDD in his family history. Ask a prospective breeder about the occurrence of CIDD in his or her lines (see Chapter 4 to find a reputable breeder who will be honest).

Most seasoned and reputable breeders have experienced CIDD at some point, so be wary of a breeder who says he's never seen it. You're looking for honest answers. Any good breeder knows not to breed a Dachshund with CIDD, but because the disease usually shows up at around 4 years of age, a Dachshund could've been bred several times before the disease manifests. The puppies of that dog, of course, shouldn't be bred.

Through hard work and careful planning, some breeders have virtually eliminated CIDD from their lines, and these are the ones to look for. Your worst bets?

- ✔ A breeder who won't show you the parents (maybe one or both are paralyzed).

- ✔ A pet store, because many of these dogs are bred with no thought to eliminating conditions like CIDD, and you don't get to see the parents.

✔ A shelter or humane society, because you can't possibly know the Dachshund's background.

That's not to say you should never adopt a needy Dachshund from a shelter or humane society. You should, however, be aware that the dog's risk of developing CIDD may be higher than average (see Chapter 5 for more on shelters).

Aside from choosing the right breeder, you can do a few more things to prevent CIDD from crashing into your world:

✔ **Choose a Dachshund that isn't so dramatically short and long.** The longer the back, the more strained it will be by any movement. An international humane organization called the Council of Europe is encouraging European breeders to breed for taller dogs with shorter backs. The Germans recently revised their standard accordingly, and many breeders in the United States are following suit — breeding for less extreme dimensions in order to ensure healthier, stronger backs.

✔ **Keep your Dachshund at a healthy weight.** Obesity puts a huge strain on your Dachshund's back (see Chapter 8).

✔ **Keep your Dachshund from engaging in any sharp twisting movements, jumping from high places, or running around sharp turns.** Avoid tricks that teach your Dachshund to beg on his hind legs or do anything else that puts his spine in a vertical position. Walks are great and exercise is great, but try to keep your Dachshund's back relatively straight when he's in motion (easier said than done, I know, but you must try).

Keep your Dachshund horizontal whenever possible, even when picking him up. Place one hand under his chest and the other under his abdomen or back legs. Lift him carefully, keeping him level, and hold him in your arms with his spine parallel to the floor. Never hold your Dachshund vertically or let his back end swing from your arms. Teach children in your household how to lift and hold your Dachshund, too. However, younger children should never lift a Dachshund and should play with your Dachsie only while sitting on the floor. (See Chapter 7 for more on teaching family members how to live with a Dachsie.)

Treating Disk Disease

Sometimes, despite all the preventive measures in the world, a Dachshund will suffer a disk herniation. If yours does, you must know what to do, and you must do it fast. However, you can't do anything if you don't know that your Dachshund is having a problem in the first place. The following sections explain the signs and what you can do to act.

Recognizing the warning signs

Dogs have high pain thresholds and an instinct not to reveal when they're in pain. After all, in the wild, the obviously injured animal is the one that gets picked off by the predators. But if you pay attention, you can tell whether your Dachshund is in pain. Look for the following signs:

- ✔ Shivering — especially when combined with unusual inactivity
- ✔ Refusal to get up and play, even for food
- ✔ A yelp when you pet your Dachshund or try to pick him up
- ✔ A pulled-in head, arched back, or any other strange position
- ✔ A refusal to bend down to the food or water dish to eat or drink
- ✔ Limping of any kind
- ✔ A "drunken" rear end, which moves but looks as if it isn't completely under control
- ✔ Dragging of the back legs

Taking emergency measures

If your Dachshund shows any of the warning signs from the previous section, call your vet immediately. In the case of dragging the back legs or showing any other signs of paralysis or severe pain, drive immediately to the vet's office or nearest pet emergency facility. Don't wait. You can call on the way.

I've talked to people whose Dachshunds showed signs of trouble on Friday but they decided to wait until Monday to act because their vets' offices were closed. Several of them now have paralyzed pets.

I've also talked to someone — a reader of the first edition of this book, in fact — who took her Dachshund to the emergency vet clinic on a Saturday, even though her regular vet was closed, just because she read this chapter. Her Dachshund underwent surgery and now has four fully functioning limbs!

Save the leaves (er, your Dachsie's mobility)!

Darryl E. McDonald, DVM — a veterinary neurosurgeon at the Dallas Veterinary Surgical Center in Dallas, Texas — has performed hundreds of disk surgeries on Dachshunds. He likes to describe the urgency of surgery with the following analogy: "When a disk ruptures and damages the spinal cord, it is analogous to a houseplant that has not been watered for three weeks. It loses half its leaves. So what do you do? You water it! If you don't, it will die. Similarly, surgery is needed to remove the spinal cord pressure. The longer you wait, the more 'leaves' are lost and the less likely your Dachshund will recover."

In short, you have just hours to act. Immediate surgery on a Dachshund with a Type I ruptured disk has a much better success rate than a similar surgery on a human. For Dachshunds still feeling pain (a good sign that the spinal cord is still functioning), the success rate for restoring function is 95 percent. The success rate is 50 percent for Dachshunds experiencing total paralysis, as long as the dog was feeling pain within the last 24 hours. But if you wait longer than 24 hours after a disk injury, the success rate plummets to a meager 5 percent. If that isn't reason enough to rush your injured Dachsie to treatment, nothing is.

Opting for surgery

Some Dachshund people are anti-surgery, but be advised: Most vets agree that surgery is the quickest and safest route to recovery in the case of a Type I disk herniation. It's a pricey, sure. But many, many Dachshund owners have paid that price and would do it again if they had to. (And a few *have* done it again when their Dachshunds had more than one disk herniation.)

Surgery is often, *very* often, successful — if done within 12 to 24 hours. Surgery has a much quicker recovery time than crate rest. And because the pressure is immediately relieved on the spinal cord, the real danger is over. Your vet still may call for a short period of post-surgery crate rest, which you should observe. After that, however, your Dachshund will probably be, for the most part, back to normal.

Don't be too quick to take your Dachshund running again, though. Don't ignore follow-up visits or the prescribed physical therapy. Your vet or veterinary surgeon can show you what to do with your Dachshund to help him regain his strength and the use of his legs. Exercises are extremely important to help your Dachshund recover.

The downsides to surgery, other than the high price tag, are the risk to your Dachshund of enduring a general anesthetic (a small but real risk) and the risk that the surgery won't be successful (a *very* small risk when the surgery is performed by an experienced, board-certified veterinary surgeon within 24 hours after the injury). If surgery is unsuccessful, your Dachshund may be paralyzed anyway or may continue to suffer pain.

If your Dachshund needs back surgery, you can't just take him to your veterinarian's office. The surgery is complicated and requires the experienced hand of a veterinary neurosurgeon or a veterinary surgeon with an emphasis in orthopedics. If you don't have a veterinary hospital in your area that specializes in back surgery — or at least one that has a surgeon with a lot of relevant experience — check out your nearest school of veterinary medicine. Chances are, the school will be associated with someone who's experienced at back surgery in dogs. The better the surgeon, the better your Dachshund's chances at recovery. No matter the distance, it will be worth the trip.

Crate-and-wait

"Waaait a minute," you may be thinking. "Just how much is this surgery going to cost me?" That depends on where you live and where you take your Dachshund, but the all-inclusive charges probably will range from $800 to over $2,000 (most are probably close to $1,500). For many Dachshund owners, surgery isn't an affordable option, so is surgery your only choice when your Dachshund's disks go bad?

No, although for severe episodes, it has the highest success rate — by a long shot. The other option is the one used more frequently for Type II herniations (see the earlier section "Understanding your chondrodystrophic canine"). In Dachshund circles, it's known as crate-and-wait, or crate rest. *Crate rest* means confining your Dachshund to his den for an extended period of time — usually between two and four weeks. Three or four times per day, you take your Dachshund out to relieve himself and then you immediately return him to his den.

Insuring your dachshund

Could pet insurance be for you? If you buy pet insurance for your Dachshund puppy before he ever has any health problems and he develops disk disease, your foresight could pay off in spades. But if you wait until your dog is full-grown and he has a disk episode, it becomes a pre-existing condition, making it too late to get insurance that would cover disk surgery. Of course, you hope that your dog won't ever have a problem. I hope so, too! But pet insurance may be a smart bargain, just in case. And even if your dog stays healthy, pet insurance could help offset the cost of regular checkups and other health maintenance (depending on the kind of plan you choose).

Put Pet Insurance into an Internet search engine to compare various plans. And if you register your purebred Dachshund with the American Kennel Club, you get a free 60-day trial of pet insurance!

At first, crate rest is easy. Your Dachshund is in pain, and he probably doesn't want to move. But by the second or third day — especially if your vet has prescribed steroids or pain medication — your Dachshund is feeling a whole lot better and is getting mighty tired of that den. He wants to get out! He'll probably whine, cry, scratch, dig at the sides, and do anything he can think of to convince you to let him out.

Keeping your Dachsie confined won't be easy, but it is essential. I repeat: *essential.* A medicated Dachshund is still extremely vulnerable to spinal cord injury. That injured disk is still soft, still ruptured, and perhaps still oozing nuclear material. Movement could cause permanent damage, and if he isn't feeling the pain due to medication, he'll be much more likely to move in ways he shouldn't. If you don't allow his spinal disks adequate healing time, he could easily wind up losing the use of his back legs. Keeping him in the den, no matter how much he begs (remember, *you* are in charge), gives him a far better chance of a full and glorious recovery.

Physical therapy is great for Dachshunds recovering from surgery and for post-crate-rest Dachshunds working to restore lost function. Commonly prescribed activities include

✔ Swimming in the bathtub (never leave your Dachshund unsupervised because if his legs don't work correctly when he needs them, he could drown)

✔ Towel walking, in which you hold up your dog's rear end with a towel sling draped under his abdomen

> ✔ Bicycling your Dachshund's limbs to exercise his full range of motion
>
> ✔ Massaging the affected areas

Also check out a unique invention called the Bottom's Up Leash (www.bottomsupleash.com). This leash holds up a weak or paralyzed rear end so your Dachshund can still go on walks with you while recuperating.

Preventive surgery: The debate

In some Dachshunds, back injury looks imminent. X-rays can reveal calcifications to the spine that may indicate impending disk trouble. For dogs with one or more parents that suffered, disk disease is likely. And what about the Dachshund that has already suffered one episode? Do you want him to endure surgery a second time?

More and more often, veterinary surgeons are performing a preventive surgery called *fenestration.* This procedure essentially drains the spinal disks of fluid to prevent any possible future herniation or rupture. Many vets agree that preventive fenestration can not only prevent a first or second disk episode from occurring, but also dramatically relieve the pain and discomfort of degenerating disks as your Dachshund ages.

The surgery isn't without risks, however. A surgery gone wrong can injure a healthy spinal cord. Recovery can be painful, too.

However, a new, experimental technique called *laser disk fenestration* shows great promise as a safer alternative with an easier recovery. Be sure to talk to your doctors about this option.

Other complications include a reaction to the anesthesia or a post-surgical infection, although these complications aren't very common. Your Dachshund could also suffer from arthritis later in life because his disks won't work to ease the friction between vertebrae.

In general, a normal, healthy Dachshund has no cause to undergo preventive fenestration. It's definitely something to consider, however, if your Dachshund is already undergoing surgery to prevent a second incident. The surgeon would fenestrate the afflicted disk as well as disks in the surrounding area. Or, if genetic or other factors make rupture particularly likely, fenestration may be a good idea. Your vet can help you evaluate the benefits and risks.

Five specific disks account for about 99 percent of disk ruptures in Dachshunds, so these five are commonly fenestrated during surgery for a ruptured disk or as a preventive.

Living with Paralysis: Is It a Quality Life?

For some Dachshunds, no matter what preventive measures have been taken, paralysis becomes an unfortunate reality. You love your pet dearly. Does paralysis really necessitate euthanasia?

This is a question many Dachshund owners struggle with, and strong opinions exist on both sides. A paraplegic Dachshund can still get around, with some help, but also requires more care than a fully functional Dachshund. Are you up for it?

You may think you can't put your Dachshund through it: the surgery, the pain, the crate rest, the suffering, and so on. This is (arguably) the least viable reason for having your Dachshund put down, however. Dogs don't have all the complicated emotional associations we do when it comes to pain and paralysis. If they can recover and live free of pain, even if paralyzed, they'll be perfectly happy — as long as they can be with you.

Many, many people have chosen to live with their paralyzed Dachsies and wouldn't have it any other way. These dogs are still capable of great love, affection, and good health apart from their paralysis. Some paralyzed Dachsies even recover full or partial use of their legs long after their owners had abandoned all hope that they would ever walk again. Many other people, on the other hand, have chosen euthanasia for their pets, for one reason or another — the desire to avoid suffering for the pet or the owners, lack of knowledge, inability to care for a paralyzed pet, and/or cost of the procedure, to name a few.

The choice, obviously, is up to you and your family. A paralyzed Dachshund and his people must endure certain challenges, even after the pain is gone. For example, he won't have bladder or bowel control and can be more susceptible to bladder infections, urine scalding (getting burned by the acid urine), and pressure sores from sitting in one place for a long time.

But remember, to a Dachshund, quality of life means a good meal, a pat on the head, and you by his side. He doesn't know to be embarrassed by lack of bladder control (although he will know something is very wrong if *you* are constantly upset because of this or other associated conditions). He doesn't care if he can't walk across the room to get his favorite ball. He'll be perfectly happy to have you do the fetching!

Of course, if your Dachshund continues to be in pain, euthanasia may be the only humane option. But if the pain resolves, your Dachshund, with your help, can find a way to have a perfectly satisfactory, rewarding life. One Dachshund owner I know said it best: If that Dachshund spirit returns, your dog is telling you he has quality of life. Period. If you're struggling with the euthanasia decision, let your Dachshund tell you what to do and don't listen to anyone else. Sometimes, humans have awfully funny ideas about things.

Life with a paralyzed Dachsie is challenging but rewarding, sometimes heartbreaking, sometimes filled with joy, but always an adventure. May you and your special Dachshund have many more happy years together.

Can't bear to look at that poor, pitiful dog with his legs dragging behind him? Carts are available for paralyzed dogs, and these wheeled contraptions allow paraplegic Dachshunds to get around quite nicely. Your Dachshund doesn't know the meaning of the word pitiful. He'll adapt, learning to pull himself with his front feet. Some tasks are more difficult, but what Dachshund isn't up for a challenge?

Considering Other Dachsie Health Issues

Because I've spent most of this chapter on it, back problems obviously are a Dachshund's number-one health concern. But Dachshunds can develop a few other health issues, as well. The following sections tell you what symptoms to look for and what warrants a call to the vet.

Bloat

Bloat, or gastric torsion, is an emergency condition that happens most often to deep-chested breeds like Dachshunds. For unknown reasons, the stomach fills with gas and then twists on itself. Without treatment, bloat is fatal. If your Dachshund suddenly starts pacing, salivating, and acting upset, nervous, or in pain — or it just seems like something is very wrong — suspect bloat. Call your vet immediately. Emergency surgery could save your dog's life.

Some experts theorize that you can prevent bloat by keeping a dog from eating too quickly or from drinking too much water right after a meal. To reduce the chance of a bloat incident, some recommend feeding two or three meals per day rather than one. This helps your Dachshund to be less hungry and less likely to gulp down his food. Preventing eating and drinking too fast immediately before or after exercise may also help, although nobody knows for sure.

Canine epilepsy

Canine epilepsy, a seizure disorder, happens in some Dachshunds, and nobody is sure why. If your Dachshund suddenly goes stiff, starts shaking, or becomes completely non-responsive or totally limp, suspect a seizure. Call your vet immediately. You can't prevent epilepsy, but it is treatable with medication.

Hypothyroidism

Hypothyroidism is a thyroid gland disorder in which the thyroid doesn't secrete enough of its hormone, slowing a dog's metabolism and resulting in weight gain, fatigue, sluggish behavior, dry skin, hair loss, and severe behavioral changes — ranging from aggression to depression. If your Dachshund exhibits these symptoms, call your vet for an appointment. Dachshunds, along with many other breeds, are particularly prone to hypothyroidism. Most dogs develop the disease in middle age. It can be successfully treated with a synthetic thyroid hormone, just like humans with the same disease.

If you have a hypothyroid condition, you may be surprised to find that your little Dachsie friend takes as much or more thyroid medication than you do. Dachshunds need more than humans per pound to manage their condition.

Progressive retinal atrophy

Some Dachshunds will develop *progressive retinal atrophy,* a degenerative eye disease that eventually results in blindness. The disease isn't painful and sometimes has no symptoms until the dog is almost completely blind; however, some dogs will show reluctance to go down stairs or go into dark areas (night blindness can be an initial stage of the disease). In some dogs, the eye lens looks more opaque or cloudy, but this isn't always the case.

In particular, longhaired Miniature Dachshunds may be prone to PRA. The good news is, a DNA test can pinpoint whether a Miniature longhaired Dachshund is a carrier for PRA, so breeders who do this test should be able to make smarter breeding decisions. Be sure to ask your breeder whether he or she tests breeding dogs for PRA.

If your breeder would like to know more about this new DNA test for PRA, send him or her here: www.dachshund-dca.org/health.html.

After a dog develops progressive retinal atrophy, no treatment can reverse it. However, blind dogs can live a happy life, with a little extra care.

Allergies

Some Dachshunds have skin problems that a veterinarian will diagnose as allergies — possibly to environmental contacts and inhalants or food. (Many pet owners think their pets have food allergies, but true food allergies account for only about 5 percent of allergic skin problems.) Allergies usually show up in the form of rashes, itchy sores, and plenty of scratching. A switch to a higher quality food with a single protein source (like lamb, fish, or venison) helps some dogs — not only with food allergies but also with lessening the severity of environmental contacts and inhalant allergies. It also boosts overall health. Be sure to consult your vet if your Dachsie shows symptoms.

A recent study suggests that Dachshunds may also be prone to vaccine-induced allergies. This ongoing study at Purdue University is exploring the link. If your Dachshund seems to be having a reaction after a vaccination, call your vet right away. For more information and updates on this study, look here: www.dachshund-dca.org/allergystudy5.07.html.

Chapter 18

Enjoying Your Senior Dachsie and Saying Goodbye

. . . .

. . . .

*W*hether your Dachsie has been your best friend for years or you've just adopted an older Dachshund, life with a senior Dachsie isn't exactly like life with a puppy. Your senior won't have quite the energy, the verve, or the capacity for destruction and mischief. On the other hand, life with a senior Dachsie isn't as different as you may imagine. Some Dachsies act downright puppylike until the end!

Aging Dachshunds have many of the same challenges as other aging breeds — and a few unique challenges as well. You want your friend to enjoy maximum longevity, of course. Knowing what's to come and taking a few precautionary measures now and later will help your Dachshund enjoy a long, healthy, happy life. This chapter is here to help. I also assist you in making the difficult euthanasia decision and coping with your loss after you say goodbye.

At What Age Is a Dachsie a Golden Oldie?

Different breeds become seniors at different ages, so just when should you consider your Dachshund a senior citizen? As you may know, dog longevity is largely based on size. Small dogs often live 14 to 16 years or longer, whereas the bigger breeds often live only half that long. Because Dachshunds are small, their longevity tends toward the high side (lucky for us owners); as long as yours is healthy, she will enjoy life to the fullest up until the very end.

But your Dachshund will begin to show signs of aging well before her final day. Dachshund owners would be wise to pay special attention to their pets' health, behavior, and appetite starting somewhere around her 7th or 8th year. You can consider your 7-year-old Dachsie middle-aged, and your 8-year-old is just entering her golden years. This is the age when your Dachshund has fully matured and is heading into the second half of her life. You may not have to do anything different right away, but do pay attention. Your Dachshund's chances of getting age-related diseases are now increasing.

Don't be alarmed if your Dachshund starts to sprout gray hair around her 7th or 8th year. This is perfectly normal — it happens to the best of us — and is no indication of ill health.

The five most common diseases of aging in dogs are kidney disease, liver disease, diabetes, cancer, and heart disease — all conditions common to humans, too. Many aging dogs also develop arthritis and canine dementia, a neurological disease similar to Alzheimer's. Ask your vet about the warning signs and symptoms for these age-related conditions so you can prepare and take action when appropriate.

Addressing a Senior Dachshund's Care Needs

The good news is, when she has passed her 7th year of life, your Dachshund's chance of developing canine intervertebral disc disease (CIDD) decreases (see Chapter 17). The bad news is, her chance of developing other conditions — such as kidney disease, liver disease, diabetes, cancer, heart disease, arthritis, cataracts, progressive retinal atrophy, and dementia — increases. Fortunately, many of these age-related conditions are treatable if caught in time.

Conditions like diabetes and liver and kidney disease often are, in the early stages, detectable only through a blood test. When your Dachshund starts showing symptoms, these diseases may be advanced and far less treatable.

Cataract is a general term often used to describe the lens of the eye gradually becoming opaque. It actually describes two separate conditions — one an age-related stiffening of the lens that causes a gradual loss of vision and a blue/white cloudiness deep in the eye.

This form usually begins around age 8 and becomes more prominent as the Dachshund gets older. It limits low-light vision but rarely leads to total blindness or the need for surgical lens replacement. True cataracts, however, are crystalline changes of the lens that happen rapidly with very obvious white alterations deep in the eye. This type can be associated with diabetes and can occur even in young dogs. It often leads to blindness but can be reversed with surgical lens replacement.

To help prevent age-related health problems, you can take some precautionary measures:

✔ **Take your Dachshund to the vet for a checkup every six months — or, at the very least, every year — after she turns 8 years old.** Technically, you should take your pet to the vet once a year anyway, but many people don't bother if their pets seem healthy. During the golden years, however, the regular vet visit is particularly critical for dogs. Only a vet can detect the diseases of aging that may not be readily apparent except through blood, urine, and heart tests. Be sure to report to your vet any changes in appetite, water consumption, bathroom habits, and behavior — all of which could signal health problems.

If you aren't already doing so, begin a Dachshund diary in which you record all daily information about your Dachshund's habits and behavior. Record what she ate, how much she drank, how much she exercised, what medications you gave her, and how she behaved. How was her mood? Later, when your vet asks you when certain changes first occurred, you'll be able to answer with authority.

✔ **Be prepared for behavioral changes, and keep your Dachshund's routine as regular as possible.** Older dogs tend to become less flexible and more resentful about changes in routine, because changes can be confusing. Feed, walk, and take your Dachshund out at the same times each day. If your Dachshund's vision or hearing declines, be sure to keep furniture and her food and water bowls in the same places so she doesn't get disoriented.

If you have an older longhaired or wirehaired Dachshund, don't yank at mats or strip hair too vigorously. Too much poking and pulling can irritate your older dog. But don't eliminate grooming, either. Keep up the daily routine but be aware that your Dachshund may be more sensitive. A gentle touch, please! She'll be comforted by the routine and your familiar touch. Frequent touching also will keep your pet prepared for more frequent vet visits and may alert you to skin or other changes.

DACHSIE MOXIE

What happens to your senior at the vet?

During a typical geriatric veterinary visit, your vet tests your Dachshund's kidney and liver function, blood sugar level, hematacrit, and protein level. Your Dachshund may receive an electrocardiogram, and the vet will check for changes in weight; look for lumps, bumps, and skin problems; ask you about your Dachshund's appetite and behavior; and take some blood.

> ✔ **If your Dachshund shows no signs of slowing down, don't curb her exercise.** If, on the other hand, she tires more easily or seems to be in pain when exercising, check with your vet and cut back on the length of your daily walks. But don't cut them out altogether unless your vet advises you to do so. Older dogs need exercise to stay healthy and in good spirits.

Looking at the senior diet

When you browse the dog-food aisles of your local pet store or supermarket, you probably notice dog foods targeted for senior dogs. Does your aging Dachshund need a change in diet? As long as her health is fine, your Dachshund can continue on her regular diet for her entire life. In fact, switching your Dachshund's diet away from the food she thrives on can actually be detrimental.

Some senior formulas are low in protein, but older dogs with healthy kidneys need protein in order to maintain muscle mass. Only dogs with kidney problems need to limit their protein intake; don't limit it in your Dachshund's diet just because she has reached middle age. If your vet tells you to limit your Dachshund's protein intake due to a specific health problem and recommends a senior diet, fine. Otherwise, forget it.

Senior diets also are lower in calories and fat, which makes sense because older dogs often are less active than younger dogs, and because Dachshunds in particular are prone to obesity. An obese, aging dog has a greater chance of developing certain problems. But you don't need to switch to a senior diet to decrease your Dachshund's caloric intake if she has decreased her level of exercise. Simply feed her a little less or cut down on the treats.

Treats often are a real problem for older dogs because of how many owners give them. A treat may be only 30 calories, but if your Dachsie gets 10 a day, that's 300 extra calories she takes in a day.

The bottom line when it comes to diet is that your healthy senior Dachsie is no different from the 4-year-old Dachsie down the street. Keep all things about your aging Dachshund's life the same unless your vet instructs you to do otherwise.

Remembering that old shouldn't equal lazy

An aging Dachshund may not be able to get around quite as quickly or spryly as she once did, but that doesn't mean she won't, or shouldn't, try. Old dogs need to keep moving. If they don't, they will experience diminished muscle tone. Moderate exercise helps keep arthritis symptoms in check and helps a Dachsie keep her weight down.

Arthritis is common in older dogs, and if your Dachshund has experienced fenestration of her spinal column during disc surgery (see Chapter 17), she may, upon aging, suffer some arthritis in her spine. Some Dachshunds also develop arthritis in their hips, shoulders, and/or leg joints. See your vet if your Dachshund appears to be in pain.

And note that although exercise shouldn't be so vigorous that it causes your Dachshund discomfort, exercise is essential to keep arthritis symptoms at bay. In the advanced stages, your Dachshund may need to cease strenuous activity. Always follow your vet's guidance.

Your older Dachshund may not show a single sign of slowing down. Age isn't a disease. If your 10-year-old Dachsie races from room to room when you say "Walk?" and still scuttles eagerly through the park sniffing for squirrels, let her go for it! Dogs have a pretty good sense, in general, of how much movement they need and how much they can handle. Unless your dog has become lazy (because you haven't kept her on a regular exercise schedule), her instincts should be sharp you can usually trust them. When it comes to exercise, age alone should have no bearing on how much your Dachshund can do.

Recognizing When Problems Aren't Just "Old Age"

It's easy to assume that if your senior dog is slowing down, becoming confused, or even occasionally yelping in pain, she's simply experiencing symptoms due to old age. Aging, however, isn't a disease. If your Dachshund displays any of the following signs or symptoms, contact your vet right away, because it isn't just old age if your pet

- ✔ **Acts confused.** This could be a sign of dementia — something dogs can develop just like people. Canine dementia is treatable.

- ✔ **Yelps in pain.** This could be a sign of arthritis, disc disease, an injury, or any number of other maladies.

- ✔ **Loses her appetite or drastically increases her appetite for more than a day or two.** Appetite changes could signal hypothyroidism (see Chapter 17), liver disease, kidney disease, depression (itself a symptom of possible illness), or something else.

- ✔ **Suddenly increases her intake of water.** Diabetes or kidney disease could be the culprit. Trouble urinating or excessive urination is a related warning sign. Increased water intake can also be a signal of other health problems that your vet can identify.

- ✔ **Quickly gains or loses weight.** Weight gain or loss — especially if you can't trace it directly to food intake — is a warning sign. Hypo- or hyperthyroidism could be the culprit, but weight changes can be a signal of many other problems, too.

- ✔ **Is excessively irritable.** If your once-placid Dachshund is suddenly growling, nipping, biting, snarling, or bearing her teeth, she could be suffering from pain, confusion, dementia, or a combination of ailments.

Losing and Mourning Your Friend

No one with a beloved dog likes to think about the fact that dogs live much shorter lives than humans. Most of the time, humans will outlive their Dachshunds, and that means having to lose a friend.

Losing a pet is a hard passage, especially in our society where pets have become increasingly meaningful in our lives. Pet owners go to such lengths to make their pets happy and healthy. When we lose them, it's heartbreaking.

In the following sections, I help you prepare for that time you and your Dachshund will someday face together.

Long live the dachshund

Amos and Archie, the Dachshunds that belonged to painter and pop-culture icon Andy Warhol, both outlived him. When Warhol died, a friend took the Dachshunds and cared for them until they died at the ripe old ages of 19 and 20.

Making the euthanasia decision

Perhaps the most difficult part of losing a pet is making the decision to euthanize. If your Dachshund is in severe pain and can't be treated or is otherwise suffering, your vet may recommend euthanasia. *Euthanasia* typically involves administering a dose of a barbiturate, which is a drug commonly used as an anesthetic. The dose is sufficient to allow the heart and the breathing to come to a gradual, peaceful stop.

Veterinary medicine has advanced to the point where much of a pet's suffering can be relieved. Some people choose to let their Dachshunds die naturally at home while treating pain and other symptoms. But in some cases, quality of life has diminished to the point that a pet owner believes his or her Dachshund really is ready to go. But how do you know for sure?

The decision is a tough one, and it's all yours. Your vet can make a recommendation, but only you can decide. That puts an awful lot of power in your hands, and sometimes the only way to make the decision is to listen to what your Dachshund is telling and showing you — and to your heart.

If you do decide that euthanasia is the best, or only, option, don't feel guilty. Sure, you'll feel a little guilty. Who wouldn't? This is a momentous decision. But remember that your Dachshund trusts you to do what's best for her. Sometimes, you have to love them more to let them go.

If your Dachshund requires an extensive, costly medical treatment that you simply can't afford, and you think your only option is euthanasia, consider contacting a local or national Dachshund rescue group (see Chapter 5 for contact information). Another person or even the rescue organization itself may be willing to adopt your Dachshund, pay for the surgery, and then place her into a good home. Surely this is a better option than euthanasia. (You can't, however, expect a rescue organization to pay for the medical treatment and then return the Dachshund to you.)

Some people struggle with the euthanasia decision more than others. If you really aren't sure what to do, wait a little longer until you are sure. Then, when it is time, if you can bear it, your Dachshund will feel safer and less stressed if you — the one she loves the most — are there to hold her, talk to her, and comfort her in her final moments.

Afterward, your veterinarian can advise you about burial, cremation, and other options. Sometimes, a memorial to your pet can help with the grieving process.

Grieving for your Dachsie

If you've ever known, loved, and lost a dog, you know how heart-breaking it can be. People don't like to admit that they're grieving over pets, but why not? Dogs are true companions to humans, and our society has evolved in such a way that many people consider their dogs to be members of their families. Of course you'll be grief-stricken when a member of your family passes away. It would be unnatural *not* to be saddened by such a loss.

Still, people feel silly. Who wants to admit to sobbing alone in a room because that warm body is no longer at your side? Yet people do it every day. Fortunately, more and more people are opening up about the grieving process as it applies to pets. You can even purchase sympathy cards for people who have lost pets. Such a gesture is usually appreciated far beyond the thank you that you may receive if you send one.

If you're the grieving one, you can do some things to help yourself get through the process. Knowing a little about the stages of the grieving process may help. You'll go through the following stages after your loss — the same stages that anyone who's lost a loved one goes through:

- ✔ **Denial:** At first, you won't quite be able to believe or accept that your pet is gone. You may forget that she is gone and call for her or look for her — even prepare her food. This is a protective mechanism. Your mind is giving you a chance to adjust to the notion before experiencing the full weight of the grief. You may also experience this stage if your pet is very ill and you don't want to admit to yourself that she probably won't pull through.

- ✔ **Bargaining:** This stage is more common in the human grieving process, but it can still happen with pets. You may make deals with yourself or with a higher power: "If she lives, I promise

never to let her escape from the backyard again." "If she pulls
through the surgery, I'll never yell at her again."

✔ **Anger:** This stage may surprise you. You aren't angry at your
pet, yet you feel abandoned. Sometimes anger manifests as
guilt: "If only I hadn't . . ." You may be angry at yourself, or
you may blame someone else — a vet or another family
member. Try not to let yourself get caught up in the guilt-and-
blame cycle. It doesn't help; it will just make you feel worse.

✔ **Grief:** After you've let go of your anger, the real grief sets in.
You feel an overwhelming sadness. This is the time when you
need support and someone to talk to. If you don't have an
understanding and sympathetic friend or family member, call
a pet support hotline. Knowing you aren't the only one who
has ever felt this badly about the loss of a pet will help; even
just talking about your pet will make you feel better. This is a
tough stage, but you can make it through. (See the section on
pet loss resources later in this chapter for more help.)

✔ **Resolution:** When your grief begins to fade (it may never go
away entirely), you'll finally come to a resolution about the
loss. Ending the grieving process doesn't mean that you've
forgotten your beloved friend. It simply means that you'll
remember the good times more than the bad and that you'll
find a sense of peace and joy in the memory of your
Dachshund. You'll recognize that your Dachshund has left you
more, in the form of memories and unconditional love, than
she took with her. You were lucky to share part of your life
with such a wonderful creature. At last, when you reach this
final stage, you'll feel lucky once again.

Holding some kind of memorial service can be of tremendous
help. Formal or informal, a memorial service allows all who knew
and loved your pet to come together and remember. Tears and
laughter are common at such events, and the final feeling is often
one of healing.

Utilizing pet-loss resources

Many excellent books and Web sites are there to help with the
subject of pet loss and bereavement. Here are a few good ones
I recommend:

✔ The Association for Pet Loss and Bereavement is a nonprofit
group of concerned people who are experienced and knowledgeable in the tender subject of pet death. Members are professional counselors as well as pet-loving people from all walks

of life; they're concerned with helping pet lovers cope with this intimate kind of loss. Anyone who's genuinely interested in this subject is invited to join them. Write, call, or check out the Web site for chat groups and extensive resources:

P.O. Box 106
Brooklyn, NY 11230
718-382-0690
www.aplb.org (Web site)
aplb@aplb.org (e-mail)

✔ *The Loss of a Pet,* a book by Wallace Sife, founder of the Association for Pet Loss and Bereavement (Howell Book House).

✔ Pet Loss Grief Support at www.petloss.com. This nurturing site includes a Monday Pet Loss Candle Ceremony, tribute pages for pets, and poetry.

✔ The Pet Loss Web site, at www.findinfo.com/petloss.htm, offers articles about pet loss, online memorials, hotlines, counselors, discussion groups, pet memorial products, stories, and poetry, among other features.

✔ In Memory of Pets is an Internet pet loss cemetery at www.in-memory-of-pets.com.

✔ The American Veterinary Medical Association's (AVMA) Grief Counseling services offers a list of pet-loss support hotlines. Look at the following link: www.avma.org/careforanimals/animatedjourneys/goodbyefriend/plhotlines.asp.

✔ Companion Animal Related Emotions' (C.A.R.E.) Pet Loss Helpline — a service offered by the University of Illinois' College of Veterinary Medicine — helps people who are dealing with grief or anticipating a loss. You can call Sunday, Tuesday, and Thursday evenings between 7 and 9 p.m. Central time at the following number: 877-394-CARE (2273). You can also check out the Web site at www.cvm.uiuc.edu/CARE.

Most of all, remember that it's okay to grieve for your lost pet. Millions of people understand and have been exactly where you are. You loved your Dachshund. Your Dachshund understood you. You're lonely without your pet. Your grief is a sign of your love, and even if you feel you made mistakes as a caretaker and Dachshund companion (we all do), remember that your love made your Dachshund's life better. Similarly, your Dachshund made your life richer and more amazing than it would've been without a Dachsie at your side.

Part V
The Part of Tens

Shoot, that ain't nothin', watch this—Roll over, Rusty. C'mon, roll over! Roll over!

In this part . . .

*E*very *For Dummies* book ends with top-ten lists, and I don't want to break with tradition! In this part, I give you ten great Dachsie books and ten useful Web sites so you can gain more information, and I outline ten people foods that are great for Dachshunds and ten bad foods you should avoid altogether.

Chapter 19

Ten Dachshund-Focused Books and Web Sites

*L*ooking for more Dachsie info? You've come to the right place! (Or at least the place that can take you to the right places.) Whether you want to delve further into training, learn more about adoption, find cool Dachshund photos, or collect children's books about Dachshunds, you'll find places to go and books to read in this chapter.

Ten Great Choices for Your Dachsie Bookshelf

Millions of dog books, so little time! Here are a few fun Dachshund books to add to your collection, if you have one (and if you don't, why not start one right now?):

The Culture Clash, by Jean Donaldson (James & Kenneth Publishers). You'll never look at training a dog the same way again. When you read this, you'll keep saying, "Ohhhh! I get it!"

Don't Shoot the Dog! The New Art of Teaching and Training, by Karen Pryor (Ringpress Books Ltd). Another really helpful book on dog training.

Dig In! Earthdog Training Made Easy, by Mario Migliorini (Howell Book House). Learn more about the sport of earthdog to help channel your Dachsie's desire to dig.

Adopting a Pet For Dummies, by Eve Adamson (Wiley). Learn more about adopting dogs from shelters and pet rescue groups.

The Ugly Dachshund, by G.B. Stern (J.N. Townsend Publishing). This classic novel from 1938 is a Dachshund story . . . and a story about people, too.

Day of the Dachshund, by Jim Dratfield (Clarkson Potter). An adorable and beautiful book of artistic Dachshund photos.

Wiener Dog Art: A Far Side Collection, by Gary Larson (Time Warner Paperbacks). You'll love these hilarious Dachshund-inspired art "reproductions."

Albert, the Dog Who Liked to Ride in Taxis, by Cynthia Zarin (Atheneume). Indispensable for the city-dwelling toddler set.

Pretzel, by H.A. Rey and Margaret Rey (Houghton Mifflin). A classic children's book from the authors of *Curious George.*

Gretchen The Bicycle Dog, by Anita Heyman (Dutton Juvenile). In this fascinating children's book, a Dachshund ruptures a spinal disk and becomes paralyzed but is determined to stay moving. Her family buys her a cart and then she lives a happy life. This book would be great for kids in a family whose Dachshund has this problem.

Ten Wiener Web Sites to Keep You Busy

If you spend time online, here's your chance to surf for Dachshund-relevant fun and information. You'll find plenty of links here to Web sites all about dogs, training, dog activities, and, of course, the wonderful Dachshund himself. Surf's up!

The American Kennel Club (www.akc.org) has quite a few sites of interest to Dachshund lovers. Have a good look around. You can find the Dachshund breed standard, information on rescue groups, information on Dachshund activities, and plenty of general dog information and news.

The Dachshund Club of America, Inc. (www.dachshund-dca.org), is the AKC parent club for the breed. You can find a good breeder, get Dachsie information, and more.

Are you all about the Mini Dachshund? Check out the **National Miniature Dachshund Club, Inc.,** a club devoted to diminutive Dachshunds, at www.dachshund-nmdc.org.

The Dachshund Friendship Club (www.dachshundfriendship club.com) is a fun and non-competitive club based in New York City. It has great resources on its fun Web site, and for those in New York, it has Dachsie events like Dachshund Octoberfest. I have so much fun looking at this site. *Great* pictures!

The Dachshund Network (www.thedachshundnetwork.com) has plenty of fun and informative dog-friendly links, as well as a bulletin board.

I would recommend **The Dachshund Rescue Web Page** (www.dachshund-rescue.org) even if I didn't know that it encourages people to buy my book! This site does a great service for rescued Dachshunds. Check it out, and follow its many links.

Able Dogs (www.abledogs.net) is an e-mail group devoted to people with disabled pets. It started specifically for people with paralyzed Dachshunds but expanded to include many other people whose pets have special needs. Check out the stories, the community, and more. You'll laugh, you'll cry, and you'll be glad you came.

DODGER (Dachshund Orthopedic Disc Group Email Resource) is a site all about Dachsund disk issues. You can find plenty of great information here, including how to find a veterinary neurologist in your area. Check it out *before* your Dachshund ever has a problem, and join their Yahoo! list, called Dodgerslist, to join up with a community of fellow Dachshund lovers dealing with orthopedic issues: www.dodgerslist.com.

The Canadian Dachshund Lovers Page (or Wienerdogs.org) was created by Bob Brennert. This Canadian site is all about Dachshunds. All the info is at www.wienerdogs.org.

You can go to the **Association of Pet Dog Trainers** (www.apdt.com) site to find a great trainer. The site is run by a group of trainers devoted to positive training methods.

Chapter 20

Ten Good Foods, Ten Bad Foods

- -

In This Chapter

▶ Feeding your Dachshund good people food (occasionally)

▶ Avoiding dangerous people foods

- -

*P*lenty of people can't resist giving their Dachshunds just a little bite of this and just a tiny smidgen of that. After all, how can you turn down those pleading, hungry faces! A little bit of healthy people food won't hurt a Dachshund, as long as your Dachsie isn't ingesting too many calories. In fact, a variety of healthy foods may actually be good for your Dachshund. (Many experts disagree, but it makes sense to me that real whole food is good for dogs on a processed kibble diet.) But you must avoid making the mistake of choosing the wrong foods — meals that could actually hurt your Dachshund. This chapter is your guide to the good foods and the bad.

Ten Great People Foods for Dachshunds

The foods in the following list may be good foods to give, but always feed these foods in moderation. Use them as a flavorful addition to your Dachshund's regular balanced diet (see Chapter 8):

✓ **Lean meat:** Dogs love meat, and some people (including this book's illustrious Technical Editor) say they don't get enough. Examples include beef, chicken, turkey, or fish. Make sure you give small pieces.

✔ **Lowfat cottage cheese:** Dish out just a spoonful to supplement meals and treats, unless this method disagrees with your dog. Many dogs think it's just great, and it adds protein.

✔ **Olive, canola, or flaxseed oil:** Drizzle a teaspoon over your Dachshund's kibble. Your dog's skin and coat will feel sooo soft.

✔ **Nonfat, plain yogurt:** One tablespoon mixed with your Dachshund's regular food should do the trick. Yogurt is especially good for dogs that are having a mild stomach issue like diarrhea. It helps replenish the gut with friendly bacteria. (Doesn't sound too appetizing, but it's true!)

✔ **Scrambled eggs:** A few bits left over from your breakfast makes for a healthy addition to your Dachshund's regular food. Some say this is the perfect protein supplement.

✔ **Broccoli florets:** Small pieces, raw or cooked, make good training treats for dogs that like broccoli.

✔ **Lettuce or other greens:** Try crunchy bits of Romaine, collards, or kale. Some Dachshunds won't eat this treat (they prefer the meat and beernuts), but some health fanatics love it. (Just kidding, don't give your dog beer nuts!)

✔ **Baby carrots:** These are great for treats — they have all the crunch of a dog cookie but none of the starch and preservatives. Cut them in half for Mini Dachshunds.

✔ **Blueberries:** These are good fresh or frozen, and they're so fun to play with before they go down the hatch. Some dogs will bat them around for hours. (And then, inevitably, you'll step on one with your bare foot, squishing it into your white carpet. But, hey, you have a dog . . . why do you have a white carpet?)

✔ **Peanut butter:** Every now and then, your Dachshund may enjoy licking a little peanut butter off a spoon. Use the natural kind of peanut butter without the added sugar and salt. Rub some on a chew toy and keep your Dachsie engaged for twice as long.

Ten Foods You Should Never Feed Your Dachshund

The foods in the following list won't necessarily harm every dog, but many dogs have developed serious illnesses after eating these seemingly harmless people foods. Why take a chance? I suggest that you never, ever feed your Dachshund any of these ten foods. If you believe your dog has ingested any of them, call your vet right away for advice.

- ✔ **Chocolate:** Both the theobromine and the caffeine in chocolate can be very harmful to dogs. Baker's chocolate is the worst, but even milk chocolate can make a dog sick.

- ✔ **Grapes and raisins:** These "treats" can cause kidney failure in some dogs — especially if they eat a lot of them. For a small dog, even a few could cause toxicity.

- ✔ **Macadamia nuts:** These yummy nuts can be very toxic for dogs, causing vomiting, pain, and neurological symptoms.

- ✔ **Onions or garlic:** Frequent ingestion of onions can cause severe anemia and even death. Small amounts can cause gastrointestinal distress, because dogs can't digest onions very well. Onions may even be more dangerous than garlic, perhaps because foods often contain more onions than garlic. In fact, many natural pet foods, treats, and homemade dog food recipes contain a little garlic. Some people believe garlic can help ward off fleas. However, neither onions nor garlic should be a daily part of your dog's diet.

- ✔ **Coffee and tea:** Don't let your Dachshund help you drink your coffee, no matter how cute that may be. The caffeine and other acids in coffee are very unhealthy for him. The same goes for your tea. Plus, dogs that eat coffee beans or coffee grounds can get very ill.

- ✔ **Alcoholic beverages:** The same goes for your beer, your wine, or your martinis. No, no, and no! (Although I know of one company that makes a non-alcoholic beer for dogs. I haven't tried it, though.)

- ✔ **High-fat foods:** Dogs don't digest high-fat foods very well, and too many fatty foods can cause pancreatitis — especially in smaller dogs. Your Dachsie may look like a hot dog, but high-fat, processed meats like hot dogs, bacon, and deli meats are dangerous because of the high sodium and nitrate content.

- ✔ **Xylitol:** This artificial sweetener, which you find in many sugar-free human foods (like sugar-free gum), is very toxic for dogs. If your Dachsie accidentally ingests something with xylitol, call your vet immediately.

- ✔ **Avocado:** Some pet foods contain avocado, but experts — including those at the ASPCA Animal Poison Control Center — say that avocado is extremely toxic to some animals, and its effects aren't fully understood in dogs and cats. Avoid avocado, just to be safe.

✔ **Milk and cheese:** Some dogs can eat small amounts of dairy products without a problem, but many can suffer from intestinal distress from dairy products (other than the fermented kinds, like yogurt and cottage cheese). Avoid the high-fat, hard cheeses. And your dog really doesn't need to finish the milk in your cereal bowl!

Index

• *U* •

SPORTS, FITNESS, PARENTING, RELIGION & SPIRITUALITY

0-471-76871-5

0-7645-7841-3

Also available:

- Catholicism For Dummies 0-7645-5391-7
- Exercise Balls For Dummies 0-7645-5623-1
- Fitness For Dummies 0-7645-7851-0
- Football For Dummies 0-7645-3936-1
- Judaism For Dummies 0-7645-5299-6
- Potty Training For Dummies 0-7645-5417-4

- Buddhism For Dummies 0-7645-5359-3
- Pregnancy For Dummies 0-7645-4483-7 †
- Ten Minute Tone-Ups For Dumm 0-7645-7207-5
- NASCAR For Dummies 0-7645-76
- Religion For Dummies 0-7645-52
- Soccer For Dummies 0-7645-522
- Women in the Bible For Dummie 0-7645-8475-8

TRAVEL

0-7645-7749-2

0-7645-6945-7

Also available:

- Alaska For Dummies 0-7645-7746-8
- Cruise Vacations For Dummies 0-7645-6941-4
- England For Dummies 0-7645-4276-1
- Europe For Dummies 0-7645-7529-5
- Germany For Dummies 0-7645-7823-5
- Hawaii For Dummies 0-7645-7402-7

- Italy For Dummies 0-7645-7386-1
- Las Vegas For Dummies 0-7645-7382-9
- London For Dummies 0-7645-427
- Paris For Dummies 0-7645-7630-
- RV Vacations For Dummies 0-7645-4442-X
- Walt Disney World & Orlando For Dummies 0-7645-9660-8

GRAPHICS, DESIGN & WEB DEVELOPMENT

0-7645-8815-X

0-7645-9571-7

Also available:

- 3D Game Animation For Dummies 0-7645-8789-7
- AutoCAD 2006 For Dummies 0-7645-8925-3
- Building a Web Site For Dummies 0-7645-7144-3
- Creating Web Pages For Dummies 0-470-08030-2
- Creating Web Pages All-in-One Desk Reference For Dummies 0-7645-4345-8
- Dreamweaver 8 For Dummies 0-7645-9649-7

- InDesign CS2 For Dummies 0-7645-9572-5
- Macromedia Flash 8 For Dummies 0-7645-9691-8
- Photoshop CS2 and Digital Photography For Dummies 0-7645-9580-6
- Photoshop Elements 4 For Dumm 0-471-77483-9
- Syndicating Web Sites with RSS F For Dummies 0-7645-8848-6
- Yahoo! SiteBuilder For Dummies 0-7645-9800-7

NETWORKING, SECURITY, PROGRAMMING & DATABASES

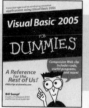

0-7645-7728-X

0-471-74940-0

Also available:

- Access 2007 For Dummies 0-470-04612-0
- ASP.NET 2 For Dummies 0-7645-7907-X
- C# 2005 For Dummies 0-7645-9704-3
- Hacking For Dummies 0-470-05235-X
- Hacking Wireless Networks For Dummies 0-7645-9730-2
- Java For Dummies 0-470-08716-1

- Microsoft SQL Server 2005 For Dummies 0-7645-7755-7
- Networking All-in-One Desk Reference For Dummies 0-7645-9939-9
- Preventing Identity Theft For Dumm 0-7645-7336-5
- Telecom For Dummies 0-471-77085-X
- Visual Studio 2005 All-in-One Desk Reference For Dummies 0-7645-9775-2
- XML For Dummies 0-7645-8845-1